THE ARMCHAIR DETECTIVE®

Book of Lists

REVISED SECOND EDITION

EDITED BY KATE STINE

OTTO PENZLER BOOKS

NEW YORK

OTTO
PENZLER
BOOKS

Otto Penzler Books
129 West 56th Street
New York, NY 10019
(Editorial offices only)

Simon & Schuster Inc.
Rockefeller Center
1230 Avenue of the Americas
New York, NY 10020

Designed by Janet Tingey

Manufactured in the United States of America
1 3 5 7 9 10 8 6 4 2

Library of Congress Cataloging-in-Publication Data
The Armchair detective book of lists/edited by Kate Stine.
Rev. 2nd ed.
p.   cm.
1. Detective and mystery stories, English—Bibliography. 2. Detective and mys-
tery stories, American—Bibliography. 3. Bibliography—Best books—Detective
and mystery stories. 4. Detective and mystery stories—Miscellanea. I. Stine,
Kate, date. II. Armchair detective.
Z2014.F4A75 1995
[PR830.D4]
016.823'087208—dc20
94-41794
CIP
ISBN 1-883402-98-0

"The Haycraft-Queen Definitive Library of Detective-Crime-Mystery Fiction"
and the "Queen's Quorum: The 125 Most Important Books of Detective-Crime-
Mystery Fiction Short Stories" are reprinted here by kind permission of the Ellery
Queen Estates and the agent for the Estates: Scott Meredith Literary Agency, Inc.,
845 Third Avenue, New York, NY 10022.
  "H. R. F. Keating's 100 Best Crime and Mystery Books" is adapted from *Crime
and Mystery: The 100 Best Books* by H. R. F. Keating. London: Xanadu; New
York: Carroll & Graf, 1987. This list is used by kind permission of the author.
  "James Sandoe's Hard-Boiled Checklist" is adapted from the pamphlet *The
Hard-Boiled Dick: A Personal Checklist* by James Sandoe. Chicago: Arthur Lovell,
1952.
  "Robin W. Winks's Personal Mystery Favorites" is adapted from one of the
appendices to *Detective Fiction: A Collection of Critical Essays, Revised Edition* by
Robin W. Winks. VT: Foul Play/Countryman, 1988. It is reprinted here by kind
permission of the author.
  "*The Sunday Times* Hundred Best Crime Stories" is reprinted by kind permission of Julian Symons.

To *Al Hubin*

WHO FOUNDED
The Armchair Detective Magazine
IN 1967

Acknowledgments

The mystery world being the genial place that it is, it's a given that I had lots of friendly help and advice on this project. Fans, writers, booksellers, and my colleagues in mystery publishing were all vital in gathering the information for this book. A few people went way beyond the call of duty and deserve special acknowledgment.

First and foremost, my grateful thanks to Priscilla Ridgway, executive director of Mystery Writers of America, for the many hours she devoted to scouring old records to make this version of the Edgar Allan Poe Awards the most accurate available. I had no idea what I was asking until I saw some of those "records" firsthand. Priscilla, you're a peach!

Bob Napier, mystery fan extraordinaire, kindly reviewed the mystery-periodicals section of this book for accuracy. Mystery writer and bookseller Jan Grape helpfully offered access to her all-encompassing Rolodex to help me reach various mystery organizations. And as the reader will see, many distinguished writers, critics, and booksellers graciously contributed material to this work.

Teresa Huddleston helped run down several elusive short-story publication dates. Keith Kahla obsessively tracked down information on some of the more obscure foreign films nominated for Edgars. Michele Slung made many excellent suggestions and Margaret Longbrake did a fantastic job of proofreading and fact-checking. Thanks to each of them.

Finally, my thanks to Otto Penzler not only for being my editor on this book but also our publisher at *The Armchair Detective*.

Contents

THE ARMCHAIR DETECTIVE®

Book of Lists

1. The Mystery Writers of America Awards

Founded in 1945, the Mystery Writers of America is the preeminent American organization of mystery writers. Each year in April, the MWA bestows the coveted Edgar Allan Poe Awards for achievement in various categories.

Edgar Allan Poe has long been acknowledged as the "father of the detective story," so it was natural that MWA would choose to name their awards after him. Although the awards criteria have reflected changing conditions over the passing years, in general the criteria are these:

THE GRAND MASTER AWARD is recognition for not only important contributions to the mystery genre over time, but also for a significant output of consistently high quality as well.

THE ELLERY QUEEN AWARD is given to writing teams and also to outstanding people in the mystery-publishing industry.

AN EDGAR is for the best work in various categories of the mystery field involving writing.

A RAVEN is for the best work in a field of the mystery *not* involving writing.

A SCROLL is recognition for being a nominee.

Mystery Writers of America presented its first Edgar Allan Poe Awards in 1946 for works published or produced in 1945. Various categories have been added or discontinued over the years. Please note that all dates in this listing designate the year the award was given. In cases where there were several nominees for a single award, the winner is in boldface.

THE GRAND MASTER AWARDS

The Grand Master Award given yearly by the MWA represents the pinnacle of achievement in the mystery field. This prestigious and highly coveted award was established to recognize not only important contributions to the mystery field over time, but a significant output of consistently high quality as well.

1994	Lawrence Block
1993	Donald E. Westlake
1992	Elmore Leonard
1991	Tony Hillerman
1990	Helen McCloy
1989	Hillary Waugh
1988	Phyllis A. Whitney
1987	Michael Gilbert
1986	Ed McBain
1985	Dorothy Salisbury Davis
1984	John le Carré
1983	Margaret Millar
1982	Julian Symons
1981	Stanley Ellin
1980	W. R. Burnett
1979	Aaron Marc Stein
1978	Daphne du Maurier
	Dorothy B. Hughes
	Ngaio Marsh
1976	Graham Greene
1975	Eric Ambler
1974	Ross Macdonald
1973	Judson Philips
	Alfred Hitchcock
1972	John D. MacDonald
1971	Mignon G. Eberhart
1970	James M. Cain
1969	John Creasey
1967	Baynard Kendrick
1966	Georges Simenon

1964 George Harmon Coxe
1963 John Dickson Carr
1962 Erle Stanley Gardner
1961 Ellery Queen (Frederic Dannay and Manfred B. Lee)
1959 Rex Stout
1958 Vincent Starrett
1955 Agatha Christie

THE EDGAR ALLAN POE AWARDS

Best Novel

1994
THE SCULPTRESS by Minette Walters (St. Martin's)
FREE FALL by Robert Crais (Bantam)
SMILLA'S SENSE OF SNOW by Peter Hoeg (Farrar, Straus & Giroux)
WOLF IN THE SHADOWS by Marcia Muller (Mysterious Press)
THE JOURNEYMAN TAILOR by Gerald Seymour (HarperCollins)

1993
BOOTLEGGER'S DAUGHTER by Margaret Maron (Mysterious Press)
BACKHAND by Liza Cody (Doubleday)
32 CADILLACS by Joe Gores (Mysterious Press)
WHITE BUTTERFLY by Walter Mosley (Norton)
POMONA QUEEN by Kem Nunn (Pocket Books)

1992
A DANCE AT THE SLAUGHTERHOUSE by Lawrence Block
  (Wm. Morrow)
DON'T SAY A WORD by Andrew Klavan (Pocket Books)
PRIOR CONVICTIONS by Lia Matera (Simon & Schuster)
I.O.U. by Nancy Pickard (Pocket Books)
PALINDROME by Stuart Woods (HarperCollins)

1991
NEW ORLEANS MOURNING by Julie Smith (St. Martin's)
FADE THE HEAT by Jay Brandon (Pocket Books)
WHISKEY RIVER by Loren Estleman (Bantam)

BONES AND SILENCE by Reginald Hill (Delacorte)
DEADFALL IN BERLIN by R. D. Zimmerman (Donald I. Fine)

1990
BLACK CHERRY BLUES by James Lee Burke (Little, Brown)
A QUESTION OF GUILT by Frances Fyfield (Pocket Books)
DEATH OF A JOYCE SCHOLAR by Batholomew Gill (Wm. Morrow)
GOLDILOCKS by Andrew Coburn (Scribners)
THE BOOSTER by Eugene Izzi (St. Martin's)

1989
A COLD RED SUNRISE by Stuart M. Kaminsky (Scribners)
A THIEF OF TIME by Tony Hillerman (Harper & Row)
IN THE LAKE OF THE MOON by David L. Lindsey (Atheneum)
JOEY'S CASE by K. C. Constantine (Mysterious Press)
SACRIFICIAL GROUND by Thomas H. Cook (Putnam)

1988
OLD BONES by Aaron Elkins (Mysterious Press)
A TROUBLE OF FOOLS by Linda Barnes (St. Martin's)
NURSERY CRIMES by B. M. Gill (Scribners)
ROUGH CIDER by Peter Lovesey (Mysterious Press)
THE CORPSE IN OOZAK'S POND by Charlotte MacLeod (Mysterious
   Press)

1987
A DARK-ADAPTED EYE by Barbara Vine (Bantam)
THE BLIND RUN by Brian Freemantle (Bantam)
COME MORNING by Joe Gores (Mysterious Press)
THE STRAIGHT MAN by Roger L. Simon (Villard)
A TASTE FOR DEATH by P. D. James (Knopf)

1986
THE SUSPECT by L. R. Wright (Viking)
CITY OF GLASS: THE NEW YORK TRILOGY, PART I by Paul Auster
   (Sun & Moon Press)
A SHOCK TO THE SYSTEM by Simon Brett (Scribners)

THE TREE OF HANDS by Ruth Rendell (Pantheon)
AN UNKINDNESS OF RAVENS by Ruth Rendell (Pantheon)

1985
BRIARPATCH by Ross Thomas (Simon & Schuster)
THE BLACK SERAPHIM by Michael Gilbert (Harper &
Row)
CHESSPLAYER by William Pearson (Viking)
EMILY DICKINSON IS DEAD by Jane Langton (St.
Martin's)
THE TWELFTH JUROR by B. M. Gill (Scribners)

1984
LA BRAVA by Elmore Leonard (Arbor House)
THE LITTLE DRUMMER GIRL by John le Carré (Knopf)
THE NAME OF THE ROSE by Umberto Eco (Harcourt Brace
Jovanovich)
THE PAPERS OF TONY VEITCH by William McIlvanney (Pantheon)
TEXAS STATION by Christopher Leach (Harcourt Brace Jovanovich)

1983
BILLINGSGATE SHOAL by Rick Boyer (Houghton Mifflin)
THE CAPTAIN by Seymour Shubin (Stein & Day)
EIGHT MILLION WAYS TO DIE by Lawrence Block (Arbor House)
KAHAWA by Donald E. Westlake (Viking)
SPLIT IMAGES by Elmore Leonard (Arbor House)

1982
PEREGRINE by William Bayer (Congdon & Lattes)
THE AMATEUR by Robert Littell (Simon & Schuster)
BOGMAIL by Patrick McGinley (Ticknor & Fields)
DEATH IN A COLD CLIMATE by Robert Barnard (Scribners)
DUPE by Liza Cody (Scribners)
THE OTHER SIDE OF SILENCE by Ted Allbeury (Scribners)

1981
WHIP HAND by Dick Francis (Harper & Row)

DEATH OF A LITERARY WIDOW by Robert Barnard (Scribners)
DEATH DROP by B. M. Gill (Scribners)
THE SPY'S WIFE by Reginald Hill (Pantheon)
MAN ON FIRE by A. J. Quinnell (Wm. Morrow)

1980
THE RHEINGOLD ROUTE by Arthur Maling (Harper & Row)
DEATH OF A MYSTERY WRITER by Robert Barnard (Scribners)
FIRE IN THE BARLEY by Frank Parrish (Dodd, Mead)
MAKE DEATH LOVE ME by Ruth Rendell (Doubleday)
A COAT OF VARNISH by C. P. Snow (Scribners)

1979
THE EYE OF THE NEEDLE by Ken Follett (Arbor House)
THE SNAKE by John Godey (Putnam)
LISTENING WOMAN by Tony Hillerman (Harper & Row)
A SLEEPING LIFE by Ruth Rendell (Doubleday)
THE SHALLOW GRAVE by Jack S. Scott (Harper & Row)

1978
CATCH ME: KILL ME by William H. Hallahan (Bobbs-Merrill)
LAIDLAW by William McIlvanney (Pantheon)
NIGHTWING by Martin Cruz Smith (Norton)

1977
PROMISED LAND by Robert B. Parker (Houghton Mifflin)
A MADNESS OF THE HEART by Richard Neely (Crowell)
THE MAIN by Trevanian (Harcourt Brace Jovanovich)
THE CAVANAUGH QUEST by Thomas Gifford (Putnam)
THE GLORY BOYS by Gerald Seymour (Random House)

1976
HOPSCOTCH by Brian Garfield (M. Evans)
THE GARGOYLE CONSPIRACY by Martin Albert (Doubleday)
THE MONEY HARVEST by Ross Thomas (Wm. Morrow)
HARRY'S GAME by Gerald Seymour (Random House)
OPERATION ALCESTIC by Maggie Rennert (Prentice-Hall)

1975
PETER'S PENCE by Jon Cleary (Wm. Morrow)
THE MAN WHO LOVED ZOOS by Malcolm Bosse (Putnam)
GOODBYE AND AMEN by Francis Clifford (Harcourt Brace
   Jovanovich)
THE SILVER BEARS by Paul E. Erdman (Scribners)
THE LESTER AFFAIR by Andrew Garve (Harper & Row)

1974
DANCE HALL OF THE DEAD by Tony Hillerman (Harper & Row)
THE RAINBIRD PATTERN by Victor Canning (Wm. Morrow)
AMIGO, AMIGO by Francis Clifford (Coward, McCann & Geoghegan)
AN UNSUITABLE JOB FOR A WOMAN by P. D. James (Scribners)
DEAR LAURA by Jean Stubbs (Stein & Day)

1973
THE LINGALA CODE by Warren Kiefer (Random House)
FIVE PIECES OF JADE by John Ball (Little, Brown)
TIED UP IN TINSEL by Ngaio Marsh (Little, Brown)
THE SHOOTING GALLERY by Hugh C. Rae (Coward, McCann &
   Geoghegan)
CANTO FOR A GYPSY by Martin Cruz Smith (Putnam)

1972
THE DAY OF THE JACKAL by Frederick Forsyth (Viking)
THE FLY ON THE WALL by Tony Hillerman (Harper & Row)
SHROUD FOR A NIGHTINGALE by P. D. James (Scribners)
SIR, YOU BASTARD by G. F. Newman (Simon & Schuster)
WHO KILLED ENOCH POWELL? by Arthur Wise (Harper & Row)

1971
THE LAUGHING POLICEMAN by Maj Sjöwall and Per Wahlöö
   (Pantheon)
THE HOUND AND THE FOX AND THE HARPER by Shaun Herron
   (Random House)
BEYOND THIS POINT ARE MONSTERS by Margaret Millar (Random
   House)

MANY DEADLY RETURNS by Patricia Moyes (Holt, Rinehart & Winston)

AUTUMN OF A HUNTER by Pat Stadley (Random House)

THE HOT ROCK by Donald E. Westlake (Simon & Schuster)

1970

FORFEIT by Dick Francis (Harper & Row)

WHERE THE DARK STREETS GO by Dorothy Salisbury Davis (Scribners)

THE OLD ENGLISH PEEP SHOW by Peter Dickinson (Harper & Row)

MIRO by Shaun Herron (Random House)

BLIND MAN WITH A PISTOL by Chester Himes (Wm. Morrow)

WHEN IN GREECE by Emma Lathen (Simon & Schuster)

Dick Francis didn't start writing fiction until he was almost forty years old; his first career was as a top jockey in British racing.

1969

A CASE OF NEED by Jeffery Hudson (World)

PICTURE MISS SEETON by Heron Carvic (Harper & Row)

GOD SPEED THE NIGHT by Dorothy Salisbury Davis and Jerome Ross (Scribners)

THE GLASS-SIDED ANTS' NEST by Peter Dickinson (Harper & Row)

THE VALENTINE ESTATE by Stanley Ellin (Random House)

BLOOD SPORT by Dick Francis (Harper & Row)

1968

GOD SAVE THE MARK by Donald E. Westlake (Random House)

LEMON IN THE BASKET by Charlotte Armstrong (Coward-McCann)

THE GIFT SHOP by Charlotte Armstrong (Coward-McCann)

A PARADE OF COCKEYED CREATURES by George Baxt (Random House)

FLYING FINISH by Dick Francis (Harper & Row)

ROSEMARY'S BABY by Ira Levin (Random House)

1967

THE KING OF THE RAINY COUNTRY by Nicolas Freeling (Harper & Row)

ODDS AGAINST by Dick Francis (Harper & Row)
KILLER DOLPHIN by Ngaio Marsh (Little, Brown)
THE BUSY BODY by Donald E. Westlake (Random House)

1966
THE QUILLER MEMORANDUM by Adam Hall (Simon & Schuster)
THE PALE BETRAYER by Dorothy Salisbury Davis (Scribners)
FUNERAL IN BERLIN by Len Deighton (Putnam)
THE PERFECT MURDER by H. R. F. Keating (Dutton)
THE FAR SIDE OF THE DOLLAR by Ross Macdonald (Knopf)
AIRS ABOVE THE GROUND by Mary Stewart (Wm. Morrow)

1965
THE SPY WHO CAME IN FROM THE COLD by John le Carré (Coward-McCann)
THE NIGHT OF THE GENERALS by Hans Hellmut Kirst (Harper & Row)
THE FIEND by Margaret Millar (Random House)
THIS ROUGH MAGIC by Mary Stewart (Wm. Morrow)

1964
THE LIGHT OF DAY by Eric Ambler (Knopf)
THE MAKE-BELIEVE MAN by Elizabeth Fenwick (Harper & Row)
GRIEVE FOR THE PAST by Stanton Forbes (Doubleday)
THE EXPENDABLE MAN by Dorothy B. Hughes (Random House)
THE PLAYER ON THE OTHER SIDE by Ellery Queen (Random House)

Eric Ambler pioneered the development of the modern, morally ambiguous novel of intrigue. He also brought a socialist sensibility to the predominately right-wing thriller fiction of the twenties and thirties.

1963
DEATH AND THE JOYFUL WOMAN by Ellis Peters (Doubleday)
THE ZEBRA-STRIPED HEARSE by Ross Macdonald (Knopf)
SÉANCE by Mark McShane (Doubleday)
THE EVIL WISH by Jean Potts (Scribners)
KNAVE OF HEARTS by Dell Shannon (Wm. Morrow)
THE BALLAD OF THE RUNNING MAN by Shelley Smith (Harper &
    Row)

1962
GIDEON'S FIRE by J. J. Marric (Harper)
NIGHTMARE by Anne Blaisdell (Harper)
NIGHT OF WENCESLAS by Lionel Davidson (Harper)
THE WYCHERLY WOMAN by Ross Macdonald (Knopf)
THE GREEN STONE by Suzanne Blanc (Harper)

1961
THE PROGRESS OF A CRIME by Julian Symons (Harper)
THE TRACES OF BRILLHART by Herbert Brean (Harper)
THE DEVIL'S OWN by Peter Curtis (Doubleday)
WATCHER IN THE SHADOWS by Geoffrey Household (Little, Brown)

1960
THE HOURS BEFORE DAWN by Celia Fremlin (Lippincott)
THE LIST OF ADRIAN MESSENGER by Philip MacDonald (Doubleday)

1959
THE EIGHTH CIRCLE by Stanley Ellin (Random House)
A GENTLEMAN CALLED by Dorothy Salisbury Davis (Scribners)
THE MADHOUSE IN WASHINGTON SQUARE by David Alexander
    (Lippincott)
THE WOMAN IN THE WOODS by Lee Blackstock (Doubleday)

1958
ROOM TO SWING by Ed Lacy (Harper)
THE LONGEST SECOND by Bill Ballinger (Harper)
THE NIGHT OF THE GOOD CHILDREN by Marjorie Carleton (Wm.
    Morrow)
THE BUSHMAN WHO CAME BACK by Arthur Upfield (Doubleday)

1957
A DRAM OF POISON by Charlotte Armstrong (Coward-McCann)
THE MAN WHO DIDN'T FLY by Margot Bennett (Harper)

1956
BEAST IN VIEW by Margaret Millar (Random House)
THE CASE OF THE TALKING BUG by The Gordons (Doubleday)
THE TALENTED MR. RIPLEY by Patricia Highsmith (Coward-McCann)

1955
THE LONG GOODBYE by Raymond Chandler (Houghton Mifflin)

1954
BEAT NOT THE BONES by Charlotte Jay (Harper)

Best First Novel by an American Author

1994
A GRAVE TALENT by Laurie King (St. Martin's)
THE LIST OF 7 by Mark Frost (Wm. Morrow)
CRIMINAL SEDUCTION by Darian North (Dutton)
THE BALLAD OF ROCKY RUIZ by Manuel Ramos (St. Martin's)
ZADDIK by David Rosenbaum (Mysterious Press)

1993
THE BLACK ECHO by Michael Connelly (Little, Brown)
TRAIL OF MURDER by Christine Andreae (St. Martin's)
TRICK OF THE EYE by Jane Stanton Hitchcock (Dutton)
LADYSTINGER by Craig Smith (Crown)

1992
SLOW MOTION RIOT by Peter Blauner (Wm. Morrow)
DEADSTICK by Terence Faherty (St. Martin's)

DEADLINE by Marcy Heidish (St. Martin's)
ZERO AT THE BONE by Mary Willis Walker (St. Martin's)
A COOL BREEZE IN THE UNDERGROUND by Don Winslow (St. Martin's)

1991
POSTMORTEM by Patricia D. Cornwell (Scribners)
COME NIGHTFALL by Gary Amo (Pinnacle)
PASSION PLAY by W. Edward Blain (Putnam)
NOBODY LIVES FOREVER by Edna Buchanan (Random House)
DEVIL IN A BLUE DRESS by Walter Mosley (Norton)

1990
THE LAST BILLABLE HOUR by Susan Wolfe (St. Martin's)
BLOOD UNDER THE BRIDGE by Bruce Zimmerman (Harper & Row)
HIDE AND SEEK by Barry Berg (St. Martin's)
THE MOTHER SHADOW by Melodie Johnson Howe (Viking)
THE STORY OF ANNIE D. by Susan Taylor Chehak (Houghton Mifflin)

1989
CAROLINA SKELETONS by David Stout (Mysterious Press)
A GREAT DELIVERANCE by Elizabeth George (Bantam)
JULIAN SOLO by Shelly Reuben (Dodd, Mead)
MURDER ONCE DONE by Mary Lou Bennett (Perseverance Press)
THE MURDER OF FRAU SCHUTZ by J. Madison Davis (Walker)

1988
DEATH AMONG STRANGERS by Deidre S. Laiken (Macmillan)
DETECTIVE by Parnell Hall (Donald I. Fine)
HEAT LIGHTNING by John Lantigua (Putnam)
LOVER MAN by Dallas Murphy (Scribners)
THE SPOILER by Domenic Stansberry (Atlantic Monthly Press)

1987
NO ONE RIDES FOR FREE by Larry Beinhart (Wm. Morrow)
DEAD AIR by Mike Lupica (Villard)
FLOATER by Joseph Koenig (Mysterious Press)

LOST by Gary Devon (Knopf)
RICEBURNER by Richard Hyer (Scribners)

1986
WHEN THE BOUGH BREAKS by Jonathan Kellerman (Atheneum)
THE ADVENTURE OF THE ECTOPLASMIC MAN by Daniel Stashower
   (Wm. Morrow)
THE GLORY HOLE MURDERS by Tony Fennelly (Carroll & Graf)
SLEEPING DOG by Dick Lochte (Arbor House)

1985
STRIKE THREE, YOU'RE DEAD by R. D. Rosen (Walker)
A CREATIVE KIND OF KILLER by Jack Early (Franklin Watts)
FOUL SHOT by Doug Hornig (Scribners)
SOMEONE ELSE'S GRAVE by Alison Smith (St. Martin's)
SWEET, SAVAGE DEATH by Orania Papazoglou (Doubleday)

1984
THE BAY PSALM BOOK MURDER by Will Harriss (Walker)
CAROLINE MINUSCULE by Andrew Taylor (Dodd, Mead)
DEAD MAN'S THOUGHTS by Carolyn Wheat (St. Martin's)
THE GOLD SOLUTION by Herbert Resnicow (St. Martin's)
RED DIAMOND, PRIVATE EYE by Mark Schorr (St. Martin's)

1983
THE BUTCHER'S BOY by Thomas Perry (Scribners)
BY FREQUENT ANGUISH by S. F. X. Dean (Walker)
IN THE HEAT OF THE SUMMER by John Katzenbach (Atheneum)
TWO IF BY SEA by Ernest Savage (Scribners)
UNHOLY COMMUNION by Richard Hughes (Doubleday)

1982
CHIEFS by Stuart Woods (Norton)
THE BLACK GLOVE by Geoffrey Miller (Viking)
GIANT KILLER by Vernon Tom Hyman (Marek)
MURDER AT THE RED OCTOBER by Anthony Olcott (Academy
   Chicago)
NOT A THROUGH STREET by Ernest Larsen (Random House)

1981
THE WATCHER by K. Nolte Smith (Coward, McCann & Geoghegan)
WINDS OF THE OLD DAYS by Betsy Aswald (Dial)
THE REMBRANDT PANEL by Oliver Banks (Little, Brown)
DOUBLE NEGATIVE by David Carkeet (Dial)
THE OTHER ANN FLETCHER by Susanne Jaffe (NAL)

1980
THE LASKO TANGENT by Richard North Patterson (Norton)
NIGHT TRAINS by Peter Heath Fine (Lippincott)
FOLLOW THE LEADER by John Logue (Crown)

1979
KILLED IN THE RATINGS by William L. DeAndrea (Harcourt Brace Jovanovich)
THE SCOURGE by Thomas L. Dunne (Coward, McCann & Geoghegan)
FALLING ANGEL by William Hjortsberg (Harcourt Brace Jovanovich)
BLOOD SECRETS by Craig Jones (Harper & Row)
THE MEMORY OF EVA RYKER by Donald A. Stanwood (Coward, McCann & Geoghegan)

1978
A FRENCH FINISH by Robert Ross (Putnam)
DEWEY DECIMATED by Charles A. Goodrun (Crown)
THE FAN by Bob Randall (Random House)

1977
THE THOMAS BERRYMAN NUMBER by James Patterson (Little, Brown)
STRAIGHT by Steve Knickmeyer (Random House)
YOUR DAY IN THE BARREL by Alan Furst (Atheneum)
FINAL PROOF by Marie R. Reno (Harper & Row)
THE BIG PAY-OFF by Janice Law (Houghton Mifflin)

1976
THE ALVAREZ JOURNAL by Rex Burns (Harper & Row)
THE DEVALINO CAPER by A. J. Russell (Random House)
HARMATTAN by Thomas Klop (Bobbs-Merrill)
WALTZ ACROSS TEXAS by Max Crawford (Farrar, Straus & Giroux)
PAPERBACK THRILLER by Lynn Meyer (Random House)

1975
FLETCH by Gregory Mcdonald (Bobbs-Merrill)
THE JONES MAN by Vern E. Smith (Henry Regnery)
THE KREUTZMAN FORMULA by Virgil Scott and Dominic Koski (Simon & Schuster)
SATURDAY GAMES by Brown Meggs (Random House)
TARGET PRACTICE by Nicholas Meyer (Harcourt Brace Jovanovich)

1974
THE BILLION DOLLAR SURE THING by Paul E. Erdman (Scribners)
KICKED TO DEATH BY A CAMEL by Clarence Jackson (Harper & Row)
MAN ON A STRING by Michael Wolfe (Harper & Row)
MANY HAPPY RETURNS by Justin Scott (David McKay)
SOMEONE'S DEATH by Charles Larson (Lippincott)

1973
SQUAW POINT by R. H. Shimer (Harper & Row)
BOX 100 by Frank Leonard (Harper & Row)
THE DEAD OF WINTER by William H. Hallahan (Bobbs-Merrill)
THE HEART OF THE DOG by Thomas A. Roberts (Random House)
A PERSON SHOULDN'T DIE LIKE THAT by Arthur Goldstein (Random House)

1972
FINDING MAUBEE by A. H. Z. Carr (Putnam)
GYPSY IN AMBER by Martin Cruz Smith (Putnam)
ASK THE RIGHT QUESTION by Michael Z. Lewin (Putnam)

TO SPITE HER FACE by Hildegarde Dolson (Lippincott)
THE STALKER by Bill Pronzini (Random House)

1971
THE ANDERSON TAPES by Lawrence Sanders (Putnam)
INCIDENT AT 125TH STREET by J. E. Brown (Doubleday)
TAKING GARY FELDMAN by Stanley Cohen (Putnam)
THE BLESSING WAY by Tony Hillerman (Harper & Row)
THE NAKED FACE by Sidney Sheldon (Wm. Morrow)

1970
A TIME FOR PREDATORS by Joe Gores (Random House)
YOU'LL LIKE MY MOTHER by Naomi Hintze (Putnam)
QUICKSAND by Myrick Land (Harper & Row)

1969
Tie: SILVER STREET by E. Richard Johnson (Harper & Row) and
THE BAIT by Dorothy Uhnak (Simon & Schuster)
THE DINOSAUR by Lawrence Kamarck (Random House)

1968
ACT OF FEAR by Michael Collins (Dodd, Mead)
MORTISSIMO by P. E. H. Dunston (Random House)
THE KILLING SEASON by John Redgate (Trident)
THE TIGERS ARE HUNGRY by Charles Early (Wm. Morrow)
HELL GATE by James Dawson (McKay)

1967
THE COLD WAR SWAP by Ross Thomas (Morrow)
A KIND OF TREASON by Robert S. Elegant (Holt, Rinehart &
   Winston)
FANCY'S KNELL by Babs Deal (Doubleday)
THE PEDESTAL by George Lanning (Harper & Row)

1966
IN THE HEAT OF THE NIGHT by John Ball (Harper & Row)
BEFORE THE BALL WAS OVER by Alexandra Roudybush (Doubleday)

THE EXPENDABLE SPY by Jack D. Hunter (Dutton)
THE FRENCH DOLL by Vincent McConner (Hill & Wang)

1965
FRIDAY THE RABBI SLEPT LATE by Harry Kemelman (Crown)
THE GRAVEMAKER'S HOUSE by Rubin Weber (Harper & Row)
IN THE LAST ANALYSIS by Amanda Cross (Macmillan)

1964
FLORENTINE FINISH by Cornelius Hirschberg (Harper & Row)
THE PROWLER by Frances Rickett (Simon & Schuster)
THE NEON HAYSTACK by James M. Ullman (Simon & Schuster)
THE FIFTH WOMAN by H. Fagyas (Doubleday)

1963
THE FUGITIVE by Robert L. Fish (Simon & Schuster)
COUNTERWEIGHT by Daniel Broun (Holt, Rinehart & Winston)
THE CHASE by Richard Unekis (Walker)

1962
THE GREEN STONE by Suzanne Blanc (Harper)
FELONY TANK by Malcolm Braley (Gold Medal)
CLOSE HIS EYES by Olivia Dwight (Harper)
THE CIPHER by Alex Gordon (Simon & Schuster)
NIGHT OF THE KILL by Breni James (Simon & Schuster)
SHOCK TREATMENT by Winfred Van Atta (Doubleday)

1961
THE MAN IN THE CAGE by John Holbrooke Vance (Random House)
THE MERCENARIES by Donald E. Westlake (Random House)
CASE PENDING by Dell Shannon (Harper)
THE KILLING AT BIG TREE by David McCarthy (Doubleday)
THE MARRIAGE CAGE by William Johnston (Lyle Stuart)

1960
THE GREY FLANNEL SHROUD by Henry Slesar (Random House)
A DREAM OF FALLING by Mary O. Rank (Houghton Mifflin)

1959
THE BRIGHT ROAD TO FEAR by Richard Martin Stern (Ballantine)
THE MAN WHO DISAPPEARED by Edgar J. Bohle (Random House)
NOW WILL YOU TRY FOR MURDER? by Harry Olesker (Simon & Schuster)
DEATH OF A SPINSTER by Frances Duncombe (Scribners)

1958
KNOCK AND WAIT A WHILE by William Rawle Weeks (Houghton Mifflin)
BAY OF THE DAMNED by Warren Carrier (John Day)
ROOT OF EVIL by James Cross (Messner)

1957
REBECCA'S PRIDE by Donald McNutt Douglass (Harper)

1956
THE PERFECTIONIST by Lane Kauffman (Lippincott)
IN HIS BLOOD by Harold R. Daniels (Dell)
MUCH ADO ABOUT MURDER by Fred Levon (Dodd, Mead)

1955
GO, LOVELY ROSE by Jean Potts (Scribners)

1954
A KISS BEFORE DYING by Ira Levin (Simon & Schuster)

1953
DON'T CRY FOR ME by William Campbell Gault and E. P. Dutton, publisher
THE INWARD EYE by Peggy Bacon (Scribners)

1952
STRANGLE HOLD by Mary McMullen and Harper Bros., publisher
CARRY MY COFFIN SLOWLY by Lee Herrington (Simon & Schuster)
THE CHRISTMAS CARD MURDERS by David William Meredith (Knopf)

CURE IT WITH HONEY by Thurston Scott (Harper)
THE ELEVENTH HOUR by Robert B. Sinclair (Mill)

1951
NIGHTMARE IN MANHATTAN by Thomas Walsh (Little, Brown)
THE HOUSE WITHOUT A DOOR by Thomas Sterling (Simon &
    Schuster)
HAPPY HOLIDAY! by Thaddeus O'Finn (Rinehart)
STRANGERS ON A TRAIN by Patricia Highsmith (Harper)

1950
WHAT A BODY by Alan Green (Simon & Schuster)
THE INNOCENT by Evelyn Piper (Simon & Schuster)
THE DARK LIGHT by Bart Spicer (Dodd, Mead)
THE SHADOW AND THE BLOT by N. D. Lobell and G. G. Lobell
    (Harper)
THE END IS KNOWN by Geoffrey Holiday Hall (Simon & Schuster)
WALK THE DARK STREETS by William Krasner (Harper)

1949
THE ROOM UPSTAIRS by Mildred Davis and Simon & Schuster, pub-
    lisher
WILDERS WALK AWAY by Herbert Brean (Wm. Morrow)
SHOOT THE WORKS by Richard Ellington (Wm. Morrow)

1948
THE FABULOUS CLIPJOINT by Fredric Brown and E. P. Dutton &
    Co., publisher

1947
THE HORIZONTAL MAN by Helen Eustis (Harper)

1946
WATCHFUL AT NIGHT by Julius Fast (Rinehart & Co.)

Best Paperback Original

1994
DEAD FOLK'S BLUES by Steven Womack (Ballantine)
THE SERVANT'S TALE by Margaret Frazer (Jove/Berkley)
TONY'S JUSTICE by Eugene Izzi (Bantam)
BEYOND SARU by T. A. Roberts (Cliffhanger)
EVERYWHERE THAT MARY WENT by Lisa Scottoline (Harper)

1993
A COLD DAY FOR MURDER by Dana
   Stabenow (Berkley)
THE GOOD FRIDAY by Lee Harris (Fawcett)
PRINCIPAL DEFENSE by Gini Hartzmark (Ivy)
SHALLOW GRAVES by William Jefferies (Avon)
NIGHT CRUISE by Billie Sue Mosiman (Jove)

1992
DARK MAZE by Thomas Adcock (Pocket
   Books)
MURDER IN THE DOG DAYS by P. M. Carlson
   (Bantam)
CRACKING UP by Ed Naha (Pocket Books)
MIDTOWN NORTH by Christopher Newman (Fawcett)
FINE DISTINCTIONS by Deborah Valentine (Avon)

1991
THE MAN WHO WOULD BE F. SCOTT FITZGERALD by David
   Handler (Bantam)
COMEBACK by L. L. Enger (Pocket Books)
NOT A CREATURE WAS STIRRING by Jane Haddam (Bantam)
DEAD IN THE SCRUB by B. J. Oliphant (Fawcett)
SPQR by John Maddox Roberts (Avon)

1990
THE RAIN by Keith Peterson (Bantam)
A COLLECTOR OF PHOTOGRAPHS by Deborah Valentine (Bantam)
HOT WIRE by Randy Russell (Bantam)

KING OF THE HUSTLERS by Eugene Izzi (Bantam)
MANHATTAN IS MY BEAT by Jeffery Wilds Deaver (Bantam)

1989
THE TELLING OF LIES by Timothy Findley (Dell)
A RADICAL DEPARTURE by Lia Matera (Bantam)
JUDGEMENT BY FIRE by Fredrick D. Huebner (Fawcett)
PREACHER by Ted Thackrey Jr. (Jove)
TRAPDOOR by Keith Peterson (Bantam)

1988
BIMBOS OF THE DEATH SUN by Sharyn McCrumb (TSR)
BULLSHOT by Gabrielle Kraft (Pocket Books)
DEADLY INTRUSION by Walter Dillon (Bantam)
THE LONG WAY TO DIE by James N. Frey (Bantam)
THE MONKEY'S RAINCOAT by Robert Crais (Bantam)

1987
THE JUNKYARD DOG by Robert Campbell (Signet)
THE CAT WHO SAW RED by Lilian Jackson Braun (Jove)
HAZZARD by R. D. Brown (Bantam)
RONIN by Nick Christian (Tor)
SHATTERED MOON by Kate Green (Dell)

1986
PIGS GET FAT by Warren Murphy (NAL)
BLACK GRAVITY by Conall Ryan (Ballantine)
BLUE HERON by Philip Ross (Tor)
BROKEN IDOLS by Sean Flannery (Charter)
POVERTY BAY by Earl W. Emerson (Avon)

1985
GRANDMASTER by Warren Murphy and Molly Cochran (Pinnacle)
BLACK KNIGHT IN RED SQUARE by Stuart M. Kaminsky (Charter)
THE KEYS TO BILLY TILLIO by Eric Blau (Pinnacle)
THE SEVENTH SACRAMENT by Roland Cutler (Dell)
WORDS CAN KILL by Kenn Davis (Fawcett Crest)

1984
MRS. WHITE by Margaret Tracy (Dell)
FALSE PROPHETS by Sean Flannery (Charter)
HUNTER by Eric Sauter (Avon)
KILL FACTOR by Richard Harper (Fawcett)
TRACE by Warren Murphy (Signet)

1983
TRIANGLE by Teri White (Ace/Charter)
CLANDESTINE by James Ellroy (Avon)
THE MISSING AND THE DEAD by Jack Lynch (Fawcett)
VITAL SIGNS by Ralph Burrows, M.D. (Fawcett)

1982
THE OLD DICK by L. A. Morse (Avon)
DEAD HEAT by Ray Obstfeld (Charter)
DEADLINE by John Dunning (Fawcett)
PIN by Andrew Neiderman (Pocket)
THE UNFORGIVEN by Patricia J. MacDonald (Dell)

1981
PUBLIC MURDERS by Bill Granger (Jove)
TOUGH LUCK, L.A. by Murray Sinclair (Pinnacle)
BLOOD INNOCENTS by Thomas H. Cook (Playboy)
LOOKING FOR GINGER NORTH by John Dunning (Fawcett)

1980
THE HOG MURDERS by William L. DeAndrea (Avon)
THE KREMLIN CONSPIRACY by Sean Flannery (Charter)
VORTEX by David Heller (Avon)
THE QUEEN IS DEAD by Glen Keger (Jove)
THE INFERNAL DEVICE by Michael Kurland (New American Library)

1979
DECEIT AND DEADLY LIES by Frank Bandy (Charter)
STUD GAME by David Anthony (Pocket Books)
THE SWITCH by Elmore Leonard (Bantam)
HEARTSTONE by Philip Margolin (Pocket Books)
CHARNEL HOUSE by Graham Masterton (Pinnacle)

1978
THE QUARK MANEUVER by Mike Jahn (Ballantine)
TIME TO MURDER AND CREATE by Lawrence Block (Dell)
THEY'VE KILLED ANNA by Mark Olden (Signet)
THE TERRORIZERS by Donald Hamilton (Gold Medal)

1977
CONFESS, FLETCH by Gregory Mcdonald (Avon)
THE CAPTIVE CITY by Daniel Da Cruz (Ballantine)
FREEZE FRAME by R. R. Irvine (Popular Library)
THE DARK SIDE by Kenn Davis and John Stanley (Avon)
THE RETALIATORS by Donald Hamilton (Fawcett)

1976
AUTOPSY by John R. Feegel (Avon)
THE ASSASSINATION by David Vowell (Bantam)
THE MIDAS COFFIN by Simon Quinn (Dell)
CHARLIE'S BACK IN TOWN by Jacqueline Park (Popular Library)
THE SET-UP by Robin Moore and Milt Machlin (Pyramid)

1975
THE CORPSE THAT WALKED by Roy Winsor (Fawcett)
FLATS FIXED—AMONG OTHER THINGS by Don Tracy (Pocket
    Books)
THE GRAVY TRAIN HIT by Curtis Stevens (Dell)
JUMP CUT by R. R. Irvine (Popular Library)
WHO KILLED MR. GARLAND'S MISTRESS? by Richard Forrest
    (Pinnacle)

1974
DEATH OF AN INFORMER by Will Perry (Pyramid)
THE BIG FIX by Roger L. Simon (Straight Arrow)
DEADLOCKED! by Leo P. Kelley (Gold Medal)
THE MEDITERRANEAN CAPER by Clive Cussler (Pyramid)
STARLING STREET by Dinah Palmtag (Dell)

1973
THE INVADER by Richard Wormser (Gold Medal)
NOT DEAD YET by Daniel Banko (Gold Medal)

POWER KILL by Charles Runyon (Gold Medal)
THE SMITH CONSPIRACY by Richard Neely (Signet)

1972
FOR MURDER I CHARGE MORE by Frank McAuliffe (Ballantine)
THE WHITE WOLVERINE CONTRACT by Philip Atlee (Gold Medal)
SPACE FOR HIRE by William F. Nolan (Lancer Books)
NOR SPELL, NOR CHARM by Alicen White (Lancer Books)
AND THE DEEP BLUE SEA by Charles Williams (Signet)

1971
FLASHPOINT by Dan J. Marlowe (Gold Medal)
THE DROWNING by Jack Ehrlich (Pocket Books)
O.D. AT SWEET CLAUDE'S by Matt Gattzden (Belmont)
AFTER THINGS FELL APART by Ron Goulart (Ace)
GRAVE DESCEND by John Lange (Signet)
MAFIOSO by Peter McCurtin (Belmont)

1970
THE DRAGON'S EYE by Scott C. S. Stone (Gold Medal)
ASSAULT ON MING by Alan Caillou (Avon)
THE SOUR LEMON SCORE by Richard Stark (Gold Medal)
THE GOVERNESS by Elsie Cromwell (Paperback Library)
A PLAGUE OF SPIES by Michael Kurland (Pyramid)

Best Short Story

1994
"Keller's Therapy" by Lawrence Block (PLAYBOY, May '93)
"The Ghost Show" by Doug Allyn (ELLERY QUEEN'S MYSTERY
    MAGAZINE, December '93)
"Mefisto in Onyx" by Harlan Ellison (OMNI, October '93)
"McIntyre's Donald" by Joseph Hansen (BOHANNON'S COUNTRY:
    MYSTERY STORIES, Viking)
"Enduring as Dust" by Bruce Holland Rogers (DANGER IN D.C,
    Donald I. Fine)

1993
"Mary, Mary, Shut the Door" by Benjamin M. Schutz (DEADLY
ALLIES, Doubleday)
"Candles in the Rain" by Doug Allyn (ELLERY QUEEN'S MYSTERY
MAGAZINE, November '92)
"Howler" by Jo Bannister (ELLERY QUEEN'S MYSTERY MAGAZINE,
October '92)
"Louise" by Max Allan Collins (DEADLY ALLIES, Doubleday)
"One Hit Wonder" by Gabrielle Kraft (SISTERS IN CRIME 5, Berkley)

1992
"Nine Sons" by Wendy Hornsby (SISTERS IN CRIME 4, Berkley)
"Sleeper" by Doug Allyn (ELLERY QUEEN'S MYSTERY MAGAZINE, May
'91)
"A Blow for Freedom" by Lawrence Block (PLAYBOY, October '91)
"Spasmo" by Liza Cody (A CLASSIC ENGLISH CRIME, Mysterious
Press)
"Dreaming in Black and White" by Susan Schwartz (PSYCHO-PATHS,
Tor)

1991
"Elvis Lives" by Lynne Barrett (ELLERY QUEEN'S MYSTERY
MAGAZINE September '90)
"Answers to Soldiers" by Lawrence Block (PLAYBOY, June '90)
"Prisoners" by Ed Gorman (NEW CRIMES, Carroll & Graf)
"A Poison That Leaves No Trace" by Sue Grafton (SISTERS IN CRIME
2, Berkley)
"Challenge the Widow-Maker" by Clark Howard (ELLERY QUEEN'S
MYSTERY MAGAZINE, August '90)

1990
"Too Many Crooks" by Donald E. Westlake (PLAYBOY, August '89)
"Afraid All the Time" by Nancy Pickard (SISTERS IN CRIME, Berkley)
"For Loyal Service" by Stephen Wasylyk (ALFRED HITCHCOCK
MYSTERY MAGAZINE, August '89)
"Ted Bundy's Father" by Ruth Graviros (ELLERY QUEEN'S MYSTERY
MAGAZINE, November '89)

"The Girl and the Gator" by Robert Halsted (ALFRED HITCHCOCK MYSTERY MAGAZINE, December '89)

1989
"Flicks" by Bill Crenshaw (ALFRED HITCHCOCK MYSTERY MAGAZINE, August '88)

"Bridey's Caller" by Judith O'Neill (ALFRED HITCHCOCK MYSTERY MAGAZINE, May '88)

"Déjà Vu" by Doug Allyn (ALFRED HITCHCOCK MYSTERY MAGAZINE, June '88)

"Incident in a Neighborhood Tavern" by Bill Pronzini (AN EYE FOR JUSTICE, Mysterious Press)

"The Alley" by Stephen Wasylyk (ALFRED HITCHCOCK MYSTERY MAGAZINE, November '88)

1988
"Soft Monkey" by Harlan Ellison (MYSTERY SCENE READER, Fedora, Inc.)

"Breakfast Television" by Robert Barnard (ELLERY QUEEN'S MYSTERY MAGAZINE, January '87)

"Mr. Felix" by Paula Gosling (ELLERY QUEEN'S MYSTERY MAGAZINE, July '87)

"Stroke of Genius" by George Baxt (ELLERY QUEEN'S MYSTERY MAGAZINE, June '87)

Harlan Ellison.

"The Au Pair Girl" by Joyce Harrington (MATTER OF CRIME #1, Harcourt Brace Jovanovich)

1987
"Rain in Pinton County" by Robert Sampson (NEW BLACK MASK, May '86)

"Body Count" by Wayne D. Dundee (MEAN STREETS, Mysterious Press)

"Christmas Cop" by Thomas Adcock (ELLERY QUEEN'S MYSTERY MAGAZINE, November '86)

"Driven" by Brendan DuBois (ELLERY QUEEN'S MYSTERY MAGAZINE, November '86)

"The Puddle Diver" by Doug Allyn (ALFRED HITCHCOCK MYSTERY MAGAZINE, October '86)

1986
"Ride the Lightning" by John Lutz (ALFRED HITCHCOCK MYSTERY MAGAZINE, January '85)

"There Goes Ravelaar" by Janwillem van de Wetering (ELLERY QUEEN'S MYSTERY MAGAZINE, January '85)

"Trouble in Paradise" by Arthur Lyons (NEW BLACK MASK, January '85)

"What's in a Name?" by Robert Barnard (ELLERY QUEEN'S MYSTERY MAGAZINE, June '85)

"Yellow One-Eyed Cat" by Robert Twohy (ELLERY QUEEN'S MYSTERY MAGAZINE, May '85)

1985
"By Dawn's Early Light" by Lawrence Block (PLAYBOY, August '84)

"After I'm Gone" by Donald E. Westlake (ELLERY QUEEN'S MYSTERY MAGAZINE, June '84)

"Breakfast at Ojai" by Robert Twohy (ELLERY QUEEN'S MYSTERY MAGAZINE, September '84)

"The Reluctant Detective" by Michael Z. Lewin (THE EYES HAVE IT, Mysterious Press)

"Season Pass" by Chet Williamson (ALFRED HITCHCOCK MYSTERY MAGAZINE, October '84)

1984
"The New Girlfriend" by Ruth Rendell (ELLERY QUEEN'S MYSTERY MAGAZINE, August '83)

"The Anderson Boy" by Joseph Hansen (ELLERY QUEEN'S MYSTERY MAGAZINE, September '83)

"Big Boy, Little Boy" by Simon Brett (ELLERY QUEEN'S MYSTERY MAGAZINE, July '83)

"Graffiti" by Stanley Ellin (ELLERY QUEEN'S MYSTERY MAGAZINE, March '83)

"Puerto Rican Blues" by Clark Howard (ELLERY QUEEN'S MYSTERY MAGAZINE, April '83)

1983
"There Are No Snakes in Ireland" by Frederick Forsyth (NO COMEBACKS, Viking)

"A Decent Price for a Painting" by James Holding (ELLERY QUEEN'S MYSTERY MAGAZINE, August '82)

"All the Heroes Are Dead" by Clark Howard (ELLERY QUEEN'S MYSTERY MAGAZINE, December '82)

"Tall Tommy and the Millionaire" by S. S. Rafferty (ALFRED HITCHCOCK MYSTERY MAGAZINE, September '82)

1982
"The Absence of Emily" by Jack Ritchie (ELLERY QUEEN'S MYSTERY MAGAZINE, January '81)

"A Token of Appreciation" by Donald Olson (ALFRED HITCHCOCK MYSTERY MAGAZINE, June '81)

"The Miracle Day" by Ernest Savage (ELLERY QUEEN'S MYSTERY MAGAZINE, February '81)

"Mousie" by Robert Twohy (ELLERY QUEEN'S MYSTERY MAGAZINE, November '81)

"Seeds of Murder" by Nan Hamilton (ALFRED HITCHCOCK MYSTERY MAGAZINE, December '81)

1981
"Horn Man" by Clark Howard (ELLERY QUEEN'S MYSTERY MAGAZINE, July '80)

"The Most Dangerous Man Alive" by Edward D. Hoch (ELLERY QUEEN'S MYSTERY MAGAZINE, May '80)

"Until You Are Dead" by John Lutz (ELLERY QUEEN'S MYSTERY MAGAZINE, January '80)

"The Choirboy" by William Bankier (ALFRED HITCHCOCK MYSTERY MAGAZINE, December '80)

1980
"Armed and Dangerous" by Geoffrey Norman (ESQUIRE, March '79)

"Used in Evidence" by Frederick Forsyth (PLAYBOY, December '79)

"Scrimshaw" by Brian Garfield (ELLERY QUEEN'S MYSTERY MAGAZINE, December '79)

"The Boiler" by Julian Symons (ELLERY QUEEN'S MYSTERY MAGAZINE, November '79)

"The Imperial Ice House" by Paul Theroux (ATLANTIC MONTHLY, April '79)

1979
"The Cloud Beneath the Eaves" by Barbara Owens (ELLERY QUEEN'S MYSTERY MAGAZINE, January '78)
"Going Backward" by David Ely (ELLERY QUEEN'S MYSTERY MAGAZINE, November '78)
"Strangers in the Fog" by Bill Pronzini (ELLERY QUEEN'S MYSTERY MAGAZINE, June '78)
"The Closed Door" by Thomas Walsh (ELLERY QUEEN'S MYSTERY MAGAZINE, May '78)
"This Is Death" by Donald E. Westlake (ELLERY QUEEN'S MYSTERY MAGAZINE, November '78)

1978
"Chance After Chance" by Thomas Walsh (ELLERY QUEEN'S MYSTERY MAGAZINE, November '77)
"The Last Rendezvous" by Jean Backus (ELLERY QUEEN'S MYSTERY MAGAZINE, September '77)
"Jode's Last Hunt" by Brian Garfield (ELLERY QUEEN'S MYSTERY MAGAZINE, January '77)
"The Problem of Li T'ang" by Geoffrey Bush (ATLANTIC MONTHLY, August '77)
"The Johore Murders" by Paul Theroux (ATLANTIC MONTHLY, March '77)

1977
"Like a Terrible Scream" by Etta Revesz (ELLERY QUEEN'S MYSTERY MAGAZINE, May '76)
"Nobody Tells Me Anything" by Jack Ritchie (ELLERY QUEEN'S MYSTERY MAGAZINE, October '76)
"Lavender Lady" by Barbara Callahan (ELLERY QUEEN'S MYSTERY MAGAZINE, April '76)
"Crazy Old Lady" by Avram Davidson (ELLERY QUEEN'S MYSTERY MAGAZINE, March '76)
"People Don't Do Such Things" by Ruth Rendell (THE FALLEN CURTAIN, Doubleday)

1976
"The Jail" by Jesse Hill Ford (PLAYBOY, March '75)

"The Fall of the Coin" by Ruth Rendell (ELLERY QUEEN'S MYSTERY MAGAZINE June '75*)*

"The Many-Flavored Crime" by Jack Ritchie (MYSTERY DIGEST MAGAZINE, December '75*)*

"Old Friends" by Dorothy Salisbury Davis (ELLERY QUEEN'S MYSTERY MAGAZINE, September '75)

"Night Crawlers" by Joyce Harrington (ELLERY QUEEN'S MYSTERY MAGAZINE, January '75)

1975
"The Fallen Curtain" by Ruth Rendell (ELLERY QUEEN'S MYSTERY MAGAZINE, August '74)

"The Cabin in the Hollow" by Joyce Harrington (ELLERY QUEEN'S MYSTERY MAGAZINE, October '74)

"The Game" by Thomasina Weber (KILLERS OF THE MIND, Random House)

"The Light in the Cottage" by David Ely (PLAYBOY, October '74)

"A Night Out with the Boys" by Elsin Ann Gardner (ELLERY QUEEN'S MYSTERY MAGAZINE, February '74)

"Screams and Echoes" by Donald Olson (ELLERY QUEEN'S MYSTERY MAGAZINE, August '74)

1974
"The Whimper of Whipped Dogs" by Harlan Ellison (BAD MOON RISING, Thomas M. Disch)

"Do with Me What You Will" by Joyce Carol Oates (PLAYBOY, June '73)

"The Ghosts at Iron River" by Chelsea Quinn Yarbro (MEN & MALICE, Doubleday)

"The O'Bannon Blarney File" by Joe Gores (MEN & MALICE, Doubleday)

"Fifty Years After" by Anthony Gilbert (ELLERY QUEEN'S MYSTERY MAGAZINE, March '73)

1973
"The Purple Shroud" by Joyce Harrington (ELLERY QUEEN'S MYSTERY MAGAZINE, September '72)

"Celestine" by George Bradshaw (LADIES' HOME JOURNAL, October '72)

"Frightened Lady" by C. B. Gilford (ALFRED HITCHCOCK MYSTERY MAGAZINE, July '72)

"Hijack" by Robert L. Fish (PLAYBOY, August '72)

"Island of Bright Birds" by John Christopher (ELLERY QUEEN'S MYSTERY MAGAZINE, February '72)

1972
"Moonlight Gardener" by Robert L. Fish (ARGOSY, December '71)

"Sardinian Incident" by Evan Hunter (PLAYBOY, October '71)

"My Daughter is Dead" by Pauline C. Smith (ALFRED HITCHCOCK MYSTERY MAGAZINE, November '71)

"The Spivvleton Mystery" by Katherine Anne Porter (LADIES' HOME JOURNAL, August '71)

1971
"In the Forests of Riga the Beasts Are Very Wild Indeed" by Margery Finn Brown (MCCALL'S, July '70)

"Miss Paisley on a Diet" by John Peirce (ELLERY QUEEN'S MYSTERY MAGAZINE, February '70)

"Door to a Different World" by Anthony Gilbert (ELLERY QUEEN'S MYSTERY MAGAZINE, March '70)

1970
"Goodbye, Pops" by Joe Gores (ELLERY QUEEN'S MYSTERY MAGAZINE, December '69)

"Double Entry" by Robert L. Fish (ELLERY QUEEN'S MYSTERY MAGAZINE, January '69)

"Death's Door" by Robert McNear (PLAYBOY, March '69)

"Poison in the Cup" by Christianna Brand (ELLERY QUEEN'S MYSTERY MAGAZINE, February '69)

"Promise of Oranges" by Duveen Polk (GOOD HOUSEKEEPING, February '69)

1969
"The Man Who Fooled the World" by Warner Law (SATURDAY EVENING POST, August 24, '68)

"The Last Bottle in the World" by Stanley Ellin (ELLERY QUEEN'S

MYSTERY MAGAZINE, February '68)
"Crooked Bone" by Gerald Kersh
   (SATURDAY EVENING POST, August 10,
   '68)
"Success of a Mission" by William Arden
   (ARGOSY, April '68)
"Moment of Power" by P. D. James (ELLERY
   QUEEN'S MYSTERY MAGAZINE, July '68)

1968
"The Oblong Room" by Edward D. Hoch
   (THE SAINT, July '67)
"Twist for Twist" by Christianna Brand
   (ELLERY QUEEN'S MYSTERY MAGAZINE,
   May '67)

Robert L. Fish
(1912–81).

"Dare I Weep? Dare I Mourn?" by John le Carré (SATURDAY EVENING
   POST, January 28, '67)
"The Salad Maker" by Robert McNear (ELLERY QUEEN'S MYSTERY
   MAGAZINE, June '67)

1967
"The Chosen One" by Rhys Davies (THE NEW YORKER, June 4, '66)
"Master of the Hounds" by Algis Budrys (SATURDAY EVENING POST,
   August 27, '66)
"The Hochmann Miniatures" by Robert L. Fish (ARGOSY, March '66)
"The Splintered Monday" by Charlotte Armstrong (ELLERY QUEEN'S
   MYSTERY MAGAZINE, March '66)

1966
"The Possibility of Evil" by Shirley Jackson (SATURDAY EVENING
   POST, December 18, '65)
"Foxer" by Brian Cleeve (SATURDAY EVENING POST, December 18,
   '65)
"The Case for Miss Peacock" by Charlotte Armstrong (ELLERY
   QUEEN'S MYSTERY MAGAZINE, February '65)
"Who Walks Behind" by Holly Roth (ELLERY QUEEN'S MYSTERY
   MAGAZINE, September '65)

1965
"H as in Homicide" by Lawrence Treat (ELLERY QUEEN'S MYSTERY MAGAZINE, March '64)

"A Soliloquy in Tongues" by William Wiser (COSMOPOLITAN, May '64)

"The Purple Is Everything" by Dorothy Salisbury Davis (ELLERY QUEEN'S MYSTERY MAGAZINE, June '64)

1964
"Man Gehorcht" by Leslie Ann Brownrigg (STORY MAGAZINE, Janauary–February '63)

"The Crime of Ezechiele Coen" by Stanley Ellin (ELLERY QUEEN'S MYSTERY MAGAZINE, November '63)

"The Ballad of Jesse Neighbors" by William Humphrey (ESQUIRE, September '63)

1963
"The Sailing Club" by David Ely (COSMOPOLITAN, October '62)

"The Terrapin" by Patricia Highsmith (ELLERY QUEEN'S MYSTERY MAGAZINE, October '62)

"An Order" by Carl Erik Soya (STORY MAGAZINE, October '62)

1962
"Affair at Lahore Cantonment" by Avram Davidson (ELLERY QUEEN'S MYSTERY MAGAZINE, June '61)

"The Children of Alda Nuova" by Robert Wallston (ELLERY QUEEN'S MYSTERY MAGAZINE, August '61)

THE ELLERY QUEEN 1962 ANTHOLOGY edited by Ellery Queen (Davis Publications, '61)

1961
"Tiger" by John Durham (COSMOPOLITAN, February '60)

"A Real Live Murderer" by Donald Honig (ALFRED HITCHCOCK MYSTERY MAGAZINE, October '60)

"Summer Evil" by Nora Kaplan (ALFRED HITCHCOCK MYSTERY MAGAZINE, October '60)

"A View From the Terrace" by Mike Marmer (COSMOPOLITAN, December '60)

"Louisa, Please" by Shirley Jackson (LADIES' HOME JOURNAL, February '60)

1960
"The Landlady" by Roald Dahl (THE NEW YORKER, November '59)
"The Day of the Bullet" by Stanley Ellin (ELLERY QUEEN'S MYSTERY MAGAZINE, October '59)

1959
"Over There, Darkness" by William O'Farrell (SLEUTH, October '58)

1958
"The Secret of the Bottle" by Gerald Kersh (SATURDAY EVENING POST, December 7, '57)
"And Already Lost" by Charlotte Armstrong (ELLERY QUEEN'S MYSTERY MAGAZINE, June '57)

1957
"The Blessington Method" by Stanley Ellin (ELLERY QUEEN'S MYSTERY MAGAZINE, June '56)
"The Gentlest of the Brothers" by David Alexander (ELLERY QUEEN'S MYSTERY MAGAZINE, February '56)
"The Last Spin" by Evan Hunter (MANHUNT, September '56)

1956
"Dream No More" by Philip MacDonald (ELLERY QUEEN'S MYSTERY MAGAZINE, November '55)
"Invitation to an Accident" by Wade Miller (ELLERY QUEEN'S MYSTERY MAGAZINE, July '55)

Stanley Ellin (1916–86).

1955

"The House Party" by Stanley Ellin (ELLERY QUEEN'S MYSTERY
MAGAZINE, May '54)

1954

SOMEONE LIKE YOU by Roald Dahl (Knopf)

1953

SOMETHING TO HIDE by Philip MacDonald (Doubleday)

1952

FANCIES AND GOODNIGHTS by John Collier (Doubleday)

TWENTY GREAT TALES OF MURDER by Helen McCloy and
Brett Halliday (Random House)

THE MEMOIRS OF SOLAR
PONS by August Derleth
(Mycroft and Moran)

HANDBOOK FOR POISONERS
by Raymond T. Bond
(Rinehart & Co.)

FULL CARGO by Wilbur
Daniel Steele (Doubleday)

1951

DIAGNOSIS: HOMICIDE by
Lawrence G. Blochman
(Lippincott)

A Scroll for excellence to
Q. Patrick

1950

Ellery Queen for ten years'
service through ELLERY
QUEEN'S MYSTERY
MAGAZINE

William Faulkner

In addition to forming one of the most
successful writing partnerships in mystery
fiction, Frederic Dannay and Manfred B.
Lee also helped found *Ellery Queen's
Mystery Magazine.*

1949
William Irish, for the sustained excellence of his short stories in magazines and DEADMAN BLUES and THE BLUE RIBBON (Lippincott)
Ellery Queen, nominee

1948
Ellery Queen for editing numerous anthologies and ELLERY QUEEN'S MYSTERY MAGAZINE

Best Fact Crime

1994
UNTIL THE TWELFTH OF NEVER by Bella Stumbo (Pocket Books)
LINDBERGH: THE CRIME by Noel Behn (Atlantic Monthly/Grove)
FINAL JUSTICE by Steven Naifeh and Gregory White Smith (Dutton)
THE MISBEGOTTEN SON by Jack Olsen (Delacorte)
GONE IN THE NIGHT by David Protess and Rob Warden (Delacorte)

1993
SWIFT JUSTICE by Harry Farrell (St. Martin's)
THE TRUNK MURDERESS: WINNIE RUTH JUDD by Jana Bommersbach (Simon & Schuster)
BLOOD ECHOES by Thomas H. Cook (Dutton)
EVERYTHING SHE EVER WANTED by Ann Rule (Simon & Schuster)
MY HUSBAND'S TRYING TO KILL ME by Jim Schutze (HarperCollins)

1992
HOMICIDE: A YEAR ON THE KILLING STREETS by David Simon (Houghton Mifflin)
WITNESSES FROM THE GRAVE: THE STORIES BONES TELL by Christopher Joyce and Eric Stover (Little, Brown)
BOSS OF BOSSES: THE FALL OF THE GODFATHER: THE FBI AND PAUL CASTELLANO by Joseph F. O'Brien and Andris Kurins (Simon & Schuster)
DEN OF THIEVES by James B. Stewart (Simon & Schuster)
DEATH OF ELVIS: WHAT REALLY HAPPENED by Charles C. Thompson II and James P. Cole (Delacorte)

1991
IN A CHILD'S NAME by Peter Maas (Simon & Schuster)
GOOMBATA by John Cummings and Ernest Volkman (Little, Brown)
BEYOND REASON by Ken Englade (St. Martin's)
A DEATH IN WHITE BEAR LAKE by Barry Siegel (Bantam)

1990
DOC: THE RAPE OF THE TOWN OF LOVELL by Jack Olsen
  (Atheneum)
THE BLOODING: THE TRUE STORY OF THE NARBOROUGH VILLAGE
  MURDERS by Joseph Wambaugh (Perigord/Morrow)
WASTED: THE PREPPIE MURDER by Linda Wolfe (Simon & Schuster)
THE DEATH SHIFT: THE TRUE STORY OF NURSE GENENE JONES AND
  THE TEXAS BABY MURDERS by Peter Elkind (Viking)
MURDER IN LITTLE EGYPT by Darcy O'Brien (Wm. Morrow)

1989
IN BROAD DAYLIGHT by Harry N. MacLean (Harper & Row)
A GATHERING OF SAINTS by Robert Lindsey (Simon & Schuster)
MONKEY ON A STICK by John Hubner and Lindsey Gruson (Harcourt
  Brace Jovanovich)
FAMILY OF SPIES: INSIDE THE JOHN WALKER SPY RING by Pete Earley
  (Bantam)
THE COCAINE WARS by Paul Eddy with Hugo Sabogal and Sara
  Walden (Norton)

1988
CBS MURDERS by Richard Hammer (Wm. Morrow)
DREAMS OF ADA by Robert Mayer (Viking)
ENGAGED TO MURDER by Loretta Schwartz-Nobel (Viking)
THE MAN WHO ROBBED THE PIERRE by Ira Berkow (Atheneum)
TALKED TO DEATH by Stephen Singular (Beechtree Books/Morrow)

1987
CARELESS WHISPERS: THE TRUE STORY OF A TRIPLE MURDER AND
  THE DETERMINED LAWMAN WHO WOULDN'T GIVE UP by Carlton
  Stowers (Taylor)
INCIDENT AT BIG SKY: SHERIFF JOHNNY FRANCE AND THE MOUNTAIN
  MEN by Johnny France and Malcolm McConnell (Norton)

THE POISON TREE: A TRUE STORY OF FAMILY VIOLENCE AND
  REVENGE by Alan Prendergast (Putnam)
UNVEILING CLAUDIA: A TRUE STORY OF SERIAL MURDER by Daniel
  Keyes (Bantam)
WISEGUY: LIFE IN A MAFIA FAMILY by Nicholas Pileggi (Simon &
  Schuster)

1986
**SAVAGE GRACE by Natalie Robins and Steven M. L. Aronson (Wm.
  Morrow)**
THE AIRMAN AND THE CARPENTER: THE LINDBERGH KIDNAPPING
  AND THE FRAMING OF RICHARD HAUPTMANN by Ludovic Kennedy
  (Viking)
AT MOTHER'S REQUEST: A TRUE STORY OF MONEY, MURDER AND
  BETRAYAL by Jonathan Coleman (Atheneum)
THE MURDER OF A SHOPPING BAG LADY by Brian Kates (Harcourt
  Brace Jovanovich)
NUTCRACKER: MONEY, MADNESS, MURDER: A FAMILY ALBUM by
  Shana Alexander (Doubleday)
SOMEBODY'S HUSBAND, SOMEBODY'S SON: THE STORY OF THE
  YORKSHIRE RIPPER by Gordon Burn (Viking)

1985
**DOUBLE PLAY: THE SAN FRANCISCO CITY HALL KILLINGS by Mike
  Weiss (Addison-Wesley)**
EARTH TO EARTH by John Cornwell (Ecco Press)
EVIDENCE OF LOVE: A TRUE STORY OF PASSION AND DEATH IN THE
  SUBURBS by John Bloom and Jim Atkinson (Texas Monthly Press)
THE MOLINEUX AFFAIR by Jane Pejsa (Kenwood Publishing)
MURDER AT THE MET by David Black (Dial Press)

1984
VERY MUCH A LADY by Shana Alexander (Little, Brown)
DEADLY FORCE by Lawrence O'Donnell, Jr. (Wm. Morrow)
JUDGEMENT DAY by Bob Lancaster and B. C. Hall (Seaview Putman)
SON by Jack Olsen (Atheneum)
THE VON BULOW AFFAIR by William Wright (Delacorte)

1983
THE VATICAN CONNECTION by Richard Hammer (Holt, Rinehart & Winston)

BIG BUCKS by Ernest Tidyman (Norton)

DEADLY INTENTIONS by William Randolph Stevens (Congdon & Weed)

INDECENT EXPOSURE by David McClintock (Wm. Morrow)

SOMEBODY IS LYING: THE STORY OF DOCTOR X. by Myron Farber (Doubleday)

1982
THE STING MAN by Robert W. Greene (Dutton)

BY REASON OF DOUBT by Ellen Godfrey (Clarke, Irwin & Co.)

THE DAY THEY STOLE THE MONA LISA by Seymour V. Reit (Summit)

THE MINDS OF BILLY MILLIGAN by Daniel Keyes (Random House)

PAPA'S GAME by Gregory Wallance (Rawson Wade)

1981
A TRUE DELIVERANCE by Fred Harwell (Knopf)

ASSASSINATION OF EMBASSY ROW by John Dinges and Saul Landeau (Pantheon)

THE TRIAL OF POLICEMAN THOMAS SHEA by Thomas Hawser (Viking)

1980
THE FALCON AND THE SNOWMAN by Robert Lindsey (Simon & Schuster)

ANYONE'S DAUGHTER by Shana Alexander (Viking)

BLOOD WILL TELL by Gary Cartwright (Harcourt Brace Jovanovich)

SENTENCED TO DIE by Stephen H. Gettinger (Macmillan)

ZEBRA by Clark Howard (Marek)

1979
TIL DEATH DO US PART by Vincent Bugliosi and Ken Hurwitz (Norton)

WHY HAVE THEY TAKEN OUR CHILDREN? by Jack W. Baugh and Jefferson Morgan (Delacorte)

CRIMINAL VIOLENCE by Charles Silberman (Random House)
PERJURY by Alan Weinstein (Knopf)

1978
BY PERSONS UNKNOWN by George Jonas and Barbara Amiel (Grove Press)
CLOSING TIME by Lacey Fosburgh (Delacorte)
SIX AGAINST THE ROCK by Clark Howard (Dial Press)
THE VOICE OF GUNS by Vin McLellan and Paul Avery (Putnam)
JUSTICE CRUCIFIED by Roberta S. Feuerlicht (McGraw-Hill)

1977
BLOOD AND MONEY by Thomas Thompson (Doubleday)
THE MICHIGAN MURDERS by Edward Keyes (Reader's Digest Press)
MURDER IN COWETA COUNTY by Margaret Anne Barnes (Reader's Digest Press)

1976
A TIME TO DIE by Tom Wicker (Quadrangle NY Times)
INVITATION TO A LYNCHING by Gene Miller (Doubleday)
THE HOUSE ON GARIBALDI STREET by Isser Harel (Viking)

1975
HELTER SKELTER by Vincent Bugliosi and Curt Gentry (Norton)
THE MEMPHIS MURDERS by Gerald Meyer (Seabury Press)
DUMMY by Ernest Tidyman (Little, Brown)

1974
LEGACY OF DEATH by Barbara Levy (Prentice-Hall)
THE IMPLOSION CONSPIRACY by Louis Nizer (Doubleday)
THE MEDICAL DETECTIVES by Paulette Cooper (David McKay)
THE PROFESSION OF VIOLENCE by John Pearson (Saturday Review Press)
BURDEN OF PROOF by Ed Cray (Macmillan)

1973
HOAX by Stephen Fay, Lewis Chester, and Magnus Linkletter (Viking)

THE SANTA CLAUS BANK ROBBERY by A. C. Greene (Knopf)

SHIPWRECK by Gordon Thomas and Max Morgan Witts (Stein & Day)

THEY GOT TO FIND ME GUILTY YET by T. P. Slattery (Doubleday)

1972
BEYOND A REASONABLE DOUBT by Sandor Frankel (Stein & Day)

THE DISAPPEARENCE OF DR. PARKMAN by Robert Sullivan (Little, Brown)

THE GIRL ON THE VOLKSWAGEN FLOOR by William A. Clark (Harper & Row)

1971
A GREAT FALL by Mildred Savage (Simon & Schuster)

THE NINTH JUROR by Girard Chester (Random House)

CRIME IN AMERICA by Ramsey Clark (Simon & Schuster)

1970
THE CASE THAT WILL NOT DIE by Herbert B. Ehrmann (Little, Brown)

SCOTTSBORO by Don T. Carter (Louisiana State University Press)

THE VICTIMS by Bernard Lefkowitz and Kenneth Gross (Putnam)

WHITMORE by Fred C. Shapiro (Bobbs-Merrill)

1969
POE THE DETECTIVE by John Walsh (Rutgers University Press)

THE MULBERRY TREE by John Frasca (Prentice-Hall)

THREE SISTERS IN BLACK by Norman Zierold (Little, Brown)

1968
A PRIVATE DISGRACE by Victoria Lincoln (Putnam)

BLACK MARKET MEDICINE by Margaret Kreig (Prentice-Hall)

JUSTICE IN THE BACK ROOM by Selwyn Raab (World Publishing Co.)

FRAME-UP by Curt Gentry (Norton)

1967
THE BOSTON STRANGLER by Gerold Frank (New American Library)

CRIME AND DETECTION by Julian Symons (Crown)
THE LAST TWO TO HANG by Elwyn Jones (Stein & Day)

1966
IN COLD BLOOD by Truman Capote (Random House)
A LITTLE GIRL IS DEAD by Harry Golden (World)
THE POWER OF LIFE AND DEATH by Michael V. DiSalle with
   Lawrence G. Blochman (Random House)
MURDERERS SANE AND MAD by Miriam Allen deFord (Abelard-
   Schuman)
THE CENTURY OF THE DETECTIVE by Jurgen Thorwald (Harcourt,
   Brace & World)

1965
GIDEON'S TRUMPET by Anthony Lewis (Random House)
THE MINISTER AND THE CHOIR SINGER by William Kunstler (Wm.
   Morrow)
THE HONORED SOCIETY by Norman Lewis (Putnam)
THE MOLLY MAGUIRES by Wayne G. Broehl Jr. (Harvard University
   Press)
LAMENT FOR THE MOLLY MAGUIRES by Arthur H. Lewis (Harcourt,
   Brace & World)

1964
THE DEED by Gerold Frank (Simon & Schuster)
FLIGHT 967 by Brad Williams (Wm. Morrow)
THE HIRED KILLERS by Peter Wyden (Wm. Morrow)

1963
TRAGEDY IN DEDHAM by Francis Russell (McGraw-Hill)

1962
**DEATH AND THE SUPREME COURT by Barrett Prettyman Jr.
   (Harcourt, Brace & World)**
THE SHEPPARD MURDER CASE by Paul Holmes (McKay)
LIZZIE BORDEN: THE UNTOLD STORY by Edward D. Radin (Simon &
   Schuster)
KIDNAP by George Waller (Dial)

1961
THE OVERBURY AFFAIR by Miriam Allen deFord (Chilton)
MOSTLY MURDER by Sir Sydney Smith (McKay)
HEAVEN KNOWS WHO by Christianna Brand (Scribners)

1960
FIRE AT SEA by Thomas Gallager (Rinehart)
GREAT TRAIN ROBBERIES OF THE WEST by Eugene B. Block (Coward-McCann)

1959
THEY DIED IN THE CHAIR by Wenzell Brown (Popular Library)
THE DEADLY REASONS by Edward D. Radin (Popular Library)
THE ROYAL VULTURES by Sam Kollman as told to Hillel Black (Pocket Books)
THE MURDER AND THE TRIAL by Edgar Lustgarten (Scribners)
THE INCURABLE WOUND by Berton Roueché (Little, Brown)

1958
THE D.A.'S MAN by Harold R. Danforth and James D. Horan (Crown)
THE GIRL IN THE BELFRY by Lenore Glen Offord and Joseph Henry Jackson (Gold Medal)
MEMOIRS OF A BOW STREET RUNNER by Henry Goddard, edited by Patrick Pringle (Wm. Morrow)

1957
NIGHT FELL ON GEORGIA by Charles and Louise Samuels (Dell)
RUBY MCCOLLUM, THE WOMAN IN THE SUWANNE JAIL by William Bradford Huie (Dutton)
HISTORICAL WHODUNITS by Hugh Ross Williamson (Macmillan)

1956
DEAD AND GONE by Manly Wade Wellman (University of North Carolina Press)
THE TRUTH ABOUT BELLE GUNNESS by Lillian de la Torre (Gold Medal)
THE ASSASSINS by Robert J. Donovan (Harper)

1955
THE GIRL WITH THE SCARLET BRAND by Charles Boswell and Lewis
   Thompson (Fawcett)

1954
WHY DID THEY KILL? by John Bartlow Martin (Ballantine)

1953
COURT OF LAST RESORT by Erle Stanley Gardner (Wm. Sloane
   Association)

1952
TRUE TALES FROM THE ANNALS OF CRIME AND RASCALITY by St.
   Clair McKelway (Random House)
LADY KILLERS by W. T. Brannon (Quinn)

1951
TWELVE AGAINST CRIME by Edward D. Radin (Putnam)
William T. Brannon for general excellence in fact crime writing

1950
BAD COMPANY by Joseph Henry Jackson (Harcourt, Brace & World)

1949
Marie Rodell for her editorship of the REGIONAL MURDER series
   (Duell, Sloan & Pearce)

1948
TWELVE AGAINST THE LAW by Edward D. Radin (Duell, Sloan &
   Pearce)

Best Critical/Biographical Work

1994
THE SAINT: A COMPLETE HISTORY by Burl Barer (McFarland &
   Co.)
THE FINE ART OF MURDER edited by Ed Gorman, Martin H.
   Greenberg, Larry Segriff with Jon L. Breen (Carroll & Graf)

A READER'S GUIDE TO THE AMERICAN NOVEL OF DETECTION by
   Marvin Lachman (G. K. Hall)
THE MAN WHO WASN'T MAIGRET by Patrick Marnham (Farrar,
   Straus & Giroux)
DOROTHY L. SAYERS: HER LIFE AND SOUL by
   Barbara Reynolds (St. Martin's)

1993
**ALIAS S. S. VAN DINE by John Loughery
(Scribners)**
DOROTHY L. SAYERS: A CARELESS RAGE FOR
   LIFE by David Coomes (Lion Publishing)
EDGAR ALLAN POE: HIS LIFE AND LEGACY
   by Jeffrey Meyers (Scribners)
DOUBLEDAY CRIME CLUB COMPENDIUM,
   1928–1991 by Ellen Nehr (Offspring
   Press)

1992
**EDGAR A. POE: MOURNFUL AND NEVER-ENDING REMEMBRANCE by
Kenneth Silverman (HarperCollins)**
OUT OF THE WOODPILE: BLACK CHARACTERS IN CRIME AND
   DETECTIVE FICTION by Frankie E. Bailey (Greenwood Press)
AGATHA CHRISTIE: MURDER IN FOUR ACTS by Peter Haining (Virgin
   Books)
TALKING MYSTERIES: A CONVERSATION WITH TONY HILLERMAN by
   Tony Hillerman and Ernie Bulow (University of New Mexico
   Press)
JIM THOMPSON: SLEEP WITH THE DEVIL by Michael J. McCauley
   (Mysterious Press)

1991
**TROUBLE IS THEIR BUSINESS: PRIVATE EYES IN FICTION, FILM, AND
   TELEVISION, 1927–1988 by John Conquest (Garland)**
JOHN DICKSON CARR: A CRITICAL STUDY by S. T. Joshi (Bowling
   Green Popular Press)
THE REMARKABLE CASE OF DOROTHY L. SAYERS by Catherine Kenney
   (Kent State University Press)

ERIC AMBLER by Peter Lewis (Continuum)
HILLARY WAUGH'S GUIDE TO MYSTERIES AND MYSTERY WRITING by
Hillary Waugh (Writer's Digest Books)

1990
THE LIFE OF GRAHAM GREENE, VOLUME I: 1904–1939 by Norman
Sherry (Viking)
FILM NOIR: REFLECTIONS IN A DARK MIRROR by Bruce Crowther
(Continuum)
MYSTERIUM AND MYSTERY: THE CLERICAL CRIME NOVEL by William
David Spencer (UMI Research Press)
THE PERFECT MURDER: A STUDY IN DETECTION by David Lehman
(Free Press/Macmillan)
MURDER ON THE AIR by Ric Meyers (Mysterious Press)

1989
CORNELL WOOLRICH: FIRST YOU DREAM, THEN YOU DIE by Francis
M. Nevins Jr. (Mysterious Press)
THE DIME DETECTIVES by Ron Goulart (Mysterious Press)
SILK STALKINGS: WHEN WOMEN WRITE OF MURDER by Victoria
Nichols and Susan Thompson (Black Lizard)
SISTERS IN CRIME: FEMINISM AND THE CRIME NOVEL by Maureen T.
Reddy (Continuum)

1988
INTRODUCTION TO THE DETECTIVE STORY by Leroy Lad Panek
(Popular Press)
CAMPION'S CAREER: A STUDY OF THE NOVELS OF MARGERY
ALLINGHAM by B. A. Pike (Bowling Green Popular Press)
CORRIDORS OF DECEIT, THE WORLD OF JOHN LE CARRÉ by Peter
Wolfe (Popular Library)
CRIME AND MYSTERY, THE 100 BEST BOOKS by H. R. F. Keating
(Carroll & Graf)

1987
HERE LIES: AN AUTOBIOGRAPHY by Eric Ambler (Farrar, Straus &
Giroux)
THE MYSTERY LOVER'S COMPANION by Art Bourgeau (Crown)

1001 MIDNIGHTS: THE AFICIONADO'S GUIDE TO MYSTERY FICTION by Bill Pronzini and Marcia Muller (Arbor House)

THE SECRET OF THE STRATEMEYER SYNDICATE: NANCY DREW, THE HARDY BOYS AND THE MILLION DOLLAR FICTION FACTORY by Carol Billman (Ungar)

13 MISTRESSES OF MURDER by Elaine Budd (Ungar)

1986

JOHN LE CARRÉ by Peter Lewis (Ungar)

AGATHA CHRISTIE by Janet Morgan (Knopf)

THE AMERICAN PRIVATE EYE: THE IMAGE IN FICTION by David Geherin (Ungar)

THE LORD PETER WIMSEY COMPANION by Stephan P. Clarke (Mysterious Press)

PRIVATE EYES: 101 KNIGHTS, A SURVEY OF AMERICAN FICTION by Robert A. Baker and Michael T. Nietzel (Bowling Green Popular Press)

1985

NOVEL VERDICTS: A GUIDE TO COURTROOM FICTION by Jon L. Breen (Scarecrow Press)

INWARD JOURNEY: ROSS MACDONALD edited by Ralph B. Sipper (Cordelia Editions)

THE JAMES BOND BEDSIDE COMPANION by Raymond Benson (Dodd, Mead)

ONE LONELY KNIGHT: MICKEY SPILLANE'S MIKE HAMMER by Max Allan Collins and James L. Traylor (Bowling Green Popular Press)

ROSS MACDONALD by Matthew J. Bruccoli (Harcourt Brace Jovanovich)

1984

THE DARK SIDE OF GENIUS: THE LIFE OF ALFRED HITCHCOCK by Donald Spoto (Little, Brown)

DASHIELL HAMMETT by Diane Johnson (Random House)

THE MYSTERY OF GEORGES SIMENON by Fenton Bresler (Beaufort)

THE POETICS OF MURDER edited by Glenn W. Most and William W. Stowe (Harcourt Brace Jovanovich)

1983
CAIN by Roy Hoopes (Holt, Rinehart & Winston)
GUN IN CHEEK by Bill Pronzini (Coward, McCann & Geoghegan)
MODUS OPERANDI by Robin W. Winks (David R. Godine)
THE POLICE PROCEDURAL by George N. Dove (Bowling Green
    Popular Press)

1982
WHAT ABOUT MURDER? by Jon L. Breen (Scarecrow Press)
THE ANNOTATED TALES OF EDGAR ALLAN POE edited by Stephen
    Peithman (Doubleday)
SELECTED LETTERS OF RAYMOND CHANDLER edited by Frank
    MacShane (Columbia University Press)
TV DETECTIVES by Richard Meyers (A. S. Barnes & Co.)
THE WHODUNIT by Stefano Benvenuti and Gianni Rizzoni
    (Macmillan)

1981
TWENTIETH CENTURY CRIME AND MYSTERY WRITERS by John Reilly
    (St. Martin's)
WATTEAU'S SHEPHERDS: THE DETECTIVE NOVEL IN BRITAIN
    1914–1940 by Leroy Lad Panek (Bowling Green Popular Press)
A TALENT TO DECEIVE: AN APPRECIATION OF AGATHA CHRISTIE by
    Robert Barnard (Dodd, Mead)

1980
DOROTHY L. SAYERS, A LITERARY BIOGRAPHY by Ralph E. Hone
    (Kent State University Press)
THE SECRETS OF GROWN-UPS by Vera Caspary (McGraw-Hill)
AS HER WHIMSEY TOOK HER edited by Margaret Hannay (Kent State
    University Press)
SHERLOCK HOLMES, THE MAN AND HIS WORLD by H. R. F. Keating
    (Scribners)

1979
THE MYSTERY OF AGATHA CHRISTIE by Gwen Robins (Doubleday)
ERLE STANLEY GARDNER: THE CASE OF THE REAL PERRY MASON by
    Dorothy B. Hughes (Wm. Morrow)

THE TELL-TALE HEART: THE LIFE AND WORK OF EDGAR ALLAN POE
by Julian Symons (Harper & Row)
THE DETECTIVE IN HOLLYWOOD by John Tuska (Doubleday)

1978
REX STOUT by John McAleer (Little, Brown)
AN AUTOBIOGRAPHY by Agatha Christie (Dodd, Mead)
THE ENCYCLOPEDIA SHERLOCKIANA by Jack Tracy (Doubleday)

1977
ENCYCLOPEDIA OF MYSTERY AND DETECTION by Chris Steinbrunner,
Otto Penzler, Marvin Lachman, and Charles Shibuk
(McGraw-Hill)
THE DANGEROUS EDGE by Gavin Lambert (Grossman)
THE LIFE OF RAYMOND CHANDLER by Frank McShane (Dutton)
THE AGATHA CHRISTIE MYSTERY by Derrick Murdoch (Pagurian
Press)
THE MYSTERY STORY edited by John Ball (University of California at
San Diego Publishers)

Best Young Adult Mystery

1994
THE NAME OF THE GAME WAS MURDER by Joan Lowery Nixon
(Delacorte)
STRANGE OBJECTS by Gary Crew (Simon & Schuster)
HELP WANTED by Richie Tankersley Cusick (Archway)
CLASS TRIP by Bebe Faas Rice (Harper)
SILENT WITNESS by Patricia H. Rushford (Bethany House)

1993
A LITTLE BIT DEAD by Chap Reaver (Delacorte)
BREAKING THE FALL by Michael Cadnum (Viking)
THE ONE WHO CAME BACK by Joann Mazzio (Houghton Mifflin)
THE WEEKEND WAS MURDER by Joan Lowery Nixon (Delacorte)
THE HIGHEST FORM OF KILLING by Malcolm Rose (Harcourt Brace
Jovanovich)

1992
THE WEIRDO by Theodore Taylor (Harcourt Brace Jovanovich)
CALLING HOME by Michael Cadnum (Viking)
WE ALL FALL DOWN by Robert Cormier (Delacorte)
SCARFACE by Peter Nelson (Archway)
THE CHRISTMAS KILLER by Patricia Windsor (Scholastic)

1991
MOTE by Chap Reaver (Delacorte)
ZACHARY by Ernest Pintoff (Eriksson)
GUILT TRIP by Stephen Schwandt (Atheneum)
THE SECRET KEEPER by Gloria Whelan (Knopf)

1990
SHOW ME THE EVIDENCE by Alane Ferguson (Bradbury Press)
FELL BACK by M. E. Kerr (Harper & Row)
REMEMBER ME by Christopher Pike (Archway Paperback)
SNIPER by Theodore Taylor (Harcourt Brace Jovanovich)
THE MAN WHO WAS POE by Avi (Orchard Books)

1989
INCIDENT AT LORING GROVES by Sonia Levitin (Dial)
SECOND FIDDLE by Ronald Kidd (Lodestar-Dutton)
SHADOW IN THE NORTH by Philip Pullman (Knopf)
THE ACCIDENT by Todd Strasser (Delacorte)
THE FALCON STING by Barbara Brenner (Bradbury)

Best Juvenile Mystery

1994
THE TWIN IN THE TAVERN by Barbara Brooks Wallace (Atheneum)
TANGLED WEBB by Eloise McGraw (Margaret K. McElderry Books)
THE FACE IN THE BESSLEDORF FUNERAL PARLOR by Phyllis Reynolds
    Naylor (Atheneum)
SPIDER KANE AND THE MYSTERY AT JUMBO NIGHTCRAWLER'S by Mary
    Pope Osborne (Knopf)
SAM THE CAT, DETECTIVE by Linda Stewart (Scholastic)

1993
COFFIN ON A CASE! by Eve Bunting (HarperCollins)
FISH AND BONES by Ray Prather (Harcourt Brace Jovanovich)
THE WIDOW'S BROOM by Chris Van Allsburg (Houghton Mifflin)
SUSANNAH AND THE PURPLE MONGOOSE by Patricia Elmore (Dutton)
THE TREASURE BIRD by Peni R. Griffin (McElderry Books)

1992
WANTED . . . MUD BLOSSOM by Betsy Byars (Delacorte)
MYSTERY ON OCTOBER ROAD by Alison Cragin Herzig and Jane
    Lawrence Mali (Viking)
DOUBLE TROUBLE SQUARED by Kathryn Lasky (Harcourt Brace
    Jovanovich)
WITCH WEED by Phyllis Reynolds Naylor (Delacorte)
FINDING BUCK MCHENRY by Alfred Slote (HarperCollins)

1991
STONEWORDS by Pam Conrad (Harper & Row)
THE MIDNIGHT HORSE by Sid Fleischman (Greenwillow)
THE TORMENTORS by Lynn Hall (Harcourt Brace Jovanovich)
TO GRANDMOTHER'S HOUSE WE GO by Willo Davis Roberts
    (Atheneum)
CAVE GHOST by Barbara Steiner (Harcourt Brace Jovanovich)

1989
MEGAN'S ISLAND by Willo Davis Roberts (Atheneum)
FOLLOWING THE MYSTERY MAN by Mary Downing Hahn (Clarion)
IS ANYBODY THERE? by Eve Bunting (Lippincott)
SOMETHING UPSTAIRS by Avi (Orchard Books)
THE LAMP FROM THE WARLOCK'S TOMB by John Bellairs (Dial)

1988
LUCY FOREVER AND MISS ROSETREE, SHRINKS by Susan Shreve
    (Henry Holt)
BURY THE DEAD by Peter Carter (Farrar, Straus & Giroux)
THE HOUSE ON THE HILL by Eileen Dunlop (Holiday House)
THE TWISTED WINDOW by Lois Duncan (Delacorte Press)
THROUGH THE HIDDEN DOOR by Rosemary Wells (Dial)

1987
THE OTHER SIDE OF DARK by Joan Lowery Nixon (Delacorte)
FLOATING ILLUSIONS by Chelsea Quinn Yarbro (Harper & Row)
THE SECRET LIFE OF DILLY MCBEAN by Dorothy Haas (Bradbury)
THE SKELETON MAN by Jay Bennett (Franklin Watts)
THE BODIES IN THE BESSLEDORF HOTEL by Phyllis Reynolds Naylor
  (Atheneum)

1986
THE SANDMAN'S EYES by Patricia Windsor (Delacorte)
LOCKED IN TIME by Lois Duncan (Little, Brown)
ON THE EDGE by Gillian Cross (Holiday House)
PLAYING MURDER by Sandra Scoppettone (Harper & Row)
SCREAMING HIGH by David Line (Little, Brown)

1985
NIGHT CRY by Phyllis Reynolds Naylor (Atheneum)
CHAMELEON THE SPY AND THE CASE OF THE VANISHING JEWELS by
  Diane R. Massie (Harper & Row)
THE GHOSTS OF NOW by Joan Lowery Nixon (Delacorte Press)
THE ISLAND ON BIRD STREET by Uri Orlev (Houghton Mifflin)
THE THIRD EYE by Lois Duncan (Little, Brown)

1984
THE CALLENDER PAPERS by Cynthia Voigt (Atheneum)
THE DOLLHOUSE MURDERS by Betty Ren Wright (Holiday House)
THE GRIFFIN LEGACY by Jan O'Donnell Klaveness (Macmillan)
SHADRACH'S CROSSING by Avi (Pantheon)
THE MAZE STONE by Eileen Dunlop (Coward-McCann)

1983
THE MURDER OF HOUND DOG BATES by Robbie Branscum (Viking)
CADBURY'S COFFIN by Glendon Swarthout and Kathryn Swarthout
  (Doubleday)
THE CASE OF THE COP CATCHERS by Terrance Dicks
  (Lodestar/Dutton)
CLONE CATCHER by Alfred Slote (Lippincott)
KEPT IN THE DARK by Nina Bawden (Lothrop, Lee & Shepard)

1982

TAKING TERRI MUELLER by **Norma Fox Mazer** (Avon)
DETECTIVE MOLE AND THE HALLOWEEN MYSTERY by Robert
  Quackenbush (Lothrop, Lee & Shepard)
DETOUR TO DANGER by Eva-Lis Wuorio (Delacorte)
HOOPS by Walter Dean Myers (Delacorte)
VILLAGE OF THE VAMPIRE CAT by Lensey Namioka (Delacorte)

1981

THE SÉANCE by **Joan Lowery Nixon** (Harcourt Brace Jovanovich)
WHEN NO ONE WAS LOOKING by Rosemary Wells (Dial Press)
WE DARE NOT GO A-HUNTING by Charlotte MacLeod (Atheneum)
MORE MINDEN CURSES by Willo Davis Roberts (Atheneum)
THE DOGGONE MYSTERY by Mary Blount Christian (Albert
  Whitman)

1980

THE KIDNAPPING OF CHRISTINA LATTIMORE by **Joan Lowery Nixon**
  (Harcourt Brace Jovanovich)
MYSTERY COTTAGE IN LEFT FIELD by Remus F. Caroselli (Putnam)
THE WHISPERED HORSE by Lynn Hall (Follett)
CHAMELEON WAS A SPY by Diane Redfield Massie (Crowell)
MYSTERY OF THE EAGLE'S CLAW by Frances Wosmek (Westminster
  Press)

1979

ALONE IN WOLF HOLLOW by **Dana Brookins** (Seabury)
THE BASSUMTYTE TREASURE by Jean Louise Curry (Atheneum)
EMILY UPHAM'S REVENGE by Avi (Pantheon)
THE HALLOWEEN PUMPKIN SMASHER by Judith St. George (Putnam)
THE CASE OF THE SECRET SCRIBBLER by E. W. Hildick (Macmillan)

1978

A REALLY WEIRD SUMMER by **Eloise Jarvis McGraw** (Atheneum)
MISS NELSON IS MISSING! by Harry Allard and James Marshall
  (Houghton Mifflin)
POOR TOM'S GHOST by Jean Louise Curry (Atheneum)
NIGHT SPELL by Robert Newman (Atheneum)

1977
ARE YOU IN THE HOUSE ALONE? by Richard Peck (Viking)
THE MASTER PUPPETEER by Katherine Peterson (Crowell)
WILEY AND THE HAIRY MAN by Molly Garrett Bang (Macmillan)
MR. MOON'S LAST CASE by Brian Patten (Scribners)
THE CHALK CROSS by Berthe Amoss (Seabury)

1976
Z FOR ZACHARIAH by Robert C. O'Brien (Atheneum)
NO MORE MAGIC by Avi (Pantheon)
GREAT STEAMBOAT MYSTERY by Richard Scarry (Random House)
THE TATTOOED POTATO AND OTHER CLUES by Ellen Raskin
(Dutton)

1975
THE DANGLING WITNESS by Jay Bennett (Delacorte)
FIRE IN THE STONE by Colin Thiele (Harper & Row)
THE GIRL IN THE GROVE by David Severn (Harper & Row)
HERE LIES THE BODY by Scott Corbett (Atlantic–Little, Brown)
THE MYSTERIOUS RED TAPE GANG by Joan Lowery Nixon
(Putnam)

1974
THE LONG BLACK COAT by Jay Bennett (Delacorte)
DREAMLAND LAKE by Richard Peck (Holt, Rinehart & Winston)
MYSTERY OF THE SCOWLING BOY by Phyllis A. Whitney (Westminster
Press)
THE SECRET OF THE SEVEN CROWS by Wylly Folk St. John (Viking)

1973
DEATHWATCH by Robb White (Doubleday)
CATCH A KILLER by George A. Woods (Harper & Row)
ELIZABETH'S TOWER by A. C. Stewart (S. G. Phillips)
UNCLE ROBERT'S SECRET by Wylly Folk St. John (Viking)

1972
NIGHTFALL by Joan Aiken (Holt, Rinehart & Winston)
THE GHOST OF BALLYHOOLY by Betty Cavanna (Wm. Morrow)

GOODY HALL by Natalie Babbitt (Farrar, Straus & Giroux)
MYSTERY IN WALES by Mabel Esther Allan (Vanguard)

1971
THE INTRUDER by John Rowe Townsend (Lippincott)
THE MYSTERY MAN by Scott Corbett (Little, Brown)
THE SECRET OF THE MISSING FOOTPRINT by Phyllis A. Whitney
  (Westminster Press)

1970
DANGER AT BLACK DYKE by Winifred Finlay (S. G. Phillips)
THEY NEVER CAME HOME by Lois Duncan (Doubleday)
SPICE ISLAND MYSTERY by Betty Cavanna (Wm. Morrow)
MYSTERY OF THE WITCH WHO WOULDN'T by Kin Platt (Chilton)

1969
THE HOUSE OF DIES DREAR by Virginia Hamilton (Macmillan)
MYSTERY OF THE FAT CAT by Frank Bonham (Dutton)
SMUGGLERS' ROAD by Hal G. Evarts (Scribners)
FORGERY! by Phyllis Bentley (Doubleday)

1968
SIGNPOST TO TERROR by Gretchen Sprague (Dodd, Mead)
THE SECRET OF THE MISSING BOAT by Paul Berna (Pantheon)
THE WITCHES' BRIDGE by Barbee Oliver Carleton (Holt, Rinehart &
  Winston)

1967
SINBAD AND ME by Kin Platt (Chilton)
RANSOM by Lois Duncan (Doubleday)
DANGER BEATS THE DRUM by Arnold Madison (Holt, Rinehart &
  Winston)
MYSTERY OF THE RED TIDE by Frank Bonham (Dutton)

1966
THE MYSTERY OF 22 EAST by Leon Ware (Westminster Press)
THE APACHE GOLD MYSTERY by Eileen Thompson (Abelard-
  Schuman)

THE SECRET OF THE SIMPLE CODE by Nancy Faulkner (Doubleday)
SECRET OF THE HAUNTED CRAGS by Lawrence J. Hunt (Funk &
  Wagnalls)

1965
MYSTERY AT CRANE'S LANDING **by Marcella Thum (Dodd, Mead)**
A SPELL IS CAST by Eleanor Cameron (Little, Brown)
TREASURE RIVER by Hal G. Evarts (Scribners)
PRIVATE EYES by Leo Kingman (Doubleday)

1964
MYSTERY OF THE HIDDEN HAND by
  Phyllis A. Whitney (Westminster
  Press)
HONOR BOUND by Frank Bonham
  (Crowell)
MYSTERY OF THE VELVET BOX by
  Margaret Scherf (Watts)

1963
CUTLASS ISLAND **by Scott Corbett
  (Little, Brown)**
THE HOUSE ON CHARLTON STREET by
  Dola de John (Scribners)
THE DIAMOND IN THE WINDOW by Jane
  Langton (Harper & Row)
THE MYSTERY OF GHOST VALLEY by
  Harriett Carr (Macmillan)

Specializing in romantic suspense, Phyllis Whitney has had great success in writing for both young people and adults.

1962
THE PHANTOM OF WALKAWAY HILL **by Edward Fenton (Doubleday)**
THE SECRET OF THE TIGER'S EYE by Phyllis A. Whitney (Westminster
  Press)

1961
THE MYSTERY OF THE HAUNTED POOL **by Phyllis A. Whitney
  (Westminster Press)**

Best Episode in a Television Series

1994
"4B or Not 4B" by David Milch (NYPD BLUE/ABC)
"Conduct Unbecoming" by Michael S. Chernuchin and Rene Balcer
(LAW & ORDER/NBC)
"Rising Sun" by Stephen Kronish (THE COMMISH/ABC)
"Turpitude" by David E. Kelley (PICKET FENCES/CBS)
"Promised Land" by Julian Mitchell (INSPECTOR
MORSE/MYSTERY!/WGBH)

1993
**"Conspiracy" by Michael S. Chernuchin and Rene Balcer (LAW &
ORDER/NBC)**
"Point of View" by Walon Green and Rene Balcer (LAW &
ORDER/NBC)
"The Dead File" by Tom Sawyer (MURDER, SHE WROTE/CBS)
"Smells Like Teen Spirit" by William Rabkin and Lee Goldberg
(LIKELY SUSPECTS/Fox)
"A Killer Book" by Paul Bernbaum (LIKELY SUSPECTS/Fox)

1992
**"Poirot: The Lost Mine" by Michael Baker and David Renwick
(MYSTERY!/WGBH)**
"Shoscombe Old Place" by Gary Hopkins (MYSTERY!/WGBH)
"Sonata for Solo Organ" by Joe Morgenstern and Michael S.
Chernuchin (LAW & ORDER/NBC)
"The Problem of Thor Bridge" by Jeremy Paul (MYSTERY!/WGBH)

1991
"Goodnight, Dear Heart" by Paul Brown (QUANTUM LEAP/NBC)
"Happily Ever After" by David Black and Robert Stuart Nathan (LAW
& ORDER/NBC)
"Justice Swerved" by David E. Kelley and Bruce Zabel (L.A.
LAW/NBC)
"Gabriel's Fire" by Jacqueline Zambrano and Coleman Luck
(GABRIEL'S FIRE/ABC)

1990
"White Noise" by David J. Burke and Alfonse Ruggiero Jr.
  (WISEGUY/CBS)
"Blues for Buder" by Robert P. Parker and Joan Parker (B.L.
  STRYKER/ABC)
"Investment in Death" by Jerry Jacobius and Nick Gore
  (HUNTER/NBC)
"Rumpole and the Bubble Reputation" by John Mortimer
  (MYSTERY!/WGBH)
"Urine Trouble Now" by David E. Kelley, William M. Finkelstein,
  Michelle Gallery, and Judith Parker (L.A. LAW/NBC)

1989
"The Devil's Foot" by Gary Hopkins (MYSTERY!/WGBH)
"Date with an Angel" by David J. Burke and Stephen Kronish
  (WISEGUY/CBS)
"May the Road Rise Up" by Richard C. Okie (SIMON & SIMON/CBS)
"Rumpole and the Bright Seraphim" by John Mortimer
  (MYSTERY!/WGBH)
"The Black Tower, Episode 1" by William Humble
  (MYSTERY!/WGBH)

1988
"The Musgrave Ritual" by Jeremy Paul (MYSTERY!/WGBH)
"Blue Movie" by Ron Hansen (PRIVATE LIVES/NBC)
"Nicky the Rose" by John Leekley and Alfonse Ruggiero Jr. (PRIVATE
  EYE/NBC)
"The Marriage of Heaven and Hell" by Eric Blakeney
  (WISEGUY/CBS)
"The Right to Remain Silent" by David Abramowitz (CAGNEY &
  LACEY/CBS)

1987
"The Cup" by David Jackson (THE EQUALIZER/CBS)
"Deirdre" by Herman Miller (THE NEW MIKE HAMMER/CBS)
"Diary of a Perfect Murder" by Dean Hargrove (MATLOCK/NBC)
"Wax Poetic" by Lee Sheldon (BLACKE'S MAGIC/NBC)

1986
"The Amazing Falsworth" by Mick Garris (AMAZING STORIES/NBC)
"The Dream Sequence Always Rings Twice" by Debra Frank and Carl
  Sautter (MOONLIGHTING/ABC)
"Wake Me When I'm Dead" by Buck Henry (ALFRED HITCHCOCK
  PRESENTS/NBC)

1985
"Deadly Lady" by Peter S. Fischer (MURDER,
  SHE WROTE/CBS)
"Miami Vice" by Anthony Yerkovich (MIAMI
  VICE/NBC)
"Seven Dead Eyes" by Joe Gores (MICKEY
  SPILLANE'S MIKE HAMMER/CBS)

1984
"The Pencil" by Jo Eisinger (PHILIP
  MARLOWE/HBO)
"Altered Steele" by Jeff Melvoin (REMINGTON
  STEELE/NBC)
"Grand Illusion" by E. Jack Kaplan (SIMON & SIMON/CBS)

Angela Lansbury in
Murder, She Wrote.

1983
"In the Steele of the Night" by Joel Steiger (REMINGTON
  STEELE/NBC)
"Ashes to Ashes, None Too Soon" by Bob Shayne (SIMON &
  SIMON/CBS)
"Matt Houston" by Ken Trevey and Richard Christian Danus (MATT
  HOUSTON/ABC)

1982
"Hill Street Station" by Steven Bochco and Michael Kozoll (HILL
  STREET BLUES/NBC)
"Stain of Guilt" by Sam Egan (QUINCY/NBC)
"Simon Eyes" by Philip DeGuere (SIMON & SIMON/CBS)

1981
"China Doll" by Donald P. Bellisario and Glen A. Larson (MAGNUM
  P.I./CBS)

"A Matter of Principle" by Aubrey Solomon and Steven Greenberg
  (QUINCY/NBC)
"Tenspeed and Brown Shoe" by Stephen Cannell (TENSPEED AND
  BROWN SHOE/ABC)

1980
**"Skin" by Robin Chapman and Roald Dahl (ROALD DAHL'S TALES
  OF THE UNEXPECTED/syndicated by Anglia Ltd.)**
"A Hollywood Whodunit" by Michele Gallery (LOU GRANT/CBS)
"Only the Pretty Girls Die" by Mark Rodgers (EISCHIED/NBC)
"Stone" by Stephen J. Cannell (STONE/ABC)

1979
"Murder Under Glass" by Robert Van Scoyk (COLUMBO/NBC)
"Vega$" by Michael Mann (VEGA$/ABC)
"Murder on the Flip Side" by Lee Sheldon (EDDIE CAPRA
  MYSTERIES/NBC)

1978
**"The Thighbone Is Connected to the Knee Bone" by Tony
  Lawrence and Lou Shaw (QUINCY/NBC)**
"In the Event of My Death" by Jerome Coopersmith (THE ANDROS
  TARGETS/ABC)
"The Deadly Maze" by Juanita Bartlett (THE ROCKFORD FILES/NBC)

1977
**"Requiem for Murder" by James J. Sweeney (STREETS OF SAN
  FRANCISCO/ABC)**
"Dear Tony" by Norman Hudis (BARETTA/ABC)
"The Oracle Wore a Cashmere Suit" by David Chase (THE
  ROCKFORD FILES/NBC)

1976
"No Immunity for Murder" by Joe Gores (KOJAK/CBS)
"The Mark of Cain" by Leonard Katzman (PETROCELLI/NBC)
"Murder Comes in Little Pills" by Robert Foster and Milt Rosen
  (KATE MCSHANE/CBS)

1975
"Requiem for C. Z. Smith" by Robert Collins (POLICE STORY/NBC)
"Gertrude" by Howard Rodman (HARRY O./ABC)
"Anatomy of Two Rapes" by Pat Fielder and Robert Bluel
    (POLICEWOMAN/NBC)

1974
"Requiem for an Informer" by Sy Salkowitz (POLICE STORY/NBC)
"Requiem for a Falling Star" by Jackson Gillis (COLUMBO/NBC)
"Here Today, Gone Tonight" by Jerome Coopersmith (HAWAII FIVE-
    O/CBS)
"One for the Morgue" by Jerrold Freedman (KOJAK/CBS)
"The Cain Connection" by Stephen J. Cannell (TOMA/ABC)

1973
"The New Mexico Connection" by Glenn A. Larson
    (McCLOUD/NBC)
"A Date With Death" by Mort Fine and Milton S. Gelman
    (BANYON/NBC)
"Bait Once, Bait Twice" by Will Lorin (HAWAII FIVE-O/CBS)
"The Crimson Halo" by Shimon Wincelberg (MANNIX/CBS)
"Victim in Shadow" by Richard Bluel (OWEN MARSHALL,
    COUNSELLOR-AT-LAW/ABC)

1972 (Until this year there was only one TV award)
"A Step in Time" by Mann Rubin (MANNIX/CBS)
"Somebody's Out to Get Jennie" by Robert Presnell Jr.
    (McCLOUD/NBC)
"Murder by the Book" by Steven Bochco (COLUMBO/NBC)
"Company Town" by Cliff Gould (CADE'S COUNTY/CBS)

1971
BERLIN AFFAIR by Richard Alan Simmons and E. Jack Neuman
    (NBC/Movie of the Week)
THE OTHER MAN by Michael Blankfort and Eric Bercovici
    (NBC/Movie of the Week)
THE OLD MAN WHO CRIED WOLF by Luther Davis (ABC/Movie of
    the Week)

"The Mouse That Died" by Chester Krumholtz (MANNIX/CBS)
"To Taste of Death but Once" by Joel Oliansky (THE SENATOR/NBC)

1970
DAUGHTER OF THE MIND by Luther Davis (ABC/Movie of the Week)
NIGHT GALLERY by Rod Serling (NBC)
"In this Corner . . ." by Sol Albert, Rita Lakin, and Harve Bennett (MOD SQUAD/ABC)
"The Sound of Darkness" by Barry Trivers (MANNIX/CBS)

1969
THE STRANGE CASE OF DR. JEKYLL AND MR. HYDE by Ian Hunter (ABC Special)
COMPANIONS IN NIGHTMARE by Robert L. Joseph (NBC World Premier Film)

1968
"Tempest in a Texas Town" by Harold Gast and Leon Tokatyan (JUDD FOR THE DEFENSE/ABC)

1967
"Operation Rogesh" by Jerome Ross (MISSION: IMPOSSIBLE/CBS)
"The Fatal Mistake" by Jacques Gillies and Oscar Millard (BOB HOPE PRESENTS/NBC)
"After the Lion, Jackals" by Stanford Whitmore (BOB HOPE PRESENTS/NBC)

1966
"An Unlocked Window" by James Bridges (ALFRED HITCHCOCK PRESENTS/NBC)
"Memorandum for a Spy" by Robert J. Joseph (BOB HOPE PRESENTS/NBC)
"Carry Me Back to Old Tsing Tao" by David Karp (I, SPY/NBC)
"The Gray Lady" by William Link and Richard Levinson (HONEY WEST/ABC)

1965
THE FUGITIVE series by Alan Armer (ABC)

1964

"The End of the World Baby" by Luther Davis (KRAFT SUSPENSE HOUR/NBC)

"To Bury Caesar" by Berkely Mather (DUPONT SHOW OF THE WEEK/NBC)

THE DEFENDERS for general excellence (CBS)

1963

"The Problem of Cell 13" by A. A. Roberts (KRAFT MYSTERY THEATRE/NBC)

"The Apostle" by Stanley R. Greenberg (THE DEFENDERS/CBS)

"Scene of the Crime" by Sidney Carroll (U.S. STEEL HOUR/CBS)

1962

"Witness in the Dark" by Leigh Vance and John Lemont (KRAFT MYSTERY THEATRE/NBC)

"The Legend of Jim Riva" by Boyd Correll and John K. Butler (THE DEFENDERS/CBS)

1961

"The Case of the Burning Court" by Kelley Roos (DOW HOUR OF GREAT MYSTERIES/NBC)

"The Day of the Bullet" by Bill Ballinger (ALFRED HITCHCOCK PRESENTS/NBC)

1960

THE EMPTY CHAIR by David Karp (ABC)

THE COMIC by Blake Edwards (NBC)

1959

"The Edge of Truth" by Adrian Spies (STUDIO ONE/CBS)

"Capital Punishment" by James Lee (OMNIBUS/NBC)

1958

MECHANICAL MANHUNT by Harold Swanton (ALCOA HOUR/NBC)

THE TRIAL OF LIZZIE BORDEN by OMNIBUS staff (ABC)

1957
THE FINE ART OF MURDER by Sidney Carroll (OMNIBUS/ABC)
PLAYHOUSE 90 was awarded a Scroll for general excellence of production and quality of its telecasts (CBS)

1956
"A Taste of Honey" by Alvin Sapinsley Jr. (ELGIN HOUR/ABC)
"Thin Air" by Ben Starr (CLIMAX/CBS)

1955
"Smoke" by Gore Vidal (SUSPENSE/CBS)
"The Long Goodbye" by E. Jack Neuman (CLIMAX/CBS)

1954
"Crime at Blossoms" by Jerome Ross (STUDIO ONE/CBS)

1953
DRAGNET by Jack Webb, writer/star, and Michael Meshekoff, producer (NBC)

1952
THE WEB by Franklin Heller, producer-director, and Goodson-Todman, package producers of the show (CBS)

Best Television Feature or Miniseries

1994
PRIME SUSPECT 2 by Allan Cubitt (MYSTERY!/WGBH)
CAUGHT IN THE ACT by Ken Hixon (USA)
1994 BAKER STREET by Kenneth Johnson (CBS)
THE LAST HIT by Walter Klenhard and Alan Sharp (USA)
12:01 by Philip Morton (Fox West Pictures)

1993
PRIME SUSPECT by Lynda La Plante (MYSTERY!/WGBH)
HONOR THY MOTHER by Richard Delong Adams and Robert L. Freedman (Creative Artists)

Helen Mirren starred in Lynda La Plante's *Prime Suspect* on PBS' *Mystery!*

MRS. CAGE by Nancy Barr (American Playhouse)
STAY THE NIGHT by Dan Freudenberger (ABC)
BURDEN OF PROOF by John Gay (ABC)

1992
MURDER 101 by Bill Condon and Roy Johansen (USA)
DEVICES AND DESIRES by Thomas Ellice (MYSTERY!/WGBH)
LOVE, LIES, AND MURDER by Danielle Hill (NBC)
A MURDER OF QUALITY by John le Carré (MASTERPIECE
    THEATRE/PBS)

1991
KILLING IN A SMALL TOWN by Cynthia Cidre (CBS)
MATHNET: CASE OF THE SWAMI SCAM by Dave Connell and Jim
    Thurman (PBS)
POLICE CHIEFS by Susan and Alan Raymond (PBS)
SHAKE HANDS FOREVER by Clive Exton (A&E)
THE INCIDENT by Michael and James Morrell (CBS)

1990
SHANNON'S DEAL by John Sayles (NBC)
GAME, SET, AND MATCH by John Howlett (PBS)
MISS MARPLE: MURDER AT THE VICARAGE by T. R. Bowen (PBS)
THE HOLLYWOOD DETECTIVE by Christopher Crowe (USA)
TURN BACK THE CLOCK by Lee Hutson and Lindsay Harrison (NBC)

1989
MAN AGAINST THE MOB by David J. Kinghorn (NBC)
A WHISPER KILLS by John Robert Bensink (ABC)
SHE WAS MARKED FOR MURDER by David Stenn (NBC)

1988
NUTCRACKER: MONEY, MURDER, AND MADNESS by William Hanley (NBC)
DEADLY DECEPTION by Gordon Cotler (CBS)
OLD DOGS by Michele Gallery (ABC)
THE HANDS OF THE STRANGER by Arthur Kopit (NBC)
THE RETURN OF SHERLOCK HOLMES by Bob Shayne (CBS)

1987
WHEN THE BOUGH BREAKS by Phil Penningroth (NBC)
THE DELIBERATE STRANGER by Hesper Anderson (NBC)
ONE POLICE PLAZA by Paul King (CBS)
PERRY MASON: THE CASE OF THE SHOOTING STAR by Anne C. Collins (NBC)
THE SWORD OF GIDEON by Chris Bryant (HBO)

1986
GUILTY CONSCIENCE by Richard Levinson and William Link (CBS)
DEADLY MESSAGES by William Bleich (ABC)
DOUBLETAKE by John Gay (CBS)
LOVE ON THE RUN by Sue Grafton and Steve Humphrey (NBC)
PERRY MASON RETURNS by Dean Hargrove (NBC)

1985
THE GLITTER DOME by Stanley Kallis (HBO)
CELEBRITY by William Hanley (NBC)
FATAL VISION by John Gay (NBC)

1984
MICKEY SPILLANE'S MURDER ME, MURDER YOU by Bill Stratton (CBS)
JANE DOE by Cynthia Mandelberg and Walter Halsey Davis (CBS)
MURDER IN COWETA COUNTY by Dennis Nemec (CBS)

1983
REHEARSAL FOR MURDER by Richard Levinson and William Link (CBS)
THE BIG EASY by Lee Hutson (ABC)
ONE SHOE MAKES IT MURDER by Felix Culver (CBS)

1982
KILLJOY by Sam H. Rolfe (CBS)
MICKEY SPILLANE'S MARGIN FOR MURDER by Calvin Clements Jr. (CBS)
A SMALL KILLING by Burt Prelutsky (CBS)

1981
CITY IN FEAR by Albert Rubin (ABC)
THE LAST SONG by Michael Berk and Douglas Schwartz (CBS)
REVENGE OF THE STEPFORD WIVES by David Wiltse (NBC)

1980
MURDER BY NATURAL CAUSES by Richard Levinson and William Link (CBS)
NERO WOLFE by Frank Gilroy (ABC)
SALEM'S LOT by Paul Monash (CBS)

1979
DASHIELL HAMMETT'S THE DAIN CURSE by Robert Lenski (CBS)
SOMEONE'S WATCHING ME! by John Carpenter (NBC)
PERFECT GENTLEMEN by Nora Ephron (CBS)
WHEN EVERY DAY WAS THE FOURTH OF JULY by Lee Hutson (NBC)

1978
MEN WHO LOVE WOMEN by Gordon Cotler and Don M. Mankiewicz (ROSETTI AND RYAN pilot/NBC)

A KILLING AFFAIR by E. Arthur Kean (CBS)
IN THE GLITTER PALACE by Jerry Ludwig (NBC)
CONTRACT ON CHERRY STREET by Edward Anhalt (NBC)

1977
HELTER-SKELTER by J. P. Miller (CBS)
ONE OF MY WIVES IS MISSING by Pierre Marton (ABC)
LAW AND ORDER by E. Jack Neuman (NBC)
SHERLOCK HOLMES IN NEW YORK by Alvin Sapinsley Jr. (NBC)

1976
THE LEGEND OF LIZZIE BORDEN by William Bast (ABC)
GUILTY OR INNOCENT: THE SAM SHEPPARD MURDER CASE by Harold
    Gast (NBC)
HUSTLING by Fay Kanin (ABC)

1975
THE LAW by Joel Oliansky (NBC)
A CASE OF RAPE by Robert E. Thompson (NBC)
JUDGE DEE IN THE MONASTERY MURDERS by Nicholas Meyer
    (ABC)

1974
ISN'T IT SHOCKING by Lane Slate (ABC)
THE BLUE NIGHT by E. Jack Neuman (NBC)
A COLD NIGHT'S DEATH by Christopher Knopf (ABC)
THE CONNECTION by Albert Ruben (ABC)
THE MARCUS-NELSON MURDERS by Abby Mann (CBS)

1973
THE NIGHT STALKER by Richard Matheson (ABC)
LT. SCHUSTER'S WIFE by Bernie Kukoff and Steven Bochco (ABC)
WHEN MICHAEL CALLS by James Bridges (ABC)
YOUR MONEY OR YOUR WIFE by J. P. Miller (CBS)

1972
THIEF by John D. F. Black (ABC)
VANISHED by Dean Riesner (NBC)

DR. COOK'S GARDEN by Art Wallace (ABC)
SEE THE MAN RUN by Mann Rubin (ABC)

Best Motion Picture

1994
FALLING DOWN by Ebbe Rose Smith (Warner Bros.)
IN THE LINE OF FIRE by Jeff Maguire (Castle Rock)
THE FUGITIVE by Jeb Stuart and David Twohy (Warner Bros.)

1993
THE PLAYER by Michael Tolkin (Fineline Features)
THE CRYING GAME by Neil Jordan (Miramax)
UNFORGIVEN by David Webb Peoples (Warner Bros.)
A FEW GOOD MEN by Aaron Sorkin (Columbia)
SNEAKERS by Phil Alden Robinson and Lawrence Lasker and Walter F.
Parkes (Universal)

1992
THE SILENCE OF THE LAMBS by Ted
Tally (Orion)
J.F.K. by Oliver Stone and Zachary
Sklar (Warner Bros.)
DEAD AGAIN by Scott Frank
(Paramount)

1991
THE GRIFTERS by Donald E.
Westlake (Miramax)
PRESUMED INNOCENT by Frank
Pierson and Alan J. Pakula
(Warner/Mirage)
GOODFELLAS by Nicholas Pileggi and
Martin Scorsese (Warner Bros.)

Jody Foster portrayed Clarice
Starling in *The Silence of the
Lambs.*

1990
HEATHERS by Daniel Waters (New World)
CRIMES AND MISDEMEANORS by Woody Allen (Orion)

LICENCE TO KILL by Richard Maibaum and Michael G. Wilson
(United Artists)
SEA OF LOVE by Richard Price (Universal)
TRUE BELIEVER by Wesley Strick (Columbia)

1989
THE THIN BLUE LINE by Errol Morris (Miramax)
A FISH CALLED WANDA by John Cleese (MGM)
DIE HARD by Jeb Stuart and Steven E. de Souza (20th Century–Fox)
MASQUERADE by Dick Wolfe (MGM)
THINGS CHANGE by David Mamet and Shel Silverstein (Columbia)

1988
STAKEOUT by Jim Kouf (Buena Vista Pictures)
BEST SELLER by Larry Cohen (Orion)
ROBOCOP by Edward Neumeir and Michael Miner (John Davison
Productions)
THE BIG EASY by Daniel Petrie Jr. (Columbia)
THE STEPFATHER by Donald E. Westlake (ITC Productions)

1987
SOMETHING WILD by E. Max Frye (Orion)
DEFENSE OF THE REALM by Martin Stellman (Hemdale Releasing)
F/X by Robert T. Megginson and Gregory Fleeman (Orion)
THE GREAT MOUSE DETECTIVE by Ron Clements, Pete Young, Vance
Gerry, Steve Hulett, John Musker, Bruce M. Morris, Matthew
O'Callaghan, Burny Mattison, Dave Michener, and Melvin Shaw
(Disney)
MANHUNTER by Michael Mann (De Laurentiis Ent.)
THE NAME OF THE ROSE by Andrew Birkin, Gerard Brach, Howard
Franklin, and Alain Godard (20th Century–Fox)

1986
WITNESS by Earl W. Wallace and William Kelley (Paramount)
BLOOD SIMPLE by Joel Coen and Ethan Coen (Circle Films)
FLETCH by Andrew Bergman (Universal)
THE HIT by Peter Prince (Island Pictures)
JAGGED EDGE by Joe Eszterhas (Columbia)

1985
A SOLDIER'S STORY by Charles Fuller (Columbia)
BEVERLY HILLS COP by Daniel Petrie Jr. (Paramount)
THE LITTLE DRUMMER GIRL by Loring Mandel (Warner Bros.)

1984
GORKY PARK by Dennis Potter (Orion)
HAMMETT by Ross Thomas and Dennis O'Flaherty (Warner Bros.)
PSYCHO II by Tom Holland (Universal)

1983
THE LONG GOOD FRIDAY by Barrie Keeffe (Handmade Films)
EVIL UNDER THE SUN by Anthony Shaffer (Universal)
48 HOURS by Roger Spottiswoode, Walter Hill, Larry Gross, and
    Steven E. de Souza (Paramount)
STILL OF THE NIGHT by Robert Benton (MGM/United Artists)

1982
CUTTER'S WAY by Jeffrey Alan Fiskin (United Artists)
BODY HEAT by Lawrence Kasdan (Warner Bros.)
THE EYE OF THE NEEDLE by Stanley Mann (United Artists)
PRINCE OF THE CITY by Jay Presson Allen and Sidney Lumet (Warner
    Bros.)

1981
THE BLACK MARBLE by Joseph Wambaugh (AVCO-Embassy)
THE FIRST DEADLY SIN by Mann Rubin (Filmways Productions)
HOPSCOTCH by Brian Garfield and Bryan Forbes (AVCO-Embassy)
THE MAN WITH BOGART'S FACE by Andrew Fenady (20th
    Century–Fox)

1980
THE GREAT TRAIN ROBBERY by Michael Crichton (United Artists)
TIME AFTER TIME by Nicholas Meyer (Orion)
MURDER BY DECREE by John Hopkins (AVCO-Embassy)

1979
MAGIC by William Goldman (20th Century–Fox)

FOUL PLAY by Collin Higgins (Paramount)
SOMEBODY KILLED HER HUSBAND by Reginald Rose (Columbia)
DEATH ON THE NILE by Anthony Shaffer (Paramount)
THE BIG FIX by Roger Simon (Universal)

1978
THE LATE SHOW by Robert Benton (Warner Bros.)
BLACK SUNDAY by Ernest Lehman, Kenneth Ross, and Ivan Moffat
    (Paramount)
TELEFON by Peter Hyams and Stirling Silliphant (MGM)

1977
FAMILY PLOT by Ernest Lehman (Universal)
CARRIE by Lawrence D. Cohen (United Artists)
MARATHON MAN by William Goldman (Paramount)
THE OMEN by David Seltzer (20th Century–Fox)

1976
**THREE DAYS OF THE CONDOR by Lorenzo Semple Jr. and David
    Rayfiel (Paramount)**
BLACK CHRISTMAS by Roy Moore (Warner Bros.)
THE DROWNING POOL by Tracy Keenan Wynn, Lorenzo Semple Jr.,
    and Walter Hill (Warner Bros.)
FAREWELL, MY LOVELY by David Zelag Goodman (AVCO-Embassy)

1975
CHINATOWN by Robert Towne (Paramount)
THE CONVERSATION by Francis Ford Coppola (Paramount)
MURDER ON THE ORIENT EXPRESS by Paul Dehn (Paramount)
THE PARALLAX VIEW by David Giler and Lorenzo Semple Jr.
    (Paramount)

1974
**THE LAST OF SHEILA by Stephen Sondheim and Anthony Perkins
    (Warner Bros.)**
DON'T LOOK NOW by Alan Scott and Cris Bryant (Paramount)
SERPICO by Waldo Salt and Norman Wexler (Paramount)
THE STING by David S. Ward (Universal)

1973

SLEUTH by Anthony Shaffer (20th Century–Fox)

THE CAREY TREATMENT by James P. Bonner (Belasco Productions)

FRENZY by Anthony Shaffer (Universal)

THE HOT ROCK by William Goldman (20th Century–Fox)

TRAVELS WITH MY AUNT by Jay Presson Allen and Hugh Wheeler (MGM)

1972

THE FRENCH CONNECTION by Ernest Tidyman (20th Century– Fox)

KLUTE by Andy and Dave Lewis (Warner Bros.)

DIRTY HARRY by Harry Julian Fink, Rita N. Fink, and Dean Riesner (Warner Bros.)

SEE NO EVIL by Brian Clemens (Columbia)

WILLARD by Gilbert A. Ralston (Cinerama)

1971

INVESTIGATION OF A CITIZEN ABOVE SUSPICION by Elio Petri and Ugo Pirro (Columbia)

THE BIRD WITH THE CRYSTAL PLUMAGE by Dario Argento (UMC Pictures)

BORSALINO by Jean Cau, Claude Sautet, Jacques Deray, and Jean-Claude Cairiere (Paramount)

THE PRIVATE LIFE OF SHERLOCK HOLMES by I. A. L. Diamond (United Artists)

RIDER ON THE RAIN by Sebastien Japrisot (Circo-Embassy)

1970

Z by Jorge Semprun and Costa Gavras (Cinema V)

HARD CONTRACT by S. Lee Pogostin (20th Century–Fox)

STILETTO by A. J. Russell (AVCO-Embassy)

PENDULUM by Stanley Niss (Columbia)

1969

BULLITT by Alan R. Trustman and Harry Kleiner, screenwriters, and Robert L. Fish, author (Warner Bros.)

THE BRIDE WORE BLACK by Jean-Louis Richard and François Truffaut (United Artists)

ROSEMARY'S BABY by Roman Polanski (Paramount)
THE BOSTON STRANGLER by Edward Anhalt (20th Century–Fox)

1968
IN THE HEAT OF THE NIGHT by Stirling Silliphant (United Artists)
BONNIE AND CLYDE by David Newman (Warner Bros.)
IN COLD BLOOD by Richard Brooks (Columbia)

1967
HARPER by William Goldman (Warner Bros.)
THE QUILLER MEMORANDUM by Harold Pinter (20th Century–Fox)
SLEEPING CAR MURDER by Costa Gavras (Seven Arts)

1966
**THE SPY WHO CAME IN FROM THE COLD by Paul Dehn and Guy
    Trosper (Paramount)**
BUNNY LAKE IS MISSING by John and Penelope Mortimer (Columbia)
THAT DARN CAT by The Gordons and Bill Walsh (Buena Vista)

1965
**HUSH, HUSH, SWEET CHARLOTTE by Henry Farrell and Lukas
    Heller (20th Century–Fox)**
IT'S A MAD, MAD, MAD, MAD WORLD by William and Tania Rose
    (United Artists)   .
FATE IS THE HUNTER by Harold Medford (20th Century–Fox)

1964
CHARADE by Peter Stone (Universal)
THE BIRDS by Evan Hunter (Universal)
THE LIST OF ADRIAN MESSENGER by Anthony Veiller (Universal)

1962
**THE INNOCENTS by Truman Capote and William Archibald (20th
    Century–Fox)**

1961
**PSYCHO by Joseph Stefano, screenwriter, and a Scroll to Robert
    Bloch as book author (Paramount)**

1960
NORTH BY NORTHWEST by Ernest
Lehman (MGM)

1959
THE DEFIANT ONES by Nathan E.
Douglas and Harold Jacob
Smith (United Artists)

1958
TWELVE ANGRY MEN by Reginald
Rose (Orion/Nova)
WITNESS FOR THE PROSECUTION
by Billy Wilder and Harry
Kurnitz (United Artists)

Anthony Perkins as Norman
Bates in *Psycho.*

1956
THE DESPERATE HOURS by Joseph
Hayes (Paramount)

1955
REAR WINDOW by John Michael Hayes (Paramount)

1954
THE BIG HEAT, Sidney Boehm, screenwriter; William P. McGivern,
author of the novel; and Columbia

1953
FIVE FINGERS by Michael Wilson and Otto Lang, producer (20th
Century–Fox)

1952
DETECTIVE STORY, Philip Yordan and Robert Wyler, screenwriters;
and Sidney Kingsley for the stage play on which the screen ver-
sion was based (Paramount)
THE PEOPLE AGAINST O'HARA, based on the novel by Eleazar Lipsky
(MGM)
THE MAN WITH A CLOAK, based on the novel by John Dickson Carr
(MGM)

1951

THE ASPHALT JUNGLE by Ben Maddow (MGM)

MR. 880, winner of a special award for the author of the novel, St. Clair McKelway (20th Century–Fox)

THE MAN ON THE EIFFEL TOWER by Harry Brown, based on the novel A BATTLE OF NERVES by Georges Simenon (A&T)

STAGE FRIGHT by Whitfield Cook, based on the novel MAN RUNNING by Selwyn Jepson (Warner)

1950

THE WINDOW by Mel Dinelli and Cornell Woolrich, author of "Fire Escape," on which the movie was based (RKO)

CRISS CROSS by Daniel Fuchs, based on the novel by Don Tracy (U-I)

CHICAGO DEADLINE by Warren Duff and Tiffany Thayer (Paramount)

THE SCENE OF THE CRIME by Charles Schnee, based on the story by John Bartlow Martin (MGM)

WHITE HEAT by Ivan Goff and Ben Roberts, based on the story by Virginia Kellogg (Warner)

1949

CALL NORTHSIDE 777 by Quentin Reynolds, Leonard Hoffman, Jay Dratler, and Jerome Cady (posthumous—accepted by Mrs. Cady), screenwriters; Henry Hathaway, director; Otto Lang, producer; and 20th Century–Fox

ROPE by Arthur Laurents, based on the play by Patrick Hamilton (Transatlantic)

SORRY, WRONG NUMBER by Lucille Fletcher, from her play (Paramount)

THE BIG CLOCK by Jonathan Latimer based on the novel by Kenneth Fearing (Paramount)

1948

CROSSFIRE, John Paxton, screenwriter; Richard Brooks, author of "The Brick Fox-Hole," on which the movie was based; Dore Schary, producer; Adrian Scott, associate producer; and Edward Dmytryk, director (RKO)

1947
THE KILLERS by Anthony Veiller, writer; Mark Hellinger, producer; and Robert Siodmak, director (Hellinger-Universal)

1946
MURDER, MY SWEET, John Paxton, screenplay; Raymond Chandler, author of FAREWELL, MY LOVELY, on which the movie was based; Dick Powell for his portrayal of a private detective; and RKO Pictures (Special Scroll)

Honorary Scroll to THE HOUSE ON 92ND ST. by Barre Lyndon, Charles G. Booth, and John Monks Jr.(20th Century–Fox)

Best Foreign Film (awarded 1949–66)

1966
THE IPCRESS FILE by Bill Canaway and James Doran (Universal)

THUNDERBALL by Richard Maibaum (United Artists)

SYMPHONY FOR A MASSACRE by Jose Giovanni, Claude Sautat, and Jacques Deray (Untra Film Co.)

1965
SÉANCE ON A WET AFTERNOON by Bryan Forbes (Artixo Productions Ltd.)

GOLDFINGER by Richard Maibaum and Paul Dehn (United Artists)

NOTHING BUT THE BEST by Frederic Raphael (Royal Films Intl.)

1964
ANY NUMBER CAN PLAY by Albert Simonin, Michael Audiard, and Henri Verneuil (MGM)

HIGH AND LOW by Ryuzo Kikiushima, Ejiro Hisaita, and Akira Kurosawa (Toho)

MURDER AT THE GALLOP by James P. Cavanagh (MGM)

1962
PURPLE NOON by Paul Degauff and Rene Clement (Paris/Panitalia/Titamus)

1960
SAPPHIRE by Janet Green (Rank/Artna)

1959
INSPECTOR MAIGRET by Georges Simenon (Intermondia/J. P. Guibert/Jolly Film)

1956
DIABOLIQUE, Henri-Georges Clouzot, writer/director (Filmsonor) (Special Edgar)

1949
JENNY LAMOUR (QUAI DES ORFÈVRES) (Vog Films)

Best Play

1991
ACCOMPLICE by Rupert Holmes

1990
CITY OF ANGELS by Larry Gelbart and Cy Coleman

1986
THE MYSTERY OF EDWIN DROOD by Rupert Holmes (New York Shakespeare Festival) (Special Edgar)

1982
A TALENT FOR MURDER by Jerome Chodorov and Norman Panama

1981
RICOCHET by Paul Nathan, for his off-Broadway show (Special Edgar)

1980
DEATH TRAP by Ira Levin

1971
SLEUTH by Anthony Shaffer, performed at the Imperial Theatre

1962
WRITE ME A MURDER by Frederick Knott
A SHOT IN THE DARK by Harry Kurnitz

1955
WITNESS FOR THE PROSECUTION by Agatha Christie (Special Edgar)

1953
DIAL M FOR MURDER by Frederick Knott (Special Edgar)

1950
DETECTIVE STORY by Sidney Kingsley (Special Edgar)

Best Radio Drama (awarded 1946–60)

1960
"Sorry, Wrong Number" by Lucille Fletcher (SUSPENSE/CBS)

1959
SUSPENSE by William N. Robson (CBS) (Raven Award)

1958
"The Galindez-Murphy Case: A Chronicle of Terror," Jay
    MacMullen, writer/producer (CBS)

1955
"The Tree" by Stanley Niss (21ST PRECINCT/CBS)

1954
"The Shot" by E. Jack Newman (SUSPENSE/CBS)

1953
THE MYSTERIOUS TRAVELER by Robert Arthur and David Kogan
    (Mutual Broadcasting System)

1952
DRAGNET, Jack Webb, producer/director; James Moser, scriptwriter
    (NBC)

1951
DRAGNET, Jack Webb, producer/director; James Moser, scriptwriter; and NBC
THE MYSTERIOUS TRAVELER by Robert Arthur and David Kogan (Mutual Broadcasting System)

1950
MURDER BY EXPERTS by Robert Arthur and David Kogan (Mutual Broadcasting System)
THIS IS YOUR FBI (ABC)
THE FAT MAN (ABC)
SUSPENSE (CBS)

1949
INNER SANCTUM, John Roeburt, writer; Himan Brown, director/producer; and CBS
THE MYSTERIOUS TRAVELER by Robert Arthur, David Kogan (Mutual Broadcasting System)

1948
SUSPENSE, William Spier, director, and CBS

1947
THE ADVENTURES OF SAM SPADE, Bob Tallman and Jason James, writers; William Spier, producer (CBS)

1946
Tie between:
ELLERY QUEEN by Frederic Dannay and Manfred B. Lee (the writing team known as Ellery Queen) (CBS)
MR. AND MRS. NORTH by Frances and Richard Lockridge (NBC)
Honorary Scroll to SUSPENSE (CBS)

Outstanding Mystery Criticism (awarded 1946–67)

1967
John T. Winterich (SATURDAY REVIEW)

1964
Hans Stefan Santesson (THE SAINT MYSTERY MAGAZINE)

1961
James Sandoe (NEW YORK HERALD-TRIBUNE)

1957
Curtis W. Casewit (DENVER POST)

1955
Drexel Drake (CHICAGO TRIBUNE)

1954
Helen McCloy and Brett Halliday
   (WESTPORT TOWN CRIER and
   other Connecticut papers)

1953
Anthony Boucher (THE NEW
   YORK TIMES and ELLERY
   QUEEN'S MYSTERY MAGAZINE)
   (Special Edgar)

1952
Lenore Glen Offord and the SAN
   FRANCISCO CHRONICLE for best
   overall mystery reviewing

The Bouchercon World
Mystery Convention was
named in honor of noted mystery critic William Anthony
Parker White, who wrote under
the name Anthony Boucher.

1951
Dorothy B. Hughes (ALBUQUERQUE
   TRIBUNE and LOS ANGELES DAILY NEWS)
Anthony Boucher (THE NEW YORK TIMES and ELLERY QUEEN'S
   MYSTERY MAGAZINE)
Elizabeth Bullock (THE NEW YORK TIMES)
Drexel Drake (CHICAGO TRIBUNE)
Hillis Mills (THE NEW YORKER)

1950

Anthony Boucher (THE NEW YORK TIMES and ELLERY QUEEN'S
MYSTERY MAGAZINE)
Elizabeth Bullock (THE NEW YORK TIMES)
James Sandoe (CHICAGO SUN-TIMES)
William Weber (SATURDAY REVIEW OF LITERATURE)
Drexel Drake (CHICAGO TRIBUNE)

1949

James Sandoe (CHICAGO SUN-TIMES)
Angelica Gibbs (THE NEW YORKER)
William McGivern (PHILADELPHIA RECORD)
Isaac Anderson (THE NEW YORK TIMES)

1948

Howard Haycraft (ELLERY QUEEN'S MYSTERY MAGAZINE **and author
of** THE ART OF THE MYSTERY STORY)

1947

William C. Weber, alias "Judge Lynch" (SATURDAY REVIEW OF
LITERATURE)

1946

Anthony Boucher (SAN FRANCISCO CHRONICLE)

Special Edgars

1991

THE ENCYCLOPEDIA OF WORLD CRIME, CRIMINAL JUSTICE,
CRIMINOLOGY, AND LAW ENFORCEMENT by Jay Robert Nash
(Crime Books, Inc.)

1989

Joan Kahn on her retirement after fifty years in mystery publishing

1986

DETECTIVE AND MYSTERY FICTION: AN INTERNATIONAL
BIBLIOGRAPHY OF SECONDARY SOURCES by Walter Albert
(Brownstone Books)

1985
THE SILENT SHAME by Mark Nykanen (NBC) news report on child-abuse crimes

1984
A BIBLIOGRAPHY OF A. CONAN DOYLE by Richard Lancelyn Green and John Michael Gibson (Oxford University Press)

1983
THE CASE OF DASHIELL HAMMETT by Stephen Talbot (PBS documentary)

1982
THE YOUNG DETECTIVE'S HANDBOOK by William Vivian Butler (Atlantic/Little, Brown)
SHERLOCK HOLMES, special HBO production of the William Gillette play

1981
MYSTERY! by Joan Wilson (PBS), best in international programming
Lawrence Spivak, founding publisher of ELLERY QUEEN'S MYSTERY MAGAZINE forty years ago
THE EDGE OF NIGHT celebrating its twenty-fifth year as a TV series

1980
DICK TRACY by Chester Gould, creator of Dick Tracy nearly fifty years ago
THE MURDERERS' WHO'S WHO by J. H. H. Gaute and Robin Odell

1979
Mignon C. Eberhart and Frederic Dannay celebrating fifty years since the publication of their first novels
Richard Levinson and William Link for their COLUMBO and ELLERY QUEEN TV series.

1978
MYSTERY WRITER'S HANDBOOK edited by Lawrence Treat
Allen J. Hubin for a decade as editor of THE ARMCHAIR DETECTIVE
MURDER INK by Dilys Winn (Workman)

1976
Jorge Luis Borges for distinguished
  contribution to the mystery genre
Donald J. Sobol for the Encyclopedia
  Brown books (juvenile mystery)

1975
Howard Haycraft for his distin-
  guished contribution to mystery
  criticism and scholarship
ROYAL BLOODLINE: ELLERY
  QUEEN, AUTHOR AND
  DETECTIVE by Francis M.
  Nevins Jr. (Bowling Green State
  University Popular Press)

Allen J. Hubin,
TAD's founder, accepts his 1978
Edgar Award.

1974
THE ONION FIELD by Joseph Wambaugh (Delacorte Press)

1973
MORTAL CONSEQUENCES: A HISTORY FROM THE DETECTIVE STORY
  TO THE CRIME NOVEL by Julian Symons (Harper & Row)
MURDER ON THE MENU by Jeanine Larmoth and Charlotte Turgeon
  (Scribners)

1972
A CATALOGUE OF CRIME by Jacques Barzun and Wendell Taylor
  (Harper & Row)

1970
John Dickson Carr in honor of his forty years as a mystery writer

1969
Ellery Queen on the fortieth anniversary of THE ROMAN HAT
  MYSTERY
Philip Wittenberg for voluntary service to MWA as general counsel
  (Special Scroll)

1967
Julius Fast as first winner of the Edgar twenty-two years ago
Clayton Rawson for decades of service to the organization

1966
"The Gospel According to 007" by the Reverend O. C. Edwards
  (THE LIVING CHURCH)

1964
DOWN THESE MEAN STREETS by Philip Durham (University of North
  Carolina Press)

1963
THE ORDEAL OF MRS. SNOW by Patrick Quentin (Random House)
  (collection of short stories)
COPS AND ROBBERS by Philip Reisman (NBC)
COMPANION TO MURDER by E. Spencer Shew (Knopf) (two-volume
  reference work)

1962
THE ANNALS OF MURDER by Thomas M. McDade (University of
  Oklahoma Press)

1961
Philip Wittenberg, legal counsel
Charles Addams, cartoonist of the macabre
Elizabeth Daly, grande dame of women mystery writers

1959
AMERICAN MURDER BALLADS by Alice Wooley Burt (Oxford
  University Press)

1957
COMPULSION by Meyer Levin (Simon & Schuster)

1954
THE FRIGHTENED WIFE AND OTHER MURDER STORIES by Mary
  Roberts Rinehart (Rinehart Publishers)

1952
QUEEN'S QUORUM: THE 125 MOST IMPORTANT BOOKS OF
   DETECTIVE-CRIME-MYSTERY SHORT STORIES compiled by Frederic
   Dannay and Manfred Lee (as Ellery Queen) (Biblo and Tannen)

1951
Franklin Heller, producer/director of MWA's television show, THE WEB

1950
THE LIFE OF SIR ARTHUR CONAN DOYLE by John Dickson Carr
   (Harper & Bros.)

1949
Peter W. Williams for creating the Edgar bust
Clayton Rawson for launching CLUE magazine
Arthur A. Stoughton, president of the Bronx Society of Arts and
   Sciences and custodian of Poe Cottage in Fordham for twenty-six
   years

THE ELLERY QUEEN AWARDS

(This award was established in 1983 to honor writing teams and outstanding people in the mystery-publishing industry.)

   1994 Otto Penzler
   1992 Margaret Norton
   1990 Joel Davis
   1989 Richard Levinson and William Link
   1988 Ruth Cavin
   1987 Eleanor Sullivan
   1985 Joan Kahn
   1983 Emma Lathen (Mary Jane Latsis and Martha Henissart)

THE ROBERT L. FISH MEMORIAL AWARDS

(This award, administered by Mystery Writers of America, is actually
sponsored by the Robert L. Fish estate. Each year the Edgar short-story

committee selects the best first short story by an American author. The author receives a plaque and a monetary award.)

1994
"Wicked Twist" by D. A. McGuire (ALFRED HITCHCOCK MYSTERY MAGAZINE, October '93)

1993
"A Will Is a Way" by Stephen Saylor (ELLERY QUEEN'S MYSTERY MAGAZINE, March '92)

1991
"Willie's Story" by Jerry F. Skarky (ALFRED HITCHCOCK MYSTERY MAGAZINE, June '90)

1990
"Hawks" by Connie Colt (ALFRED HITCHCOCK MYSTERY MAGAZINE, June '89)

1989
"Different Drummers" by Linda O. Johnston (ELLERY QUEEN'S MYSTERY MAGAZINE, July '88)

1988
"Roger, Mr. Whilkie!" by Eric M. Heideman (ALFRED HITCHCOCK MYSTERY MAGAZINE, July '87)

1987
"Father to the Man" by Mary Kittredge (ALFRED HITCHCOCK MYSTERY MAGAZINE, November '86)

1986
"Final Rites" by Doug Allyn (ALFRED HITCHCOCK MYSTERY MAGAZINE, December '85)

1985
"Poor Dumb Mouths" by Bill Crenshaw (ALFRED HITCHCOCK MYSTERY MAGAZINE, May '84)

1984
"Locked Doors" by Lilly Carlson (ELLERY QUEEN'S MYSTERY MAGAZINE, October '83)

THE RAVEN AWARDS

(A special award given for outstanding achievement in the mystery field outside the realm of creative writing)

1993
President Bill Clinton, Reader of the Year

1992
Harold Q. Masur for his years of service to MWA as general counsel

1990
Sarah Booth Conroy, Reader of the Year
Carol Brener for her skill in selling books to the public

1989
The Bouchercon Annual World Mystery Convention
SHEAR MADNESS by Marilyn Abrams and Bruce Jordan (Cranberry Productions) for longest-running off-Broadway play

1988
Angela Lansbury
Vincent Price

1986
Suzi Oppenheimer, Reader of the Year

1985
Eudora Welty, Reader of the Year

1984
Sylvia Porter, Reader of the Year

1983
Isaac Bashevis Singer, Reader of the Year

1980
"Muppet Murders" (MUPPET SHOW)

1979
Alberto Tedeschi (Mondadori), publisher of the most succesful Italian
  series of mysteries

1978
I AM MY BROTHER'S KEEPER by Richard N. Hughes (WPIX) for
  being the best showcase for mystery stories
Danny Arnold (ABC) as the executive producer of BARNEY MILLER,
  TV police series
Edwin Gorey for the sets he designed for DRACULA on Broadway

1976
Eddie Lawrence, Reader of the Year
Leo Margolies as editor of MIKE SHAYNE MYSTERY MAGAZINE

1975
ABC-TV for its WORLD WIDE MYSTERY series
Royal Shakespeare Company for the company's revival of the play
  SHERLOCK HOLMES.
RADIO MYSTERY THEATRE (CBS) for the Hy Brown nightly mysteries
Hardcover Book Jacket
  Doubleday (TALES OF THE BLACK WIDOWERS)
  Harper & Row (FERAL)
  Harper & Row (THEY CAN'T HANG ME)
  Putnam (NELLA WAITS)
Softcover Book Jacket
  Pocket Books (THE HUBSCHMANN EFFECT)
  Dell (THE MOUSETRAP)
  Fawcett-Crest (ANIMA)

1974
Hardcover Book Jacket
  Dodd, Mead (REPRISAL)
  Random House (HAIL TO THE CHIEF)
  Simon & Schuster (THE COLD ONES)
Softcover Book Jacket
  Curtis Books (THE ABDUCTOR)
  Curtis Books (INSPECTOR MAIGRET AND THE MADWOMAN)
  Dell (DAUGHTER OF DARKNESS)

1973
Hardcover Book Jacket
  E. P. Dutton (THE ERECTION SET)
  G. P. Putnam's Sons (TRICKS OF THE TRADE)
  McKay (MRS. KNOX'S PROFESSION)
  Random House (DEAD SKIP)
Softcover Book Jacket
  Ace (FETISH MURDERS)
  Dell (DEATH CAN BE BEAUTIFUL)
  Dell (ROLLING GRAVESTONES)

1972
Hardcover Book Jacket
  G. P. Putnam's Sons (IF YOU WANT TO SEE YOUR WIFE AGAIN)
  Wm. Morrow (WHIM TO KILL)
  Random House (THE STALKER)
Softcover Book Jacket
  Ace (BLACK MAN, WHITE MAN)
  Avon (THE SHADOWS OF THE HOUSE)
  Ballantine (THE LADY OF THE LAKE)

1971
Judith Crist, Reader of the Year
Hardcover Book Jacket
  Dodd, Mead (ACT OF VIOLENCE)
  Doubleday (IF LAUREL SHOT HARDY THE WORLD WOULD END)
  Inner Sanctum (IF THE SHROUD FITS)

Softcover Book Jacket
Avon Classic Crime Collection (LAST CASE)
Avon (ONE MAN SHOW)
Popular Library (PICTURE MISS SEETON)

1970
Hardcover Book Jacket
E. P. Dutton (THE SPANISH PRISONER)
Doubleday (TALES OF UNEASE)
Wm. Morrow (THE BLACK GENERAL)
Softcover Book Jacket
Avon for Classic Crime Collection

1969
Hardcover Book Jacket
Scribners (GOD SPEED THE NIGHT)
Doubleday (DIE QUICKLY, DEAR MOTHER)
Wm. Morrow (SINGAPORE WINK)
Softcover Book Jacket
Ballantine (THE DRESDEN GREEN)
Ballantine (NOTHING IS THE NUMBER WHEN YOU DIE)
Berkley Books (A TANGLED WEB)

1968
Joey Adams, Reader of the Year
Hardcover Book Jacket
Doubleday (PERTURBING SPIRIT)
Doubleday (THE RELUCTANT MEDIUM)
A. A. Mills (RAIN WITH VIOLENCE)
Softcover Book Jacket
Ballantine (JOHNNY UNDERGROUND)
Ballantine (MALICE MATRIMONIAL)
Pyramid Books (A DOLL FOR THE TOFF)

1967
Richard Watts Jr., Reader of the Year
ELLERY QUEEN'S MYSTERY MAGAZINE on its twenty-sixth anniversary
and as the best showcase for mystery stories

Hardcover Book Jacket
Wm. Morrow (LET SLEEPING GIRLS LIE)
Doubleday (THE CRIMSON MADNESS OF LITTLE DOOM)
Scribners (THE BARON AND THE MOGUL SWORDS)
Harper & Row
Softcover Book Jacket
Ballantine (SOME OF YOUR BLOOD)
Crowell-Collier
Bantam Books
Collier (I AM THE CAT)

1966
Hardcover Book Jacket
Random House
Doubleday (GIRL ON THE RUN)
Simon & Schuster
Viking
Softcover Book Jacket
Bantam (KNOCK AND WAIT A WHILE)
Dell
Popular Library

1965
Dr. Milton Helpern for his work in forensic medicine
Philip Wittenberg for his long years of voluntary service (Scroll)
Hardcover Book Jacket
Doubleday
Simon & Schuster's Inner Sanctum Mysteries
Walker & Co.
Softcover Book Jacket
Bantam Books
Dell
Popular Library

1964
Hardcover Book Jacket
Harper & Row
Simon & Schuster

Softcover Book Jacket
  Berkley Medallion Books
  Popular Library

1963
Hardcover Book Jacket
  Doubleday
Softcover Book Jacket
  Collier Books

1962
Book Jacket
  Walker & Co.
  Doubleday
  Harper Bros.
THE DEFENDERS, a TV show in its first year

1961
Ilka Chase, Reader of the Year
Hardcover Book Jacket
  Scribners (A MARK OF DISPLEASURE)
Paperback Book Jacket
  Dell (THE THREE COFFINS)

1960
Ray Brennan for crime reporting
David C. Cook for BEST DETECTIVE STORIES OF THE YEAR
Phyllis McGinley, Mystery Fan of the Year
Alfred Hitchcock for his contribution to the mystery
Gail Jackson, producer of PERRY MASON TV series

1959
Franklin Delano Roosevelt (posthumous), Reader of the Year (Scroll
  accepted by Eleanor Roosevelt)
Lawrence G. Blochman for long and distinguished service to MWA
  and THE THIRD DEGREE
Frederic G. Melcher on his retirement after thirty-five years with
  PUBLISHERS WEEKLY

Western Printing & Lithographing Co. for Dell book jackets

1958
Harper & Bros. for general excellence
Dell, a Scroll for their Great Mystery Series book jackets

1957
Miss Dorothy Kilgallen, Reader of the Year
Hardcover Book Jacket
  Doubleday (INSPECTOR MAIGRET AND THE BURGLAR'S WIFE)

1956
Book Jacket
  Scribners

1955
Softcover Book Jacket
  Dell (BERTON ROUECHÉ)
  Little, Brown (ELEVEN BLUE MEN)

1954
Dr. Harrison Martland, retiring medical examiner, Essex County,
    New Jersey
Dr. Thomas A. Gonzales, retiring medical examiner, New York City
Tom Lehrer for his mystery parodies

1953
E. T. Guymon Jr. for his outstanding library of mystery literature

2. The Crime Writers' Association of Great Britain Awards

The Crime Writers' Association of Great Britain has presented an award for the best crime novel of the year since 1955. Originally the Crossed Red Herring Award, this award is now known as the Gold Dagger. The Silver Dagger goes to the runner-up. Since 1978, a Gold Dagger has also been awarded to the year's best nonfiction crime book.

The John Creasey Memorial Award, instituted in 1973, is for the best first crime novel by an author who has not previously published a full-length work of fiction.

The Diamond Dagger, sponsored by Cartier since 1986, goes to a writer, not a book, and is awarded annually for outstanding contribution to the genre.

From 1985 to 1987, *The Police Review* sponsored an award for the crime novel that best portrayed police work and procedure.

In 1988, for one year only, *Punch* magazine sponsored a Punch Prize for the funniest crime book of the year. It was superseded by the Last Laugh Award.

In 1990, Hazel Wyn Jones instituted the CWA '92 Award to run for a period of three years for a crime novel partly or wholly set in Europe.

Also in 1990, the *New Law Journal* sponsored the biennial Rumpole Award for a crime novel with a British legal setting.

The CWA/The Macallan Short Story Award was instituted in 1993 for the best short story of the year and is sponsored by The Macallan Whisky Distillery.

1993
Gold Dagger: Patricia D. Cornwell, CRUEL AND UNUSUAL
Nonfiction Gold Dagger: Alexandra Artley, MURDER IN THE HEART
Silver Dagger: Sarah Dunant, FATLANDS
John Creasey Award: None
Diamond Dagger: Edith Pargeter (aka Ellis Peters)
Last Laugh Award: Michael Pearce, THE MAMUR ZAPT & THE SPOILS
    OF EGYPT
CWA/The Macallan Short Story Award: Julian Rathbone, "Some
    Sunny Day"

1992
Gold Dagger: Colin Dexter, THE WAY THROUGH THE WOODS
Nonfiction Gold Dagger: Charles Nicholl, THE RECKONING
Silver Dagger: Liza Cody, BUCKET NUT
John Creasey Award: Minette Walters, THE ICE HOUSE
Diamond Dagger: Leslie Charteris
Last Laugh Award: Carl Hiaasen, NATIVE TONGUE
CWA '92 Award: Timothy Williams, BLACK AUGUST
CWA Rumpole Award: Peter Rawlinson, HATRED AND CONTEMPT

1991
Gold Dagger: Barbara Vine (aka Ruth Rendell), KING SOLOMON'S
    CARPET
Nonfiction Gold Dagger: John Bossy, GIORDANO BRUNO AND THE
    EMBASSY AFFAIR
Silver Dagger: Frances Fyfield, DEEP SLEEP
John Creasey Award: Walter Mosley, DEVIL IN A BLUE DRESS
Diamond Dagger: Ruth Rendell
Last Laugh Award: Mike Ripley, ANGELS IN ARMS
CWA '92 Award: Barbara Wilson, GAUDI AFTERNOON

1990
Gold Dagger: Reginald Hill, BONES AND SILENCE
Nonfiction Gold Dagger: Jonathan Goodman, THE PASSING OF STARR
    FAITHFULL
Silver Dagger: Mike Phillips, THE LATE CANDIDATE
John Creasey Award: Patricia D. Cornwell, POSTMORTEM

Diamond Dagger: Julian Symons
Last Laugh Award: Simon Shaw, KILLER CINDERELLA
CWA '92 Award: Michael Dibdin, VENDETTA
Rumpole Award: Frances Fyfield, TRIAL BY FIRE

1989

Gold Dagger: Colin Dexter, THE WENCH IS DEAD
Nonfiction Gold Dagger: Robert Lindsey, A GATHERING OF SAINTS
Silver Dagger: Desmond Lowden, THE SHADOW RUN
John Creasey Award: Annette Roome, A REAL SHOT IN THE ARM
Diamond Dagger: Dick Francis
Last Laugh Award: Mike Ripley, ANGEL TOUCH
Red Herring Special Awards: Glyn Hardwicke (posthumously) for
 redrafting the constitution and John Kennedy Melling for editing
 THE CRIME WRITERS' PRACTICAL HANDBOOK

1988

Gold Dagger: Michael Dibdin, RATKING
Nonfiction Gold Dagger: Bernard Wasserstein, THE SECRET LIVES OF
 TREBITSCH LINCOLN
Silver Dagger: Sara Paretsky, TOXIC SHOCK
John Creasey Award: Janet Neel, DEATH'S BRIGHT ANGEL
Diamond Dagger: John le Carré
Punch Prize: Nancy Livingston, DEATH IN A DISTANT LAND

1987

Gold Dagger: Barbara Vine (aka Ruth
 Rendell), A FATAL INVERSION
Nonfiction Gold Dagger: Bernard Tay-
 lor and Stephen Knight, PERFECT
 MURDER
Silver Dagger: Scott Turow, PRESUMED
 INNOCENT
John Creasey Award: Denis Kilcom-
 mons, DARK APOSTLE
Diamond Dagger: P. D. James
Police Review Award: Roger Busby,
 SNOWMAN

Ruth Rendell also writes under the name Barbara Vine.

1986
Gold Dagger: Ruth Rendell, LIVE FLESH
Nonfiction Gold Dagger: John Bryson, EVIL ANGELS
Silver Dagger: P. D. James, A TASTE FOR DEATH
John Creasey Award: Neville Steed, TINPLATE
Diamond Dagger: Eric Ambler
Police Review Award: Bill Knox, THE CROSSFIRE KILLINGS
Red Herring Special Award: Beatrice Taylor, for fourteen years as the
   Association's treasurer

1985
Gold Dagger: Paula Gosling, MONKEY PUZZLE
Nonfiction Gold Dagger: Brian Masters, KILLING FOR COMPANY
Silver Dagger: Dorothy Simpson, LAST SEEN ALIVE
John Creasey Award: Robert Richardson, THE LATIMER MERCY
Police Review Award: Andrew Arncliffe, AFTER THE HOLIDAY
Red Herring Special Award: Marian Babson for "ten years of magnifi-
   cent secretaryship"

1984
Gold Dagger: B. M. Gill, THE TWELFTH JUROR
Nonfiction Gold Dagger: David Yallop, IN GOD'S NAME
Silver Dagger: Ruth Rendell, THE TREE OF HANDS
John Creasey Award: Elizabeth Ironside, A VERY PRIVATE ENTERPRISE

1983
Gold Dagger: John Hutton, ACCIDENTAL CRIMES
Nonfiction Gold Dagger: Peter Watson, DOUBLE DEALER
Silver Dagger: William McIlvanney, THE PAPERS OF TONY VEITCH
John Creasey Award: tie—Carol Clemeau, THE ARIADNE CLUE, and
   Eric Wright, THE NIGHT THE GODS SMILED
Red Herring Special Award: F. E. Pardoe for serving twenty-five years
   on the Fiction Panel

1982
Gold Dagger: Peter Lovesey, THE FALSE INSPECTOR DEW
Nonfiction Gold Dagger: John Cornwell, EARTH TO EARTH
Silver Dagger: S. T. Haymon, RITUAL MURDER
John Creasey Award: Andrew Taylor, CAROLINE MINUSCULE

1981
Gold Dagger: Martin Cruz Smith, GORKY PARK
Nonfiction Gold Dagger: Jacobo Timerman, PRISONER WITHOUT A
NAME, CELL WITHOUT A NUMBER
Silver Dagger: Colin Dexter, THE DEAD OF JERICHO
John Creasey Award: James Leigh, THE LUDI VICTOR
Red Herring Special Award: Martin Russell for his work in editing RED
HERRINGS

1980
Gold Dagger: H. R. F. Keating, THE MURDER
OF THE MAHARAJAH
Nonfiction Gold Dagger: Anthony Summers,
CONSPIRACY
Silver Dagger: Ellis Peters, MONK'S HOOD
John Creasey Award: Liza Cody, DUPE
Special Silver Dagger: Elizabeth Ferrars, in
recognition of her publication of fifty
outstanding books

H. R. F. Keating.

1979
Gold Dagger: Dick Francis, WHIP HAND
Nonfiction Gold Dagger: Shirley Green, RACHMAN
Silver Dagger: Colin Dexter, SERVICE OF ALL THE DEAD
Nonfiction Silver Dagger: Jon Connell and Douglas Sutherland,
FRAUD
John Creasey Award: David Serafin, SATURDAY OF GLORY
Red Herring Special Award: Madelaine Duke and Frank Arthur "for
services to the Association"

1978
Gold Dagger: Lionel Davidson, THE CHELSEA MURDERS
Nonfiction Gold Dagger: Audrey Williamson, THE MYSTERY OF THE
PRINCES
Silver Dagger: Peter Lovesey, WAXWORK
Nonfiction Silver Dagger: Harry Hawkes, THE CAPTURE OF THE BLACK
PANTHER
John Creasey Award: Paula Gosling, A RUNNING DUCK
Red Herring Special Awards: Alberto Tedeschi of Mondadori Publish-

ers, Italy, Frederic Dannay, and Nigel Morland "for services to crime fiction"

1977
Gold Dagger: John le Carré, THE HONOURABLE SCHOOLBOY
Silver Dagger: William McIlvanney, LAIDLAW
John Creasey Award: Jonathan Gash, THE JUDAS PAIR

1976
Gold Dagger: Ruth Rendell, A DEMON IN MY VIEW
Silver Dagger: James McClure, ROGUE EAGLE
John Creasey Award: Patrick Alexander, DEATH OF A THIN-SKINNED ANIMAL

1975
Gold Dagger: Nicholas Meyer, THE SEVEN PER CENT SOLUTION
Silver Dagger: P. D. James, THE BLACK TOWER
John Creasey Award: Sara George, ACID DROP
Special Award: Gladys Mitchell in honor of fifty outstanding books
Special Award: Anne Britton for ten years of editing RED HERRINGS
Special Awards: Jean Bosden and Penelope Wallace for their valuable services in connection with the first Crime Writers' International Congress

1974
Gold Dagger: Anthony Price, OTHER PATHS TO GLORY
Silver Dagger: Francis Clifford, THE GROSVENOR SQUARE GOODBYE
John Creasey Award: Roger Simon, THE BIG FIX

1973
Gold Dagger: Robert Littell, THE DEFECTION OF A. J. LEWINTER
Silver Dagger: Gwendoline Butler, A COFFIN FOR PANDORA
John Creasey Award: Kyril Bonfiglioli, DON'T POINT THAT THING AT ME

1972
Gold Dagger: Eric Ambler, THE LEVANTER
Silver Dagger: Victor Canning, THE RAINBIRD PATTERN

1971
Gold Dagger: James McClure, THE STEAM PIG
Silver Dagger: P. D. James, SHROUD FOR A NIGHTINGALE
Special Award: Alex Clark Smith for his services as treasurer

1970
Gold Dagger: Joan Fleming, YOUNG MAN, I THINK YOU'RE DYING
Silver Dagger: Anthony Price, THE LABYRINTH MAKERS
Special Award: Gavin Lyall for his work in editing the CRIME BACK-
GROUND pamphlets

1969
Gold Dagger: Peter Dickinson, A PRIDE OF HEROES
Silver Dagger: Francis Clifford, ANOTHER WAY OF DYING
Best Foreign: Rex Stout, THE FATHER HUNT

1968
Gold Dagger: Peter Dickinson, SKIN DEEP
Runner-up: Nicholas Blake, THE PRIVATE WOUND
Best Foreign: Sebastien Japrisot, THE LADY IN THE CAR WITH GLASSES
AND A GUN

1967
Gold Dagger: Emma Lathen, MURDER AGAINST THE GRAIN
Runner-up: Colin Watson, LONELYHEART 4122
Best British: Eric Ambler, DIRTY STORY
Special Award: Charles Franklin for his work as editor of the CRIME
WRITER

1966
Gold Dagger: Lionel Davidson, A LONG WAY TO SHILOH
Runner-up: John Bingham, THE DOUBLE AGENT
Best Foreign: John Ball, IN THE HEAT OF THE NIGHT
Special Merit Award: Julian Symons for CRIME AND DETECTION: AN
ILLUSTRATED HISTORY FROM 1840

1965
Gold Dagger: Ross Macdonald, THE FAR SIDE OF THE DOLLAR

Runners-up: Dick Francis, FOR KICKS, and Emma Lathen, ACCOUNT-
ING FOR MURDER
Best British: Gavin Lyall, MIDNIGHT PLUS ONE

1964
Gold Dagger: H. R. F. Keating, THE PERFECT MURDER
Runners-up: Gavin Lyall, THE MOST DANGEROUS GAME, and Ross
    Macdonald, THE CHILL
Best Foreign: Patricia Highsmith, THE TWO FACES OF JANUARY
Special Merit Award: Herbert Harris for his valuable services in editing
    RED HERRINGS

1963
Gold Dagger: John le Carré, THE
SPY WHO CAME IN FROM THE
COLD
Runners-up: Nicolas Freeling,
GUN BEFORE BUTTER, and
William Haggard, THE HIGH
WIRE
Special Merit Award: Allan Prior
for his outstanding television
crime plays

1962
Gold Dagger: Joan Fleming,
    WHEN I GROW RICH
Runners-up: Eric Ambler, THE
LIGHT OF DAY, and Colin
Watson, HOPJOY WAS HERE

John le Carré's most recent book is
The Night Manager.

1961
Gold Dagger: Mary Kelly, THE SPOILT KILL
Runners-up: John le Carré, CALL FOR THE DEAD, and Allan Prior, ONE
AWAY
Special Merit Award: Berkley Mather for the outstanding quality of his
television crime plays

1960
Gold Dagger: Lionel Davidson, THE NIGHT OF WENCESLAS
Runners-up: Mary Stewart, MY BROTHER MICHAEL, and Julian
Symons, PROGRESS OF A CRIME

1959
Gold Dagger: Eric Ambler, PASSAGE OF ARMS
Runners-up: James Mitchell, A WAY BACK, and Menna Gallie, STRIKE
FOR A KINGDOM
Special Merit Awards: Roy Vickers for his many outstanding contribu-
tions to crime fiction, and Janet Green for her original film script
of SAPPHIRE

1958
Gold Dagger: Margot Bennett, SOMEONE FROM THE PAST
Runners-up: Margery Allingham, HIDE MY EYES, James Byrom, OR
BE HE DEAD, and John Sherwood, UNDIPLOMATIC EXIT

1957
Gold Dagger: Julian Symons, THE COLOUR OF MURDER
Runners-up: Ngaio Marsh, OFF WITH HIS HEAD, George Milner,
YOUR MONEY AND YOUR LIFE, and Douglas Rutherford, THE
LONG ECHO

1956
Gold Dagger: Edward Grierson, THE SECOND MAN
Runners-up: Sarah Gainham, TIME RIGHT DEADLY, Arthur Upfield,
MAN OF TWO TRIBES, and J. J. Marric (aka John Creasey),
GIDEON'S WEEK

1955
Gold Dagger: Winston Graham, THE LITTLE WALLS
Runners-up: Leigh Howard, BLIND DATE, Ngaio Marsh, SCALES OF
JUSTICE, and Margot Bennett, THE MAN WHO DIDN'T FLY

3. Crime Writers of Canada's Arthur Ellis Awards

The Arthur Ellis Awards, established in 1984 and named after the *nom de travail* of Canada's official hangman, are awarded annually by the Crime Writers of Canada, Canada's national association of authors and industry professionals active in the field of crime writing.

The CWC's special award, the Chairman's citation, was given the first year to Derrick Murdoch, who helped found the CWC and was the most active reviewer of crime fiction in Canada in 1983. After his death the following year the award was renamed in his honor and presented for outstanding service to the mystery genre. Dates denote the year the award was given.

1994

Best Novel: John Lawrence Reynolds, GYPSY SINS
Best First Novel: Gavin Scott, MEMORY TRACE
Best Short Story: Robert J. Sawyer, "Just Like Old Times"
Best True Crime: David R. Williams, WITH MALICE AFORETHOUGHT: SIX SPECTACULAR CANADIAN TRIALS
Best Juvenile: John Dowd, ABALONE SUMMER
Best Play: Timothy Findley, THE STILLBORN LOVER

1993

Best Novel: Carsten Stroud, LIZARDSKIN
Best First Novel: Sean Stewart, PASSION PLAY
Best Short Story: Nancy Kilpatrick, "Mantrap"
Best Nonfiction: Kirk Makin, REDRUM THE INNOCENT

1992

Best Novel: Peter Robinson, PAST
REASON HATED
Best First Novel: Paul Grescoe,
FLESH WOUND
Best Short Story: Eric Wright, "Two
in the Bush"
Best Nonfiction: William Lowther,
ARMS AND THE MAN
Best Genre Criticism: Wesley K.
Wark, ed., SPY FICTION: SPY
FILMS AND REAL INTELLIGENCE

1991

Best Novel: L. R. Wright, A CHILL
RAIN IN JANUARY
Best First Novel: Carsten Stroud,
SNIPER'S MOON
Best Short Story: Peter Robinson,
"Innocence"
Best Nonfiction: Susan Mayse, GIN-
GER: THE LIFE AND DEATH OF ALBERT GOODWIN
Best Genre Criticism: Donald A. Redmond, SHERLOCK HOLMES
AMONG THE PIRATES

Now living in Canada, Peter
Robinson grew up in Yorkshire,
England, where his Inspector
Banks mysteries are set.

1990

Best Novel: Laurence Gough, HOT SHOTS
Best First Novel: John Lawrence Reynolds, THE MAN WHO MUR-
DERED GOD
Best Short Story: Josef Skvorecky, "Humbug"
Best Nonfiction: Lisa Priest, CONSPIRACY OF SILENCE
Derrick Murdoch Award: Eric Wilson

1989

Best Novel: Chris Scott, JACK
Best First Novel: John Brady, A STONE OF THE HEART
Best Short Story: Jas R. Petrin, "Killer in the House"
Best Nonfiction: Mick Lowe, CONSPIRACY OF BROTHERS

1988

Best Novel: Carol Shields, SWANN: A MYSTERY
Best First Novel: Laurence Gough, THE GOLDFISH BOWL
Best Short Story: Eric Wright, "Looking for an Honest Man"
Best Nonfiction: Gary Ross, STUNG
Derrick Murdoch Awards: J. D. Singh, of Sleuth of Baker Street Books, Toronto, and Jim Reicker, of Prime Crime Books, Ottawa

1987

Best Novel: Edward O. Phillips, BURIED ON SUNDAY
Best First Novel: Medora Sale, MURDER ON THE RUN
Best Nonfiction: Elliot Layton, HUNTING HUMANS
Derrick Murdoch Award: Canadian Broadcasting Corporation, Drama Department

1986

Best Novel: Eric Wright, DEATH IN THE OLD COUNTRY
Best Nonfiction: Maggie Siggins, A CANADIAN TRAGEDY
Derrick Murdoch Award: Margaret Millar

1985

Best Novel: Howard Engel, MURDER SEES THE LIGHT
Best Nonfiction: Martin Friedland, THE TRIALS OF ISRAEL LIPSKY
Derrick Murdoch Award: Tony Aspler

1984

Best Novel: Eric Wright, THE NIGHT THE GODS SMILED
Chairman's Award for Lifetime Achievement: Derrick Murdoch

4. Independent Mystery Booksellers Association's Dilys Winn Awards

Named in honor of the first mystery bookstore owner, Dilys Winn of Murder Ink, this award is given by independent mystery booksellers, who select the books they had the most fun selling to their customers throughout the year. These awards are announced in February at the annual Left Coast Crime Convention. Dates are for the year the award was given.

1994
Winner: SMILLA'S SENSE OF SNOW, Peter Hoeg
Runner-up: THE SCULPTRESS, Minette Walters
Short List: WOLF IN THE SHADOWS, Marcia Muller
DEATH COMES AS EPIPHANY, Sharan Newman
BY EVIL MEANS, Sandra Prowell
CATALINA'S RIDDLE, Steven Saylor
WAY DOWN ON THE HIGH LONELY, Don Winslow

1993
Winner: BOOKED TO DIE, John Dunning
Short List: BLACK ECHO, Michael Connelly
BOOTLEGGER'S DAUGHTER, Margaret Maron
THE ICE HOUSE, Minette Walters

1992
Winner: NATIVE TONGUE, Carl Hiaasen
Short List: SUITABLE VENGEANCE, Elizabeth George
                BOOK CASE, Stephen Greenleaf
                HOUR OF THE HUNTER, J. A. Jance
                WE WISH YOU A MERRY MURDER, Valerie Wolzien

5. International Association of Crime Writers' Hammett Awards

First presented by the North American branch of the International Association of Crime Writers in 1992, the Hammett Award recognizes works of literary excellence by an American or Canadian writer in the mystery field. Dates are the year the award was given.

1994
MEXICAN TREE DUCK, James Crumley

1993
TURTLE MOON, Alice Hoffman

1992
MAXIMUM BOB, Elmore Leonard

6. The Wolfe Pack's Nero Wolfe Awards

The Wolfe Pack is a group of aficionados of the works of Rex Stout. Stout's most enduring creation, of course, was the incomparable Nero Wolfe, America's foremost armchair detective. The Nero Wolfe Award is presented annually for the novel that best captures the spirit and fair-play aspects of the Nero Wolfe novels. Dates are the year the award was given.

1994	OLD SCORES by Aaron Elkins
1993	BOOKED TO DIE by John Dunning
1992	A SCANDAL IN BELGRAVIA by Robert Barnard
1991	COYOTE WAITS by Tony Hillerman
1988–90	No award given
1987	THE CORPSE IN OOZAK'S POND by Charlotte MacLeod
1986	MURDER IN E MINOR by Robert Goldsborough
1985	SLEEPING DOG by Dick Lochte
1984	EMILY DICKINSON IS DEAD by Jane Langton
1983	THE ANODYNE NECKLACE by Martha Grimes
1982	PAST, PRESENT AND MURDER by Hugh Pentecost
1981	DEATH IN A TENURED POSITION by Amanda Cross
1980	BURN THIS by Helen McCloy
1979	THE BURGLAR WHO LIKED TO QUOTE KIPLING by Lawrence Block

7. The Bouchercon World Mystery Convention Anthony Awards

The Anthony Awards are voted on by fans attending the Bouchercon World Mystery Convention, which is held annually in October. Dates are for the year the award was given.

1994 SEATTLE
Best Novel: WOLF IN THE SHADOWS, Marcia Muller
Best First Novel: TRACK OF THE CAT, Nevada Barr
Best Critical Work: THE FINE ART OF MURDER, edited be Ed Gorman, Martin H Greenberg, Larry Segriff, with Jon L. Breen
Best True Crime: A ROSE FOR HER GRAVE, Ann Rule
Best Individual Short Story: "Chckout," Susan Dunlap (in MALICE DOMESTIC 2)
Best Short Story Collection/Anthology: MALICE DOMESTIC 2, edited by Mary Higgins Clark

1993 OMAHA
Best Novel: BOOTLEGGER'S DAUGHTER, Margaret Maron
Best First Novel: BLANCHE ON THE LAM, Barbara Neely
Best Critical Work: DOUBLEDAY CRIME CLUB COMPENDIUM, Ellen Nehr
Best True Crime: THE DOCTOR, THE MURDER, THE MYSTERY, Barbara D'Amato
Best Individual Short Story: "Cold Turkey," Diane Mott Davidson (in SISTERS IN CRIME 5)

1992 TORONTO
Best Novel: THE LAST DETECTIVE, Peter Lovesey
Best First Novel: MURDER ON THE IDITAROD TRAIL, Sue Henry
Best True Crime: HOMICIDE: A YEAR ON THE KILLING STREETS, David Simon
Best Short Story: "Lucky Dip," Liza Cody (in A WOMAN'S EYE)
Best Short Story Collection/Anthology: A WOMAN'S EYE, edited by Sara Paretsky
Best Critical Work: 100 GREAT DETECTIVES, Maxim Jakubowski

1991 PASADENA
Best Novel: "G" IS FOR GUMSHOE, Sue Grafton
Best First Novel: POSTMORTEM, Patricia D. Cornwell
Best Paperback Original: tie— GRAVE UNDERTAKING, James McCahery, and WHERE'S MOMMY NOW?, Rochelle Krich
Best Short Story: "The Celestial Buffet," Sue Dunlap (SISTERS IN CRIME 2)
Best Critical Work: SYNOD OF SLEUTHS, Jon L. Breen and Martin H. Greenberg
Best Motion Picture: PRESUMED INNOCENT
Best TV Series: MYSTERY! (PBS)

1990 LONDON
Best Novel: THE SIRENS SANG OF MURDER, Sarah Caudwell
Best First Novel: KATWALK, Karen Kijewski
Best Paperback Original: HONEYMOON FOR MURDER, Carolyn G. Hart
Best Short Story: "Afraid All the Time," Nancy Pickard
Best TV Series: INSPECTOR MORSE
Best Movie: CRIMES AND MISDEMEANORS

1989 PHILADELPHIA
Best Novel: THE SILENCE OF THE LAMBS, Thomas Harris
Best First Novel: A GREAT DELIVERANCE, Elizabeth George
Best Paperback Original: SOMETHING WICKED, Carolyn Hart

1988 SAN DIEGO

Best Novel: SKINWALKERS, Tony Hillerman
Best Paperback Original: THE MONKEY'S RAINCOAT, Robert Crais
Best First Novel: CAUGHT DEAD IN PHILADELPHIA, Gillian Roberts
Best Short Story: "Television Breakfast," Robert Barnard (ELLERY QUEEN'S MYSTERY MAGAZINE)
Best TV Series: MYSTERY!
Best Movie: THE BIG EASY

1987 MINNEAPOLIS

Best Novel: "C" IS FOR CORPSE, Sue Grafton
Best Paperback Original: JUNKYARD DOG, Robert Campbell
Best First Novel: TOO LATE TO DIE, Bill Crider
Best Short Story: "The Parker Shotgun," Sue Grafton (MEAN STREETS)

Sue Grafton, author of the immensely popular Kinsey Milhone private-eye novels, is the daughter of C. W. Grafton, who wrote legal mysteries in the forties.

1986 BALTIMORE

Best Novel: "B" IS FOR BURGLAR, Sue Grafton
Best First Novel: WHEN THE BOUGH BREAKS, Jonathan Kellerman
Best Paperback Original: SAY NO TO MURDER, Nancy Pickard
Best Short Story: "Lucky Penny," Linda Barnes
Best TV Series: MURDER, SHE WROTE
Best Movie: WITNESS

8. *Private Eye Writers of America Shamus Awards*

The Shamus Awards are presented annually to honor writers of private-eye mystery fiction. PWA's executive director, Robert J. Randisi, created the Shamus Awards in 1982, the same year he began PWA. Winners are selected by committees of writers; THE EYE Life Achievement Award is voted on by the general membership which includes fans and publishing professionals. Years denote when the award was given.

1994

Best Novel: THE DEVIL KNOWS YOU'RE DEAD, Lawrence Block

Best Paperback Original: BROTHERS AND SINNERS, Rodman Philbrick

Best Short Story: "The Merciful Angel of Death," Lawrence Block (THE NEW MYSTERY)

Best First Novel: SATAN'S LAMBS, Lynne Hightower

THE EYE Life Achievement Award: Stephen J Cannell, creator of THE ROCKFORD FILES

1993

Best Novel: THE MAN WHO WAS TALLER THAN GOD, Harold Adams

Best Paperback Original: THE LAST TANGO OF DELORES DELGADO, Marele Day

Best Short Story: "Mary, Mary, Shut the Door," Benjamin Schutz
Best First Novel: THE WOMAN WHO MARRIED A BEAR, James Straley
THE EYE Life Achievement Award: Marcia Muller

1992
Best Novel: STOLEN AWAY, Max Collins
Best Paperback Original: COOL BLUE TOMB, Paul Kemprecos
Best Short Story: "Dust Devils," Nancy Pickard
Best First Novel: SUFFER LITTLE CHILDREN, Thomas D. Davis
THE EYE Life Achievement Award: Joseph Hansen

1991
Best Novel: "G" IS FOR GUMSHOE, Sue Grafton
Best Paperback Original: RAFFERTY: FATAL SISTERS, W. Glenn Duncan
Best Short Story: "Final Resting Place," Marcia Muller
Best First Novel: DEVIL IN A BLUE DRESS, Walter Mosley
THE EYE Life Achievement Award: Roy Huggins

1990
Best Novel: EXTENUATING CIRCUMSTANCES, Jonathan Valin
Best Paperback Original: HELL'S ONLY HALF FULL, Rob Kantner
Best Short Story: "The Killing Man," Mickey Spillane
Best First Novel: KATWALK, Karen Kijewski
THE EYE Life Achievement Award: None

1989
Best Novel: KISS, John Lutz
Best Paperback Original: DIRTY WORK, Rob Kantner
Best Short Story: "The Crooked Way," Loren Estleman
Best First Novel: FEAR OF THE DARK, Gar Anthony Haywood
THE EYE Life Achievement Award: None

1988
Best Novel: A TAX IN BLOOD, Benjamin Schutz
Best Paperback Original: WILD NIGHT, L. J. Washburn
Best Short Story: "Turn Away," Ed Gorman
Best First Novel: DEATH ON THE ROCKS, Michael Allegretto
THE EYE Life Achievement Award: Michael Collins and Robert Wade

1987

Best Novel: STAKED GOAT, Jeremiah Healy
Best Paperback Original: THE BACK DOOR MAN, Rob Kantner
Best Short Story: "Fly Away Home," Rob Kantner
Best First Novel: JERSEY TOMATOES, J. W. Ryder
THE EYE Life Achievement Award: Bill Pronzini

1986

Best Novel: "B" IS FOR BURGLAR, Sue Grafton
Best Paperback Original: POVERTY BAY, Earl Emerson
Best Short Story: "Eight Mile and Dequindre," Loren Estleman
Best First Novel: HARDCOVER, Wayne Warga
THE EYE Life Achievement Award: Richard S. Prather

1985

Best Novel: SUGARTOWN, Loren Estleman
Best Paperback Original: THE CEILING OF HELL, Warren Murphy
Best Short Story: "By Dawn's Early Light," Lawrence Block
Best First Novel: A CREATIVE KIND OF KILLER, Jack Early
THE EYE Life Achievement Award: Howard Browne

1984

Best Novel: TRUE DETECTIVE, Max Allan Collins
Best Paperback Original: DEAD IN CENTER FIELD, Paul Engleman
Best Short Story: "Cat's Paw," Bill Pronzini
THE EYE Life Achievement Award: William Campbell Gault

1983

Best Novel: EIGHT MILLION WAYS TO DIE, Lawrence Block
Best Paperback Original: THE CANA DIVERSION, William Campbell
   Gault
Best Short Story: "What You Don't Know Can't Hurt You," John Lutz
THE EYE Life Achievement Award: Mickey Spillane

1982

Best Novel: HOODWINK, Bill Pronzini
Best Paperback Original: CALIFORNIA THRILLER, Max Byrd
THE EYE Life Achievement Award: Ross Macdonald

9. Mystery Readers International's Macavity Awards

Nominees for and the winners of the Macavity Awards are voted on by the members of Mystery Readers International, the largest fan organization in existence. (See the "Mystery Organizations" section for more information.) The year listed is when the award was given.

1994
Best Novel: THE SCULPTRESS, Minette Walters
Best First Novel: DEATH COMES AS EPIPHANY, Sharan Newman
Best Critical/Biographical: THE FINE ART OF MURDER, edited by Ed Gorman, Martin H. Greenberg and Larry Segriff with Jon L. Breen
Best Short Story: "Checkout," Susan Dunlap (MALICE DOMESTIC 2)

1993
Best Novel: BOOTLEGGER'S DAUGHTER, Margaret Maron
Best First Novel: BLANCHE ON THE LAM, Barbara Neely
Best Critical/Biographical: DOUBLEDAY CRIME CLUB COMPENDIUM, Ellen Nehr
Best Short Story: "Henrie O's Holiday," Carolyn G. Hart (MALICE DOMESTIC)

1992
Best Novel: I.O.U., Nancy Pickard
Best First Novel: tie—MURDER ON THE IDITAROD TRAIL, Sue Henry, and ZERO AT THE BONE, Mary Willis Walker

Best Short Story: "Deborah's Judgement," Margaret Maron
(A WOMAN'S EYE)
Best Critical/Biographical: TALKING MYSTERIES: A CONVERSATION
WITH TONY HILLERMAN, Tony Hillerman and Ernie Bulow

1991
Best Novel: IF EVER I RETURN PRETTY PEGGY-O, Sharyn McCrumb
Best First Novel: POSTMORTEM, Patricia D. Cornwell
Best Critical/Biographical: AGATHA CHRISTIE: THE WOMAN AND HER
MYSTERIES, Gillian Gill.
Best Short Story: "Too Much to Bare," Joan Hess (SISTERS IN CRIME 2)

1990
Best Novel: A LITTLE CLASS ON MURDER, Carolyn Hart
Best First Novel: GRIME AND PUNISHMENT, Jill Churchill
Best Critical/Biographical: THE BEDSIDE COMPANION TO CRIME,
H. R. F. Keating
Best Short Story: "Afraid All the Time," Nancy Pickard (SISTERS IN
CRIME)

1989
Best Novel: A THIEF OF TIME, Tony Hillerman
Best First Novel: THE KILLINGS AT BADGER'S DRIFT, Caroline Graham
Best Nonfiction/Critical: SILK STALKINGS, Victoria Nichols and Susan
Thompson
Best Short Story: "Déjà Vu," Doug Allyn (ALFRED HITCHCOCK MYS-
TERY MAGAZINE)

1988
Best Novel: MARRIAGE IS MURDER, Nancy Pickard
Best First Novel: THE MONKEY'S RAINCOAT, Robert Crais
Best Nonfiction/Critical: SON OF GUN IN CHEEK, Bill Pronzini
Best Short Story: "The Woman in the Wardrobe," Robert Barnard
(ELLERY QUEEN'S MYSTERY MAGAZINE)

1987

Best Novel: A TASTE FOR DEATH, P. D. James

Best First Novel: tie—RITUAL BATH, Fay Kellerman, and A CASE OF LOYALTIES, Marilyn Wallace

Best Nonfiction/Critical: 1001 MIDNIGHTS, Marcia Muller and Bill Pronzini

Best Short Story: "The Parker Shotgun," Sue Grafton (MEAN STREETS)

10. The Malice Domestic Agatha Awards

Given annually at the Malice Domestic conference for the best "cozy" mystery in each category. The year is when the awards were given, for works of the previous year.

1994
Best Novel: DEAD MAN'S ISLAND, Carolyn Hart
Best First Novel: TRACK OF THE CAT, Nevada Barr
Best Short Story: "Kim's Game," M. D. Lake
Best Nonfiction: THE DOCTOR, THE MURDER, THE MYSTERY, Barbara D'Amato
Lifetime Achievement: Mignon G. Eberhart

1993
Best Novel: BOOTLEGGER'S DAUGHTER, Margaret Maron
Best First Novel: BLANCHE ON THE LAM, Barbara Neely
Best Short Story: "Nice Gorilla," Aaron and Charlotte Elkins (MALICE DOMESTIC I)

1992
Best Novel: I.O.U., Nancy Pickard
Best First Novel: ZERO AT THE BONE, Mary Willis Walker
Best Short Story: "Deborah's Judgement," Margaret Maron

1991
Best Novel: BUM STEER, Nancy Pickard

Best First Novel: THE BODY IN THE BELFRY, Katherine Hall Page
Best Short Story: "Too Much to Bare," Joan Hess

1990
Best Novel: NAKED ONCE MORE,
  Elizabeth Peters
Best First Novel: GRIME AND
  PUNISHMENT, Jill Churchill
Best Short Story: "A Wee Doch
  and Doris," Sharyn McCrumb
  (MISTLETOE MYSTERIES)
Lifetime Achievement: Phyllis A.
  Whitney

1989
Best Novel: SOMETHING WICKED,
  Carolyn Hart
Best First Novel: A GREAT DELIV-
  ERANCE, Elizabeth George
Best Short Story: "More Final
  Than Divorce," Robert
  Barnard (ELLERY QUEEN'S
  MYSTERY MAGAZINE)

Elizabeth Peters (aka Barbara
Michaels) dressed in the style of one
of her most popular characters—
Amelia Peabody Emerson, Victorian
Egyptologist.

The Critics Have Their Say

11. The Haycraft-Queen Definitive Library of Detective-Crime-Mystery Fiction

This list was initially compiled by Howard Haycraft, who provided the scholarly foundation for the mystery genre in his landmark 1941 book, *Murder for Pleasure: The Life and Times of the Detective Story.* Originally titled "A Reader's List of Detective Story 'Cornerstones,'" it was updated several times by Ellery Queen (the writing team of Frederic Dannay and Manfred B. Lee) and the criteria expanded to include a broader range of crime and mystery fiction. Although Haycraft was very straightforward in stating that this list was originally compiled for "unpretentious detective-story fans who may care to assemble for their own pleasure 'cornerstone' libraries of the best and most influential writing in the medium," versions of this list are a standard tool of mystery collectors and rare-book dealers. It is often referred to as the "Haycraft-Queen Cornerstones."

This is the final version of this celebrated list and covers books published from 1748 through 1952. Asterisks denote titles added to the list by Ellery Queen. Author names in parentheses denote the true name of the writer if he used a pseudonym; names in brackets denote the lesser-known pseudonym the book was published under, if the writer used a more generally known nom de plume. All the comments following titles and in the section introducing the 1948–52 suggested additions were made by Ellery Queen.

1748   *Voltaire, ZADIG. The Great-Great-Grandfather of the Detective Story.

1794   *William Godwin, THINGS AS THEY ARE; OR, THE ADVEN-
          TURES OF CALEB WILLIAMS. The Great-Grandfather of the
          Detective Story.

1828–29   *François Eugène Vidocq, MEMOIRES DE VIDOCQ. The
          Grandfather of the Detective Story.

1845   Edgar Allan Poe, TALES. The Father of the Modern Detec-
          tive Story.

1852–53   Charles Dickens, BLEAK HOUSE
          THE MYSTERY OF EDWIN DROOD, 1870

1856   *"Waters" (William Russell), RECOLLECTIONS OF A DETEC-
          TIVE POLICE OFFICER. The first English detective yellow-
          back.

1860   *Wilkie Collins, THE
          WOMAN IN WHITE.
          An important transi-
          tional book.

1862   *Victor Hugo, LES
          MISÉRABLES (first edi-
          tion in English, also
          1862)

1866   *Fyodor Dostoyevsky,
          CRIME AND PUNISH-
          MENT (first edition in
          English, 1886)

1866   Émile Gaboriau,
          L'AFFAIRE LEROUGE
          (THE WIDOW LER-
          OUGE)
          *LE DOSSIER NO.   Frederick Walker's 1871 poster for the
          113, 1867 (FILE NO.   London stage dramatization of *The
          113)   Woman in White* delighted the author
          *LE CRIME D'ORCI-   Wilkie Collins.
          VAL, 1868 (THE MYS-
          TERY OF ORCIVAL)
          MONSIEUR LECOQ, 1869. The Father of the Detective
          Novel.

1866   *Seeley Regester (Mrs. M. V. Victor), THE DEAD LETTER.
          An example of the pioneer American detective novel—pub-

lished twelve years before Anna Katharine Green's THE
LEAVENWORTH CASE. Detective: Mr. Burton.

1868   Wilkie Collins, THE MOONSTONE. The Father of the English Detective Novel.

1872   *(Harlan Page Halsey), OLD SLEUTH, THE DETECTIVE. The
first dime-novel detective story. Old Cap Collier made his
debut in 1882, Old King Brady in 1885, and Nick Carter
in 1889.

1874   *Allan Pinkerton, THE EXPRESSMAN AND THE DETECTIVE.

1878   Anna Katharine Green, THE LEAVENWORTH CASE. Generally conceded to be the Mother of the American Detective
Novel.

1882   *Robert Louis Stevenson, NEW ARABIAN NIGHTS
*THE STRANGE CASE OF DR. JEKYLL AND MR. HYDE, 1886.
Was it Maurice Richardson who said of this book that it is
the only detective-crime story he knows in which the solution is more terrifying than the problem?

1887   *Fergus W. Hume, THE MYSTERY OF A HANSOM CAB

1887   A. Conan Doyle, A STUDY IN SCARLET
THE SIGN OF FOUR, 1890
THE ADVENTURES OF SHERLOCK HOLMES, 1892
THE MEMOIRS OF SHERLOCK HOLMES, 1894
THE HOUND OF THE BASKERVILLES, 1902
THE RETURN OF SHERLOCK HOLMES, 1905
THE VALLEY OF FEAR, 1915
HIS LAST BOW, 1917
THE CASE-BOOK OF SHERLOCK HOLMES, 1927

The listing of all the Sherlock Holmes books—the complete works—is
sheer idolatry. Surely, the first Holmes story, A Study in Scarlet, is an
undeniable cornerstone; also The Adventures and The Memoirs; and the
best of the novels should also be present in any definitive detective
library. Most critics would probably select The Hound as the best
novel; John Dickson Carr's choice is The Valley of Fear.

1892   Israel Zangwill, THE BIG BOW MYSTERY
1894   *Mark Twain, THE TRAGEDY OF PUDD'NHEAD WILSON
1894   Arthur Morrison, MARTIN HEWITT, INVESTIGATOR

1895   *M. P. Shiel, PRINCE ZALESKI
1897   *Bram Stoker, DRACULA. A classic mystery—interpreting
        mystery in its broadest sense.
1899   *E. W. Hornung, THE AMATEUR CRACKSMAN. The first Raf-
        fles book—"Detection in Reverse."
1903   *Erskine Childers, THE RIDDLE OF THE SANDS. Recom-
        mended by Christopher Morley as the Classic Secret Service
        Novel.
1905   *Baroness Orczy, THE SCARLET PIMPERNEL
        THE OLD MAN IN THE CORNER, 1909
1906   Godfrey R. Benson, TRACKS IN THE SNOW
1906   Robert Barr, THE TRIUMPHS OF EUGÈNE VALMONT
1907   Jacques Futrelle, THE THINKING MACHINE
1907   *Maurice Leblanc, ARSÈNE LUPIN, GENTLEMAN-CAMBRI-
        OLEUR
        "813," 1910 (the
        Leblanc-Lupin Master-
        piece)
        LES HUITS COUPS DE
        L'HORLOGE, 1922 (THE
        EIGHT STROKES OF THE
        CLOCK)
1907   Gaston Leroux, LE
        MYSTÈRE DE LA CHAM-
        BRE JAUNE (THE MYS-
        TERY OF THE YELLOW
        ROOM)
        *LE PARFUM DE LA
        DAME EN NOIR, 1908–9
        (THE PERFUME OF THE
        WOMAN IN BLACK)
1907   R. Austin Freeman, THE
        RED THUMB MARK. The
        first Dr. Thorndyke
        book.
        *JOHN THORNDYKE'S
        CASES, 1909

Mary Roberts Rinehart
(1876–1958), founder of the Had-
I-But-Known school of mystery
fiction.

*THE EYE OF OSIRIS, 1911

THE SINGING BONE, 1912. The first "inverted" detective stories.

1907   *Joseph Conrad, THE SECRET AGENT. Said to be a favorite with both Eric Ambler and Graham Greene.

1908   Mary Roberts Rinehart, THE CIRCULAR STAIRCASE. The founding of the Had-I-But-Known school.

1908   *O. Henry, THE GENTLE GRAFTER

1908   *G. K. Chesterton, THE MAN WHO WAS THURSDAY

THE INNOCENCE OF FATHER BROWN, 1916

1909   *Cleveland Moffett, THROUGH THE WALL. A neglected high spot.

1909   Carolyn Wells, THE CLUE. The first Fleming Stone book.

1910   A. E. W. Mason, AT THE VILLA ROSE. The first Hanaud book.

THE HOUSE OF THE ARROW, 1924

1910   *William MacHarg and Edwin Balmer, THE ACHIEVE-MENTS OF LUTHER TRANT. The first book of short stories to make scientific use of psychology as a method of crime detection.

1912   Arthur B. Reeve, THE SILENT BULLET. The first Craig Kennedy book.

1913   Mrs. Belloc Lowndes, THE LODGER. One of the earliest "suspense" stories.

1913   *Sax Rohmer, THE MYSTERY OF DR. FU-MANCHU.

1913   E. C. Bentley, TRENT'S LAST CASE. (First U.S. title: THE WOMAN IN BLACK.) The birth of naturalism in characterization.

1914   Ernest Bramah, MAX CARRADOS. The first blind detective.

1914   *Louis Joseph Vance, THE LONE WOLF

1915   *John Buchan, THE THIRTY-NINE STEPS

1916   *Thomas Burke, LIMEHOUSE NIGHTS

1918   Melville Davisson Post, UNCLE ABNER

1918   J. S. Fletcher, THE MIDDLE TEMPLE MURDER

1920   *Agatha Christie, THE MYSTERIOUS AFFAIR AT STYLES. The first Hercule Poirot book.

THE MURDER OF ROGER ACKROYD, 1926

1920   Freeman Wills Crofts, THE CASK
        INSPECTOR FRENCH'S GREATEST CASE, 1924
1920   H. C. Bailey, CALL MR. FORTUNE
        THE RED CASTLE, 1932
1920   *"Sapper" (Cyril McNeile), BULL-DOG DRUMMOND
1920   *Arthur Train, TUTT AND MR. TUTT
1920   *E. Phillips Oppenheim, THE GREAT IMPERSONATION.
1921   Eden Phillpotts, THE GREY ROOM
1922   A. A. Milne, THE RED HOUSE MYSTERY
1923   G. D. H. Cole, THE BROOKLYN MURDERS
1923   *Dorothy L. Sayers, WHOSE BODY? The first Lord Peter
        Wimsey book.
        THE NINE TAILORS, 1934
        —with Robert Eustace, THE DOCUMENTS IN THE CASE,
        1930
1924   Philip MacDonald, THE RASP. The first Col. Anthony
        Gethryn book.
        *WARRANT FOR X, 1938 (English title: THE NURSEMAID
        WHO DISAPPEARED)
1925   Edgar Wallace, THE MIND OF MR. J. G. REEDER
1925   John Rhode, THE PADDINGTON MYSTERY. The first Dr.
        Priestley book.
        *THE MURDERS IN PRAED STREET, 1928
1925   Earl Derr Biggers, THE HOUSE WITHOUT A KEY. The first
        Charlie Chan book.
1925   *Theodore Dreiser, AN AMERICAN TRAGEDY
1925   *Liam O'Flaherty, THE INFORMER
1925   Ronald A. Knox, THE VIADUCT MURDER
1926   S. S. Van Dine, THE BENSON MURDER CASE. The first
        Philo Vance book.
        THE "CANARY" MURDER CASE, 1927
1926   *C. S. Forester, PAYMENT DEFERRED
1927   Frances Noyes Hart, THE BELLAMY TRIAL
1928   *W. Somerset Maugham, ASHENDEN
1928   *Leslie Charteris, MEET THE TIGER (U.S. Title: MEET—
        THE TIGER! 1929). The first Simon Templar (the Saint)
        book.
1929   Anthony Berkeley, THE POISONED CHOCOLATES CASE

	TRIAL AND ERROR, 1937

TRIAL AND ERROR,
1937
BEFORE THE FACT,
1932 (as Frances Iles)

1929   Ellery Queen, THE
ROMAN HAT MYS-
TERY. The first Ellery
Queen book.
*CALAMITY TOWN,
1942
THE TRAGEDY OF X,
1932 (as Barnaby
Ross). The first
Drury Lane book.

A. B. Cox (1893–1971), who wrote as both Anthony Berkeley and Francis Iles.

*THE TRAGEDY OF Y, 1932 (as Barnaby Ross)

1929   *Rufus King, MURDER BY THE CLOCK. The first Lieutenant Valcour book.

1929   *W. R. Burnett, LITTLE CAESAR

1929   *T. S. Stribling, CLUES OF THE CARIBBEES. The only Professor Poggioli book.

1929   *Harvey J. O'Higgins, DETECTIVE DUFF UNRAVELS IT. The first psychoanalyst detective.

1929   Mignon G. Eberhart, THE PATIENT IN ROOM 18

1930   Frederick Irving Anderson, BOOK OF MURDER

1930   Dashiell Hammett, THE MALTESE FALCON. The first Sam Spade book.
*THE GLASS KEY, 1931
*THE ADVENTURES OF SAM SPADE, 1944

1930   David Frome, THE HAMMERSMITH MURDERS. The first Mr. Pinkerton book.

1931   *Stuart Palmer, THE PENGUIN POOL MURDER. The first Hildegarde Withers book.

1931   *Francis Beeding, DEATH WALKS IN EASTREPPS. Vincent Starrett considers this book "one of the ten greatest detective novels."

1931   *Glen Trevor (James Hilton), MURDER AT SCHOOL (U.S. title: WAS IT MURDER? 1933)

1931   *Damon Runyon, GUYS AND DOLLS

1931   Phoebe Atwood Taylor, THE CAPE COD MYSTERY. The first Asey Mayo book.

1932   R. A. J. Walling, THE FATAL FIVE MINUTES

1932   Clemence Dane and Helen Simpson, RE-ENTER SIR JOHN

1933   *Erle Stanley Gardner, THE CASE OF THE VELVET CLAWS. The first Perry Mason book.
THE CASE OF THE SULKY GIRL, 1933

1934   Margery Allingham, DEATH OF A GHOST

1934   *James M. Cain, THE POSTMAN ALWAYS RINGS TWICE

1934   Rex Stout, FER-DE-LANCE. The first Nero Wolfe book.
*THE LEAGUE OF FRIGHTENED MEN, 1935

1935   Richard Hull, THE MURDER OF MY AUNT

1935   *John P. Marquand, NO HERO. The first Mr. Moto book.

1938   John Dickson Carr [Carter Dickson], THE CROOKED HINGE
THE JUDAS WINDOW, 1938
*THE CURSE OF THE BRONZE LAMP, 1945 (English title: LORD OF THE SORCERERS, 1946)

1938   Nicholas Blake, THE BEAST MUST DIE

1938   Michael Innes, LAMENT FOR A MAKER

1938   *Clayton Rawson, DEATH FROM A TOP HAT. The first Great Merlini book.

1938   *Graham Greene, BRIGHTON ROCK

1938   *Daphne du Maurier, REBECCA

1938   Mabel Seeley, THE LISTENING HOUSE

1939   Ngaio Marsh, OVERTURE TO DEATH

1939   Eric Ambler, A COFFIN FOR DIMITRIOS (English title: THE MASK OF DIMITRIOS).

1939   Raymond Chandler, THE BIG SLEEP. The first Philip Marlowe book.
FAREWELL, MY LOVELY, 1940

1939   Georges Simenon, THE PATIENCE OF MAIGRET

1939   *Elliot Paul, THE MYSTERIOUS MICKEY FINN. The first Homer Evans book.

1940   Raymond Postgate, VERDICT OF TWELVE

1940   Frances and Richard Lockridge, THE NORTHS MEET MURDER

1940   Dorothy B. Hughes, THE SO BLUE MARBLE (or IN A LONELY PLACE, 1947)

1940   *Cornell Woolrich [William Irish], THE BRIDE WORE BLACK PHANTOM LADY, 1942

1940   Manning Coles, DRINK TO YESTERDAY A TOAST TO TOMORROW, 1941 (English title: PRAY SILENCE, 1940). The first two Tommy Hambledon books.

1941   *H. F. Heard, A TASTE FOR HONEY

1941   Craig Rice, TRIAL BY FURY (or HOME SWEET HOMICIDE, 1944)

1942   *H. H. Holmes [Anthony Boucher], ROCKET TO THE MORGUE

1942   *James Gould Cozzens, THE JUST AND THE UNJUST

1943   *Vera Caspary, LAURA. A modern "psychothriller."

Cornell Woolrich (1903–68). Many of his short stories and novels were adapted for radio, television, and film, perhaps the best-known being Hitchcock's *Rear Window*.

1944   Hilda Lawrence, BLOOD UPON THE SNOW

1946   Helen Eustis, THE HORIZONTAL MAN

1946   *Charlotte Armstrong, THE UNSUSPECTED

1946   *Lillian de la Torre, DR. SAM JOHNSON, DETECTOR

1946   Edmund Crispin, THE MOVING TOYSHOP (or LOVE LIES BLEEDING, 1948)

1947   Edgar Lustgarten, ONE MORE UNFORTUNATE (English title: A CASE TO ANSWER)

1947   *Roy Vickers, THE DEPARTMENT OF DEAD ENDS

1948   Josephine Tey, THE FRANCHISE AFFAIR

1948   *William Faulkner, INTRUDER IN THE DUST

Ellery Queen notes: "Undoubtedly Howard Haycraft would give serious consideration, as new selections or as possible replacement of earlier selections, to the following dozen books, which appeared in the lustrum of 1948 to 1952."

1948   Robert M. Coates, WISTERIA COTTAGE. Strongly recommended by Anthony Boucher.

1948   Stanley Ellin, DREADFUL SUMMIT

1949   John [Ross] Macdonald, THE MOVING TARGET

1950   Eleazar Lipsky, THE PEOPLE AGAINST O'HARA. Rated by Dorothy B. Hughes as the best detective novel of the year.

1950   Evelyn Piper, THE MOTIVE. Anthony Boucher considers this book a "major milestone" in the history of the whydunit, as opposed to the whodunit and howdunit.

1950   Thomas Walsh, NIGHTMARE IN MANHATTAN

1950   Helen McCloy, THROUGH A GLASS, DARKLY

1950   Bart Spicer, BLUES FOR THE PRINCE

1950   Charlotte Armstrong, MISCHIEF. Possibly to replace THE UNSUSPECTED, 1946.

1950   Raymond Chandler, THE SIMPLE ART OF MURDER. To replace an earlier choice or to be added.

1951   Dorothy Salisbury Davis, A GENTLE MURDERER

1952   Lord Dunsany, THE LITTLE TALES OF SMETHERS. In Queen's opinion, the outstanding book of detective short stories in the lustrum.

12. Queen's Quorum: The 125 Most Important Books of Detective-Crime-Mystery Short Stories, Selected by Ellery Queen

1. Edgar Allan Poe, TALES, 1845
2. "Waters," RECOLLECTIONS OF A DETECTIVE POLICE OFFICER, 1856
3. Wilkie Collins, THE QUEEN OF HEARTS, 1859
4. Charles Dickens, HUNTED DOWN, 1860
5. "Anonyma," THE EXPERIENCES OF A LADY DETECTIVE, 1861
6. Thomas Bailey Aldrich, OUT OF HIS HEAD, 1862
7. Mark Twain, THE CELEBRATED JUMPING FROG OF CALAVERAS COUNTY, 1867
8. Emile Gaboriau, THE LITTLE OLD MAN OF BATIGNOLLES, 1876
9. James M'Govan, BROUGHT TO BAY, 1878
10. DETECTIVE SKETCHES by a New York Detective, 1881
11. Robert Louis Stevenson, NEW ARABIAN NIGHTS, 1882
12. Frank R. Stockton, THE LADY, OR THE TIGER?, 1884
13. Eden Phillpotts, MY ADVENTURE IN THE FLYING SCOTSMAN, 1888
14. Dick Donovan, THE MAN-HUNTER, 1888
15. Israel Zangwill, THE BIG BOW MYSTERY, 1892
16. A. Conan Doyle, THE ADVENTURES OF SHERLOCK HOLMES, 1892
17. L. T. Meade and Dr. Clifford Halifax, STORIES FROM THE DIARY OF A DOCTOR, 1894

18. Arthur Morrison, MARTIN HEWITT, INVESTIGATOR, 1894
19. M. P. Shiel, PRINCE ZALESKI, 1895
20. Melville Davisson Post, THE STRANGE SCHEMES OF RANDOLPH MASON, 1896
21. Grant Allen, AN AFRICAN MILLIONAIRE, 1897
22. George R. Sims, DORCAS DENE, DETECTIVE, 1897
23. M. Mcdonnell Bodkin, PAUL BECK, THE RULE OF THUMB DETECTIVE, 1898
24. Rodrigues Ottolengui, FINAL PROOF, 1898
25. Nicholas Carter, THE DETECTIVE'S PRETTY NEIGHBOR, 1899
26. E. W. Hornung, THE AMATEUR CRACKSMAN, 1899
27. L. T. Meade and Robert Eustace, THE BROTHERHOOD OF THE SEVEN KINGS, 1899
28. Herbert Cadett, THE ADVENTURES OF A JOURNALIST, 1900
29. Richard Harding Davis, IN THE FOG, 1901
30. Clifford Ashdown, THE ADVENTURES OF ROMNEY PRINGLE, 1902
31. Bret Harte, CONDENSED NOVELS, 1902
32. Percival Pollard, LINGO DAN, 1903
33. B. Fletcher Robinson, THE CHRONICLES OF ADDINGTON PEACE, 1905
34. Arnold Bennett, THE LOOT OF CITIES, 1905 (actually 1904)
35. Rovert Barr, THE TRIUMPHS OF EUGENE VALMONT, 1906
36. Alfred Henry Lewis, CONFESSIONS OF A DETECTIVE, 1906
37. Maurice Leblanc, THE EXPLOITS OF ARSENE LUPIN, 1907
38. Jacques Futrelle, THE THINKING MACHINE, 1907
39. George Randolph Chester, GET-RICH-QUICK WALLINGFORD, 1908
40. O. Henry, THE GENTLE GRAFTER, 1908
41. Baroness Orczy, THE OLD MAN IN THE CORNER, 1909
42. R. Austin Freeman, JOHN THORNDYKE'S CASES, 1909
43. J. S. Fletcher, THE ADVENTURES OF ARCHER DAWE SLEUTH-HOUND, 1909
44. Balduin Groller, DETECTIVE DAGOBERT'S DEEDS AND ADVENTURES, 1910
45. T. W. Hanshew, THE MAN OF THE FORTY FACES, 1910
46. William MacHarg and Edwin Balmer, THE ACHIEVEMENTS OF LUTHER TRANT, 1910

47. G. K. Chesterton, THE INNOCENCE OF FATHER BROWN, 1911
48. Samuel Hopkins Adams, AVERAGE JONES, 1911
49. Arthur B. Reeve, THE SILENT BULLET, 1912
50. Gelett Burgess, THE MASTER OF MYSTERIES, 1912
51. Victor L. Whitechurch, THRILLING STORIES OF THE RAILWAY, 1912
52. R. Austin Freeman, THE SINGING BONE, 1912
53. William Hope Hodgson, CARNACKI THE GHOST-FINDER, 1913

Father Brown, detective creation of G. K. Chesterton (1874–1936).

54. Anna Katharine Green, MASTERPIECES OF MYSTERY, 1913
55. Hesketh Prichard, NOVEMBER JOE, 1913
56. Ernest Bramah, MAX CARRADOS, 1914
57. Arthur Sherburne Hardy, DIANE AND HER FRIENDS, 1914
58. Thomas Burke, LIMEHOUSE NIGHTS, 1916
59. A. E. W. Mason, THE FOUR CORNERS OF THE WORLD, 1917
60. Melville Davisson Post, UNCLE ABNER, 1918
61. Ellis Parker Butler, PHILO GUBB, 1918
62. John Russell, THE RED MARK, 1919
63. William Le Queux, MYSTERIES OF A GREAT CITY, 1920
64. Sax Rohmer, THE DREAM-DETECTIVE, 1920
65. J. Storer Clouston, CARRINGTON'S CASES, 1920
66. Vincent Starrett, THE UNIQUE HAMLET, 1920
67. Arthur Train, TUTT AND MR. TUTT, 1920
68. H. C. Bailey, CALL MR. FORTUNE, 1920
69. Maurice Leblanc, THE EIGHT STROKES OF THE CLOCK, 1922
70. Octavius Roy Cohen, JIM HANVEY, DETECTIVE, 1923
71. Agatha Christie, POIROT INVESTIGATES, 1924
72. Edgar Wallace, THE MIND OF MR. J. G. REEDER, 1925
73. Louis Golding, PALE BLUE NIGHTGOWN, 1926

74. Anthony Wynne, SINNERS GO SECRETLY, 1927
75. Susan Glaspell, A JURY OF HER PEERS, 1927
76. Dorothy L. Sayers, LORD PETER VIEWS THE BODY, 1928
77. G. D. H. and M. I. Cole, SUPERINTENDENT WILSON'S HOLIDAY, 1928
78. W. Somerset Maugham, ASHENDEN, 1928
79. Percival Wilde, ROGUES IN CLOVER, 1929
80. T. S. Stribling, CLUES OF THE CARIBBEES, 1929
81. Harvey J. O'Higgins, DETECTIVE DUFF UNRAVELS IT, 1929
82. Frederick Irving Anderson, BOOK OF MURDER, 1930
83. F. Tennyson Jesse, THE SOLANGE STORIES, 1931
84. Damon Runyon, GUYS AND DOLLS, 1931
85. Georges Simenon, THE THIRTEEN CULPRITS, 1932
86. Leslie Charteris, THE BRIGHTER BUCCANEER, 1933
87. Henry Wade, POLICEMAN'S LOT, 1933
88. Mignon G. Eberhart, THE CASES OF SUSAN DARE, 1934
89. Irvin S. Cobb, FAITH, HOPE AND CHARITY, 1934
90. Ellery Queen, THE ADVENTURES OF ELLERY QUEEN, 1934
91. C. Daly King, THE CURIOUS MR. TARRANT, 1935
92. Margery Allingham, MR. CAMPION AND OTHERS, 1939
93. E. C. Bentley, TRENT INTERVENES, 1938
94. Carter Dickson, THE DEPARTMENT OF QUEER COMPLAINTS, 1940
95. William MacHarg, THE AFFAIRS OF O'MALLEY, 1940
96. H. Bustos Domecq, SIX PROBLEMS FOR DON ISIDRO PARODI, 1942
97. William Irish, AFTER-DINNER STORY, 1944
98. Dashiell Hammett, THE ADVENTURES OF SAM SPADE, 1944
99. Raymond Chandler, FIVE MURDERS, 1944
100. Lillian De La Torre, DR. SAM JOHNSON, DETECTOR, 1946
101. Rafael Sabatini, TURBULENT TALES, 1946
102. Antonio Helé, THE COMPULSION TO MURDER, 1946
103. Stuart Palmer, THE RIDDLES OF HILDEGARDE WITHERS, 1947
104. Roy Vicker, THE DEPARTMENT OF DEAD ENDS, 1947
105. William Faulkner, KNIGHT'S GAMBIT, 1949
106. Lawrence G. Blochman, DIAGNOSIS: HOMICIDE, 1950
107. John Collier, FANCIES AND GOODNIGHTS, 1950
108. Philip MacDonald, SOMETHING TO HIDE, 1952

109. Lord Dunsany, THE LITTLE TALES OF SMETHERS, 1952
110. Edmund Crispin, BEWARE OF THE TRAINS, 1953
111. Roald Dahl, SOMEONE LIKE YOU, 1953
112. Michael Innes, APPLEBY TALKING, 1954
113. Stanley Ellin, MYSTERY STORIES, 1956
114. Evan Hunter, THE JUNGLE KIDS, 1956
115. Charlotte Armstrong, THE ALBATROSS, 1957
116. Craig Rice, THE NAME IS MALONE, 1958
117. Rufus King, MALICE IN WONDERLAND, 1958
118. Georges Simenon, THE SHORT CASES OF INSPECTOR MAIGRET, 1959

Evan Hunter, author of *The Blackboard Jungle* and screenwriter of the Hitchcock classic *The Birds,* is equally successful under his other pseudonym of Ed McBain.

119. Patrick Quentin, THE ORDEAL OF MRS. SNOW, 1961
120. Stuart Palmer and Craig Rice, PEOPLE VS. WITHERS & MALONE, 1963
121. Helen McCloy, SURPRISE, SURPRISE! 1965
122. Robert L. Fish, THE INCREDIBLE SCHLOCK HOMES, 1966
123. Miriam Allen deFord, THE THEME IS MURDER, 1967
124. Michael Gilbert, GAME WITHOUT RULES, 1967
125. Harry Kemelman, THE NINE MILE WALK, 1967

13. Otto Penzler's Top 100 Sherlock Holmes Books

Frederic Dorr Steele

Otto Penzler, in addition to being a noted Sherlockian, is something of a mystery Renaissance man. An acknowledged mystery authority, he is also a collector, bookseller, and publisher of Otto Penzler Books and *The Armchair Detective* magazine.

Otto Penzler comments: "Since 1887, when *A Study in Scarlet* first appeared, there have been over thirty thousand novels, short stories, parodies, burlesques, pastiches, critical studies, reviews, essays, appreciations and scholarly examinations devoted to Sherlock Holmes. Virtually all the material is important in that it refers to the world's greatest detective; however, life being short, the Holmesian collector may never be able to possess all of it. This Holmesian shopping list itemizes the one hundred indispensables. To amass them requires only three things: fabulous wealth, infinite patience, and divine intervention."

1. 1887   Doyle, Arthur Conan: A STUDY IN SCARLET. Contained in BEETON'S CHRISTMAS ANNUAL (London: Ward, Lock), $100,000.

First book edition (London: Ward, Lock, 1888), $50,000. First American edition (Philadelphia: Lippincott, 1890), $7,500.

2. 1890   Doyle, Arthur Conan: THE SIGN OF THE FOUR. Contained in LIPPINCOTT'S MONTHLY MAGAZINE for February 1890, London, Philadelphia, $5,000. Also of importance is the first book edition (London: Spencer Blackett, 1890,) $7,500—the spine of the earliest issue has Spencer Blackett's name and the later issue has the imprint of Griffith Farrano—and the first American edition (New York: Collier's Once a Week Library, 1891), $6,000.

3. 1892   Doyle, Arthur Conan: THE ADVENTURES OF SHERLOCK HOLMES (London: Newnes), $3,000. Also the first American edition (New York: Harper, 1892), $1,500. The first short-story collection.

4. 1894   Doyle, Arthur Conan: THE MEMOIRS OF SHERLOCK HOLMES (London: Newnes), $2,000. Also first American edition (New York: Harper, 1894), $1,500. The English edition contains twelve tales; the American, thirteen.

5. 1894   Barr, Robert: THE FACE AND THE MASK (London: Hutchinson), $250. Contains "The Great Pegram Mystery"—the first parody, originally published as "Detective Stories Gone Wrong: The Adventures of Sherlaw Kombs" by Luke Sharp in THE IDLER MAGAZINE, May 1892.

6. 1897   Bangs, John Kendrick: THE PURSUIT OF THE HOUSE-BOAT: BEING SOME FURTHER ACCOUNT OF THE DIVERS DOINGS OF THE ASSOCIATED SHADES, UNDER THE LEADERSHIP OF SHERLOCK HOLMES, ESQ. (New York: Harper), $50. The first American book containing a Holmes parody.

7. 1901   Lehmann, R. C.: THE ADVENTURES OF PICKLOCK HOLES (London: Bradbury, Agnew), $1,000. The first Holmes parody cycle.

8. 1902   Doyle, Arthur Conan: THE HOUND OF THE BASKERVILLES (London: Newnes), $2,500. Also the first American edition (New York: McClure, Phillips), $300. The most famous mystery ever written.

9. 1902   Twain, Mark: A DOUBLE-BAR-RELLED DETECTIVE STORY (New York: Harper), $100. A book-length satire on detective fiction, particularly Holmes.

10. 1902   Harte, Bret: CONDENSED NOV-

ELS SECOND SERIES NEW BURLESQUES (London: Chatto & Windus), $100. Also the first American edition (Boston, New York: Houghton Mifflin), $100. Contains "The Stolen Cigar Case" about Hemlock Jones. Ellery Queen considers this the best Holmes parody.

11. 1905   Doyle, Arthur Conan: THE RETURN OF SHERLOCK HOLMES (London: Newnes), $2,500. Also the first American edition (New York: McClure, Phillips), $300. The sixth Holmes book.

12. 1907   Leblanc, Maurice: THE EXPLOITS OF ARSENE LUPIN (New York, London: Harper), $75. Translated from the French edition of the same year by Alexander Teixeira de Mattos. Contains "Holmlock Shears Arrives Too Late," the first of several confrontations between Holmes and France's great rogue.

13. 1909   Dunbar, Robin: THE DETECTIVE BUSINESS (Chicago: Charles H. Kerr), $350. The first book of mainly nonfiction writings about Holmes.

14. 1911   Henry, O.: SIXES AND SEVENS (New York: Doubleday, Page), $75. Contains "The Adventures of Shamrock Jolnes" and "The Sleuths" by America's master of the short story.

15. 1912   Doyle, Arthur Conan: THE SPECKLED BAND: AN ADVENTURE OF SHERLOCK HOLMES (London, New York: Samuel French), $5,000. (Note that the earliest state has green paper covers; later states have light brown covers.) The first published play.

16. 1912   Holmes, Sherlock: PRACTICAL HANDBOOK OF BEE CULTURE, WITH SOME OBSERVATIONS UPON THE SEGREGATION OF THE QUEEN (Sussex: privately printed), $2,500. The author's magnum opus.

17. 1913   Saxby, Jessie M. E.: JOSEPH BELL, M.D., F.R.C.S., J.P., D.L., ETC.: AN APPRECIATION BY AN OLD FRIEND (Edinburgh and London: Oliphant, Anderson & Ferrier), $250. The first book about the man who was Doyle's professor in medical school and the model for Sherlock Holmes.

18. 1913   Doyle, Arthur Conan: SHERLOCK HOLMES: THE ADVENTURE OF THE DYING DETECTIVE (New York: Collier), $4,000. The only Sherlock Holmes story to be printed separately in book form before appearing in a collection.

19. 1915   Doyle, Arthur Conan: THE VAL-

LEY OF FEAR (London: Smith, Elder), $500. Also the first American edition (New York: Doran), $250. The last Holmes novel, called the best of the four by John Dickson Carr.

20. 1917 Doyle, Arthur Conan: HIS LAST BOW (London: Murray), $350. Also the first American edition (New York: Doran), $100.

21. 1918 Thierry, James Francis: THE ADVENTURE OF THE ELEVEN CUFF BUTTONS (New York: Neale), $400. An early book-length parody.

22. 1920 Starrett, Vincent: THE UNIQUE HAMLET: A HITHERTO UNCHRONICLED ADVENTURE OF MR. SHERLOCK HOLMES (Chicago: privately printed), $3,000. A rare book, issued in a very limited edition of indeterminate number. Although Starrett said 200, and De Waal, 33, it is probably 110, of which 100 have the imprint of Walter H. Hill and 10 of Starrett. The best Holmes pastiche.

23. 1920 Clouston, J. Storer: CARRINGTON'S CASES (Edinburgh: Blackwood), $150. Contains "The Truthful Lady," a parody about Watson.

24. 1922 Gillette, William: SHERLOCK HOLMES: A DRAMA IN FOUR ACTS (London, New York: Samuel French), $150. Although Arthur Conan Doyle is credited with coauthorship, he had nothing to do with writing the play. The best Holmes play.

25. 1924 Lucas, E. V., ed.: THE BOOK OF THE QUEEN'S DOLL HOUSE LIBRARY, 2 vols. (London: Methuen), $1,000. Contains "How Watson Learned the Trick," a parody by Arthur Conan Doyle. Limited to 1,500 copies.

26. 1924 Doyle, Arthur Conan: MEMORIES AND ADVENTURES (London: Hodder & Stoughton), $250. Contains "The Adventure of the Two Collaborators" by James M. Barrie. In the opinion of Doyle, it is the best of the many burlesques of Holmes.

William Gillette wrote the stage drama *Sherlock Holmes: A Drama in Four Acts*. Gillette's portrayal of Holmes received international acclaim.

27. 1927 Doyle, Arthur Conan: THE CASEBOOK OF SHERLOCK HOLMES (London: Murray), $300. Also the first American edition (New York: Doran), $100. Last book in the canon.

28. 1928   Knox, Ronald A.: ESSAYS IN SATIRE (London: Sheed & Ward), $50. Contains "Studies in the Literature of Sherlock Holmes," regarded as the first essay of "higher criticism".

29. 1929   Fuller, William O.: A NIGHT WITH SHERLOCK HOLMES (Cambridge, Mass.: privately printed), $750. A handsomely printed pastiche, limited to 200 copies.

30. 1929   Christie, Agatha: PARTNERS IN CRIME (London: Collins, $1,000). Also the first American edition (New York: Dodd, Mead), $400. Contains "The Case of the Missing Lady," a parody by the first lady of crime.

31. 1930   Morley, Christopher, ed.: THE COMPLETE SHERLOCK HOLMES, 2 vols. (New York: Doubleday, Doran), $200. Contains "In Memoriam: Sherlock Holmes," the first printing of the widely published essay on Holmes. The first complete American edition of the canon.

32. 1931   Roberts, S. C.: DOCTOR WATSON: PROLEGOMENA TO THE STUDY OF A BIOGRAPHICAL PROBLEM (London: Faber & Faber), $75. The standard life of Watson.

33. 1932   Blakeney, T. S.: SHERLOCK HOLMES: FACT OF FICTION? (London: Murray), $350. The first book-length biography of Holmes.

34. 1932   Bell, H. W.: SHERLOCK HOLMES AND DR. WATSON: THE CHRONOLOGY OF THEIR ADVENTURES (London: Constable), $150. The first attempt to date all of Holmes's adventures, recorded and unrecorded. 500 copies.

35. 1933   Starrett, Vincent: THE PRIVATE LIFE OF SHERLOCK HOLMES (New York: Macmillan), $300. The standard biography of Holmes.

36. 1934   Bell, H. W., ed.: BAKER STREET STUDIES (London: Constable), $200. The first critical anthology devoted to Holmes.

37. 1934   Smith, Harry B.: HOW SHERLOCK HOLMES SOLVED THE MYSTERY OF EDWIN DROOD (Glen Rock, Pa: Walter Klinefelter), $1,000. A rare pastiche, limited to 33 copies.

38. 1934   Clendening, Logan: THE CASE OF THE MISSING PATRI-ARCHS (Yselta, Tex: privately printed for Edwin B. Hill), $250. With a note by Vincent Starrett. Posthumous adventure of Holmes, limited to 30 copies.

39. 1934 Doyle, Arthur Conan: THE FIELD BAZAAR (London: Athenaeum Press), $250. Holmes parody written by Doyle in 1896. 100 copies.

40. 1938 Morley, Frank V.: A SHERLOCK HOLMES CROSS-WORD PUZZLE (New York: privately printed), $1,000. Often credited to Christopher Morley. The original test for membership in the Baker Street Irregulars. Rare; limited to 38 copies.

41. 1938 Smith, Edgar W.: APPOINTMENT IN BAKER STREET (Maplewood, N.J.: Pamphlet House), $200. Profiles of everyone who had dealings with Holmes. Limited to 250 copies.

42. 1938 Honce, Charles: A SHERLOCK HOLMES BIRTHDAY (New York: privately printed), $500. Reminiscences of the 1937 semicentennial. The first of his Christmas books. 100 copies.

43. 1938 Klinefelter, Walter: EX LIBRIS A. CONAN DOYLE SHERLOCK HOLMES (Chicago: Black Cat Press), $100. Sherlockian essays. 250 copies.

44. 1940 Starrett, Vincent, ed.: 221B: STUDIES IN SHERLOCK HOLMES (New York: Macmillan), $250. The first American anthology of essays.

45. 1940 Smith, Edgar W.: BAKER STREET AND BEYOND (Maplewood, N.J.: Pamphlet House), $200. The first Sherlockian gazetteer. 300 copies ($75), the first 100 in deluxe binding.

46. 1940 Boucher, Anthony: THE CASE OF THE BAKER STREET IRREGULARS (New York: Simon & Schuster), $150. A mystery novel involving many Sherlockians.

47. 1941 Heard, H. F.: A TASTE FOR HONEY (New York: Vanguard), $150. A detective novel about "Mr. Mycroft," a pseudonymous, reclusive Holmes.

48. 1941 McKee, Wilbur K.: SHERLOCK HOLMES IS MR. PICKWICK (Brattleboro, Vt.: privately printed), $250. A whimsical pamphlet. Limited to 300 copies.

49. 1941 Wilde, Percival: DESIGN FOR MURDER (New York: Random House), $50. A detective novel with Sherlockian overtones.

50. 1943 Officer, Harvey: A BAKER STREET SONG BOOK (Maplewood, N.J.: Pamphlet House), $200.

51. 1944 Ellery Queen, ed.: THE MISADVENTURES OF SHERLOCK HOLMES (Boston: Little, Brown), $400. The best anthology of paro-

dies and pastiches. A special edition of 125 copies was distributed at the 1944 BSI dinner ($750).

52. 1944   Smith, Edgar W., ed.: PROFILE BY GASLIGHT (New York: Simon & Schuster), $200. A large collection about Holmes. A special edition of approximately 125 copies was distributed at the BSI dinner in 1944 ($500).

53. 1945   Roberts, S. C.: THE STRANGE CASE OF THE MEGATHERI-UM THEFTS (Cambridge: privately printed), $600. A flavorful pastiche. Limited to 125 copies.

54. 1945   Smith, Edgar W.: BAKER STREET INVENTORY (Summit, N.J.: Pamphlet House), $50. The first bibliography of the canon and the writings about the writings. A preliminary pamphlet appeared in 1944. Limited to 300 copies.

55. 1945   Derleth: "IN RE: SHERLOCK HOLMES": THE ADVEN-TURES OF SOLAR PONS (Sauk City, Wis.: Mycroft & Moran), $125. The first Pons book, with an introduction by Vincent Starrett.

56. 1946   Yuhasova, Helene: A LAURISTON GARDEN OF VERSES (Summit, N.J.: Pamphlet House), $75. Attributed to Edgar W. Smith. 250 copies.

57. 1946–49   Smith, Edgar W., ed.: THE BAKER STREET JOURNAL. The official publication of the Baker Street Irregulars; thirteen issues were published ($350).

58. 1947   Cutter, Robert A., ed.: SHERLOCKIAN STUDIES (Jackson Heights, N.Y.: Baker Street Press), $75. Seven essays, sponsored by The Three Students of Long Island. 200 copies.

59. 1947   Williamson, J. N. and H. B. Williams, eds.: ILLUSTRI-OUS CLIENT'S CASE-BOOK (Indianapolis, Ind.: The Illustrious Clients), $125.

60. 1947   Keddie, James Jr., ed.: THE SECOND CAB (Boston: pri-vately printed), $100. Essays, ephemera by The Speckled Band of Boston. 300 copies.

61. 1947   Christ, Jay Finley: AN IRREGULAR GUIDE TO SHERLOCK HOLMES OF BAKER STREET (New York: Argus Books; Summit, N.J.: Pamphlet House), $100. A concordance.

62. 1948   Bayer, Robert John: SOME NOTES ON A MEETING AT CHISAM (Chicago: Camden House,) $200. Father Brown and Sherlock Holmes. Limited to 60 copies.

63. 1949   Carr, John Dickson: THE LIFE OF SIR ARTHUR CONAN

DOYLE (New York: Harper), $45. The standard life of Watson's agent.

64. 1949 Grazebrook, O. F.: STUDIES IN SHERLOCK HOLMES, 7 vols. (London: privately printed), $700.

65. 1950 Smith, Edgar W.: A BAKER STREET QUARTETTE (New York: The Baker Street Irregulars), $200. Four Sherlockian tales in verse. 221 copies.

Frederic Dorr Steele

66. 1950-52 Doyle, Sir Arthur Conan: SHERLOCK HOLMES, 8 vols. (New York: Limited Editions Club), $1,000. The ultimate edition of the canon, edited by Edgar W. Smith and profusely illustrated. Limited to 1,500 sets.

67. 1951 Brend, Gavin: MY DEAR HOLMES (London: Allen & Unwin), $45.

68. 1951 Smith, Edgar W. (followed by Julian Wolff, M.D.), ed.: THE BAKER STREET JOURNAL (New Series). The quarterly publication of the Baker Street Irregulars ($1,750).

69. 1952 Donegall, Marquess of, ed.: THE SHERLOCK HOLMES JOURNAL. Semiannual publication of the Sherlock Holmes Society of London ($1,000).

70. 1952 Peterson, Robert Storm, and Tage La Cour: TOBACCO TALK IN BAKER STREET (New York: Baker Street Irregulars), $100. Contains an essay and a burlesque.

71. 1952 Wolff, Julian, M.D.: THE SHERLOCKIAN ATLAS (New York: privately printed), $200. Thirteen detailed maps of Holmes's world. 400 copies.

72. 1953 Smith, Edgar W.: THE NAPOLEON OF CRIME (Summit, N.J.: Pamphlet House), $75. The standard life of Professor Moriarty. Limited to 221 copies.

73. 1953 Zeisler, Ernest Bloomfield: BAKER STREET CHRONOLOGY (Chicago: Alexander J. Isaacs), $350. A new dating of Holmes's adventures. Limited to 200 copies.

74. 1953–71 Simpson, A. Carson: SIMPSON'S SHERLOCKIAN STUDIES, 9 vols. (Philadelphia: privately printed), $850. The first eight

pamphlets limited to 221 copies; the last was reproduced from the unpublished manuscript in 1971.

75. 1954   Montgomery, James: A STUDY IN PICTURES (Philadelphia: privately printed), $100. The first guide to the illustrators of Holmes. The most elaborate of the author's six Christmas annuals (1950–55). 300 copies.

76. 1954   Doyle, Adrian Conan, and John Dickson Carr: THE EXPLOITS OF SHERLOCK HOLMES (New York: Random House), $75. Twelve pastiches by the agent's son and a brilliant writer.

77. 1955   Gillette, William: THE PAINFUL PREDICAMENT OF SHERLOCK HOLMES: A FANTASY IN ONE ACT (Chicago: Ben Abranson), $35. Introduction by Vincent Starrett. Gillette's other Sherlock Holmes play, first performed in 1905. 500 copies.

78. 1955   Clarke, Richard W., ed.: THE BEST OF THE PIPS (New York: The Five Orange Pips of Westchester County), $50. Called by Edgar W. Smith "the most erudite" essays.

79. 1955   Mitchell, Gladys: WATSON'S CHOICE (London: Michael Joseph), $65. A novel with Sherlockian flavorings.

80. 1957   Wolff, Julian, M.D.: A RAMBLE IN BOHEMIA (New York: U.N. Philatelic Chronicle [sic]), $45. A report on the commemorative Holmes stamp issued by the Republic of Bohemia in 1988. A stamp accompanies some copies of the pamphlet.

81. 1957   Warrack, Guy: SHERLOCK HOLMES AND MUSIC (London: Faber & Faber), $50. The definitive guide to Holmes's life as a musician.

82. 1958   Doyle, Arthur Conan: THE CROWN DIAMOND: AN EVENING WITH SHERLOCK HOLMES. A PLAY IN ONE ACT (New York: privately printed), $450. A very short play written just after the turn of the century and published for the first time. With an introduction by Edgar W. Smith. 59 copies.

83. 1958   Harrison, Michael: IN THE FOOTSTEPS OF SHERLOCK HOLMES (London: Cassell), $65. An authoritative geographical examination of Holmes's world.

84. 1958   Titus, Eve: BASIL OF BAKER STREET (New York: Whittlesey House), $35. The first of the best series of juveniles for Sherlockians; illustrated by Paul Galdone.

85. 1959   Starr, H. W., ed.: LEAVES FROM THE COPPER BEECHES (Narberth, Pa.: The Sons of the Copper Beeches), $75. Mostly humorous essays. 500 copies.

86. 1959   Holroyd, James Edward: BAKER STREET BY-WAYS (London: Allen & Unwin), $50. A commentary by the chairman of the Sherlock Holmes Society of London.

87. 1962   Baring-Gould, William S.: SHERLOCK HOLMES OF BAKER STREET (New York: Clarkson N. Potter), $35. The most authoritative life of Holmes.

88. 1962   Smith, Edgar W.: SHERLOCK HOLMES: THE WRITINGS OF JOHN H. WATSON, M.D. (Morristown, N.J.: Baker Street Irregulars), $40. A comprehensive bibliography of Holmes's adventures.

89. 1963   Klinefelter, Walter: SHERLOCK HOLMES IN PORTRAIT AND PROFILE (New York: Syracuse University Press), $35. Introduction by Vincent Starrett. The definitive study of illustrations.

90. 1964   Kahn, William B.: AN ADVENTURE OF OILOCK COMBS: THE SUCCORED BEAUTY (San Francisco: The Beaune Press), $100. A parody originally published in the October 1905 issue of THE SMART SET MAGAZINE. The first of the Christmas keepsakes of Dean and Shirley Dickensheet. 222 copies.

91. 1964   Klinefelter, Walter: A PACKET OF SHERLOCKIAN BOOK-PLATES (Nappanee, Ind.: privately printed), $125. A compendium of the bookplates of eminent Sherlockians, extensively illustrated in color. 150 copies.

92. 1966   Fish, Robert L.: THE INCREDIBLE SCHLOCK HOMES (New York: Simon & Schuster), $75. The funniest series of Sherlockian parody-pastiches.

93. 1966   Queen, Ellery: A STUDY IN TERROR (New York: Lancer, $20). Also the first English edition, and the first in hardcover, retitled SHERLOCK HOLMES VERSUS JACK THE RIPPER (London: Gollancz), 1967. A novelization of the film, with added material, which records Holmes's encounter with the Harlot Killer.

94.   1967   Baring-Gould, William S.: THE ANNOTATED SHERLOCK HOLMES, 2 vols. (New York: Clarkson N. Potter),

Frederic Dorr Steele

$125. The definitive edition of the canon, heavily illustrated and annotated by a preeminent author.

95. 1968   Wincor, Richard: SHERLOCK HOLMES IN TIBET (New York: Weybright & Talley), 50 cents. Noteworthy as probably the worst book about Holmes.

96. 1974   Meyer, Nicholas: THE SEVEN-PERCENT SOLUTION (New York: Dutton), $25. The book largely responsible for a new Sherlockian boom.

97. 1974   Gardner, John: THE RETURN OF MORIARTY (London: Weidenfeld & Nicholson), $35. The most literate, enthralling, and atmospheric pastiche in half a century.

98. 1974   De Waal, Ronald Burt: THE WORLD BIBLIOGRAPHY OF SHERLOCK HOLMES AND DR. WATSON (Boston: New York Graphic Society), $75. A monumental reference book and a prodigious achievement, listing 6,221 items relating to Holmes.

99. 1976   Todd, Peter: THE ADVENTURES OF HERLOCK SHOLMES (New York: The Mysterious Press), with an introduction by Philip Jose Farmer. Contains eighteen parodies by Charles Hamilton under the Todd pseudonym. Published originally in a British periodical, 1915–16, they are the first of the longest Holmes parody cycle (one hundred stories). Limited to 1,250 copies ($25), 250 deluxe ($75).

100.   (In preparation) Holmes, Sherlock: THE WHOLE ART OF DETECTION. In preparation for more than fifty years and will contain everything learned in the preceding fifty years. Priceless.

14. Robin W. Winks's
Personal Mystery Favorites

Robin W. Winks, professor of history and former master of Berkeley College, Yale University, is a distinguished writer, essayist, and historian of crime fiction. This list was adapted from his *Detective Fiction,* revised edition (Countryman Press, 1988).

Robin W. Winks notes: "Those who are basically unacquainted with detective fiction must begin somewhere. As Edmund Wilson noted, friends tend to recommend books they have enjoyed with little regard to the reading tastes of the recipient of such advice. Among the many thousands of books into which the novice might stumble, there must nonetheless be some way of deciding where to start. The following list of titles is provided, therefore, as a point of entry; authors are limited to no more than three titles. The editor regards all of the books as good, although for a variety of reasons. Not all have contributed to the history of the field and not all are written with equal grace, but each has substantial merit, whether for plot, well-realized setting, characterization, detection, or even trickery. For the most part, books from the early classic period (pre-1930) are omitted."

COBALT, Nathan Aldyne, 1982
A CHOICE OF ENEMIES, Ted Allbeury, 1973
THE CRIME AT BLACK DUDLEY, Margery Allingham, 1929
DANCERS IN MOURNING, Margery Allingham, 1937
THE TIGER IN THE SMOKE, Margery Allingham, 1952
GODEY'S LAST STAND, Charles Alverson, 1975
BACKGROUND TO DANGER, Eric Ambler, 1937

A COFFIN FOR DIMITRIOS, Eric Ambler, 1939
JOURNEY INTO FEAR, Eric Ambler, 1940
THE AFFAIR OF THE BLOOD-STAINED EGG COSY, James Anderson, 1975
DEATH OF A HITTITE, Sylvia Angus, 1969
MURDER AT THE ABA, Isaac Asimov, 1976
HIGH CITADEL, Desmond Bagley, 1965
RUNNING BLIND, Desmond Bagley, 1970
THE ENEMY, Desmond Bagley, 1977
IN THE HEAT OF THE NIGHT, John Ball, 1965
THE REMBRANDT PANEL, Oliver Banks, 1980
DEATH OF AN OLD GOAT, Robert Barnard, 1974
DEATH OF A LITERARY WIDOW, Robert Barnard, 1979
THE KREMLIN LETTER, Noel Behn, 1966
THE RUNNING MAN, Ben Benson, 1957
TRENT'S LAST CASE, E. C. Bentley, 1913
THE BIG KISS OFF OF 1944, Andrew Bergman, 1974

TRIAL AND ERROR, Anthony Berkeley, 1937
REPEAT THE INSTRUCTIONS, R. Vernon Beste, 1967
THE CASE OF THE ABOMINABLE SNOWMAN, Nicholas Blake, 1941
MINUTE FOR MURDER, Nicholas Blake, 1947
THE SINS OF THE FATHER, Lawrence Block, 1976
FICCIONES, Jorge Luis Borges, 1962
THE CASE OF THE SEVEN OF CALVARY, Anthony Boucher, 1937
DEATH IN THE FIFTH POSITION, Edgar Box (Gore Vidal), 1952
GREEN FOR DANGER, Christianna Brand, 1944
WILDERS WALK AWAY, Herbert Brean, 1948
THE FABULOUS CLIPJOINT, Fredric Brown, 1947
THE LENIENT BEAST, Fredric Brown, 1956
THE THIRTY-NINE STEPS, John Buchan, 1915
JOHN MACNAB, John Buchan, 1925
MOUNTAIN MEADOW, John Buchan, 1941
SAVING THE QUEEN, William F. Buckley Jr., 1976
MONGOOSE R.I.P., William F. Buckley Jr., 1987
THE PYX, John Buell, 1959

Tremor of Intent, Anthony Burgess, 1966
Angle of Attack, Rex Burns, 1979
Ground Money, Rex Burns, 1986
Or Be He Dead, James Byrom, 1958
The Postman Always Rings Twice, James M. Cain, 1934
Double Indemnity, James M. Cain, 1935
Finding Maubee, A. H. Z. Carr, 1970
The Three Coffins, John Dickson Carr, 1935
The Case of the Constant Suicides, John Dickson Carr, 1941
Thus Was Adonis Murdered, Sarah Caudwell, 1981
The Big Sleep, Raymond Chandler, 1939
Farewell, My Lovely, Raymond Chandler, 1940
The Lady in the Lake, Raymond Chandler, 1943
The Innocence of Father Brown, G. K. Chesterton, 1911
The Riddle of the Sands, Erskine Childers, 1903
The Murder of Roger Ackroyd, Agatha Christie, 1926
And Then There Were None, Agatha Christie, 1939
The Patriotic Murders, Agatha Christie, 1940
The Hunt for Red October, Tom Clancy, 1985
The Third Side of the Coin, Francis Clifford, 1965
All Men Are Lonely Now, Francis Clifford, 1967
Wisteria Cottage, Robert M. Coates, 1948
Bad Company, Liza Cody, 1982
Drink to Yesterday, Manning Coles, 1940
A Toast to Tomorrow, Manning Coles, 1940
The Blank Page, K. C. Constantine, 1974
The Man Who Liked Slow Tomatoes, K. C. Constantine, 1982
Murder's Burning, S. H. Courtier, 1967
Gideon's Week, John Creasey (as J. J. Marric) 1956
Gideon's River, John Creasey (as J. J. Marric) 1968
The Trial of Lobo Icheka, David Creed, 1971
The Moving Toy Shop, Edmund Crispin, 1946
The Cheyne Mystery, Freeman Wills Crofts, 1926
Death of a Train, Freeman Wills Crofts, 1946
Poetic Justice, Amanda Cross, 1970
The Last Good Kiss, James Crumley, 1978
Sylvia, E. V. Cunningham, 1960
Out of the Dark, Ursula Curtiss, 1964

NIGHT OF WENCESLAS, Lionel Davidson, 1960
THE ROSE OF TIBET, Lionel Davidson, 1962
KILLED IN THE RATINGS, William L. DeAndrea, 1978
THE IPCRESS FILE, Len Deighton, 1962
SS-GB, Len Deighton, 1978
THE SUNLIT AMBUSH, Mark Derby, 1955
THE SILENT WORLD OF NICHOLAS QUINN, Colin Dexter, 1977
THE GLASS-SIDED ANTS' NEST, Peter Dickinson, 1968
ONE FOOT IN THE GRAVE, Peter Dickinson, 1979
HINDSIGHT, Peter Dickinson, 1983
THE LONG ESCAPE, David Dodge, 1948
REBECCA'S PRIDE, Donald McNutt Douglass, 1956
THE Q DOCUMENT, Robert Duncan (as James Hall Roberts), 1964
THE NAME OF THE ROSE, Umberto Eco, 1983
THE EIGHTH CIRCLE, Stanley Ellin, 1958
VERY OLD MONEY, Stanley Ellin, 1985
THE GLASS HIGHWAY, Loren D. Estleman, 1983
THE HORIZONTAL MAN, Helen Eustis, 1946
THE BIG CLOCK, Kenneth Fearing, 1946
PURSUIT, Robert L. Fish, 1978
I WAKE UP SCREAMING, Steve Fisher, 1941
FROM RUSSIA WITH LOVE, Ian Fleming, 1957
EYE OF THE NEEDLE, Ken Follett, 1978
PAYMENT DEFERRED, C. S. Forester, 1926
THE DAY OF THE JACKAL, Frederick Forsyth, 1971
DEAD CERT, Dick Francis, 1962
BLOOD SPORT, Dick Francis, 1967
FORFEIT, Dick Francis, 1969
LOVE IN AMSTERDAM, Nicolas Freeling, 1962
AUPRÈS DE MA BLONDE, Nicolas Freeling, 1972
THE CASE OF THE CARETAKER'S CAT, Erle Stanley Gardner, 1935
THE D.A. DRAWS A CIRCLE, Erle Stanley Gardner, 1939
THE CASE OF THE CROOKED CANDLE, Erle Stanley Gardner, 1944
THE LIQUIDATOR, John Gardner, 1964
THE CUCKOO-LINE AFFAIR, Andrew Garve, 1953
THE GALLOWAY CASE, Andrew Garve, 1958
THE ASCENT OF D-13, Andrew Garve, 1969

THE JUDAS PAIR, Jonathan Gash, 1977
THE DAY OF THE RAM, William Campbell Gault, 1956
THE WIND CHILL FACTOR, Thomas Gifford, 1975
DEATH HAS DEEP ROOTS, Michael Gilbert, 1951
DEATH IN CAPTIVITY, Michael Gilbert, 1952
DEATH DROP, B. M. Gill, 1979
MARATHON MAN, William Goldman, 1974
THE RIVER GETS WIDER, R. L. Gordon, 1974
STAMBOUL TRAIN, Graham Greene, 1932
BRIGHTON ROCK, Graham Greene, 1938
THE MINISTRY OF FEAR, Graham Greene, 1943
FATAL OBSESSION, Stephen Greenleaf, 1983
THE DIRTY DUCK, Martha Grimes, 1984
THE NIGHT OF THE HUNTER, Davis Grubb, 1953
WILD PITCH, A. B. Guthrie Jr., 1973
THE TELEMANN TOUCH, William Haggard, 1958
VENETIAN BLIND, William Haggard, 1959
THE SCORPION'S TAIL, William Haggard, 1975
THE QUILLER MEMORANDUM, Adam Hall, 1965
THE TANGO BRIEFING, Adam Hall, 1973
THE MANDARIN CYPHER, Adam Hall, 1975
EXIT SHERLOCK HOLMES, Robert Lee Hall, 1977
THE SEARCH FOR JOSEPH TULLY, William Hallahan, 1974
DEATH OF A CITIZEN, Donald Hamilton, 1960
THE RAVAGERS, Donald Hamilton, 1964
RED HARVEST, Dashiell Hammett, 1929
THE MALTESE FALCON, Dashiell Hammett, 1930
EARLY GRAVES, Joseph Hansen, 1987
AN ENGLISH MURDER, Cyril Hare, 1951
THE BELLAMY TRAIL, Frances Noyes Hart, 1927
RITUAL MURDER, S. T. Haymon, 1982
THE STAKED GOAT, Jeremiah Healy, 1986
A TASTE FOR HONEY, H. F. Heard, 1941
THROUGH THE DARK AND HAIRY WOOD, Shaun Herron, 1972
A BLUNT INSTRUMENT, Georgette Heyer, 1938
THE FRIENDS OF EDDIE COYLE, George V. Higgins, 1972
RULING PASSION, Reginald Hill, 1973
DEADHEADS, Reginald Hill, 1984

THE BLESSING WAY, Tony Hillerman, 1970

THE GHOSTWAY, Tony Hillerman, 1984

COTTON COMES TO HARLEM,
Chester Himes, 1965

FLORENTINE FINISH, Cornelius
Hirschberg, 1963

ROGUE MALE, Geoffrey Household, 1939

A ROUGH SHOOT, Geoffrey
Household, 1951

DANCE OF THE DWARFS, Geoffrey Household, 1968

OSSIAN'S RIDE, Fred Hoyle,
1959

TROTSKY'S RUN, Richard Hoyt,
1982

RIDE THE PINK HORSE, Dorothy
B. Hughes, 1946

Chester Himes (1909–84), creator
of Harlem policemen Coffin Ed
Johnson and Grave Digger Jones.

FROM CUBA, WITH LOVE, E. Howard Hunt, 1964

MURDER ON SAFARI, Elspeth Huxley, 1938

BEFORE THE FACT, Francis Iles, 1932

THE WRECK OF THE MARY DEARE, Hammond Innes, 1956

HAMLET, REVENGE!, Michael Innes, 1937

COVER HER FACE, P. D. James, 1962

SHROUD FOR A NIGHTINGALE, P. D. James, 1971

AN UNSUITABLE JOB FOR A WOMAN, P. D. James, 1972

BEAT NOT THE BONES, Charlotte Jay, 1952

THE YELLOW TURBAN, Charlotte Jay, 1955

A RUSH ON THE ULTIMATE, H. R. F. Keating, 1961

THE PERFECT MURDER, H. R. F. Keating, 1964

THE SPOILT KILL, Mary Kelly, 1961

FRIDAY THE RABBI SLEPT LATE, Harry Kemelman, 1964

COURT OF CROWS, Robert A. Knowlton, 1961

FLOATER, Joseph Koenig, 1986

EMILY DICKINSON IS DEAD, Jane Langton, 1984

DEATH SHALL OVERCOME, Emma Lathen, 1966

MURDER AGAINST THE GRAIN, Emma Lathen, 1967
PASSPORT TO OBLIVION, James Leasor, 1964
THE SPY WHO CAME IN FROM THE COLD, John le Carré, 1963
TINKER, TAILOR, SOLDIER, SPY, John le Carré, 1974
SWAG, Elmore Leonard, 1976
LA BRAVA, Elmore Leonard, 1983
NIGHT COVER, Michael Z. Lewin, 1976
THE MAN IN THE MIDDLE, Norman Lewis, 1984
THE DEFECTION OF A. J. LEWINTER, Robert Littell, 1973
THE DEBRIEFING, Robert Littell, 1979
THE AMATEUR, Robert Littell, 1981
WOBBLE TO DEATH, Peter Lovesey, 1970
THE FALSE INSPECTOR DEW, Peter Lovesey, 1982
ONE MORE UNFORTUNATE, Edgar Lustgarten, 1947
THE MOST DANGEROUS GAME, Gavin Lyall, 1963
MIDNIGHT PLUS ONE, Gavin Lyall, 1965
CASTLES BURNING, Arthur Lyons, 1980
HAIL TO THE CHIEF, Ed McBain, 1973
ICE, Ed McBain, 1983
THE MIERNIK DOSSIER, Charles McCarry, 1973
THE STEAM PIG, James McClure, 1971
THE ARTFUL EGG, James McClure, 1985
FLETCH'S FORTUNE, Gregory Mcdonald, 1978
DEAD LOW TIDE, John D. MacDonald, 1953
THE DROWNER, John D. MacDonald, 1963
THE QUICK RED FOX, John D. MacDonald, 1964
THE LIST OF ADRIAN MESSENGER, Philip MacDonald, 1959
THE GALTON CASE, Ross Macdonald, 1959
THE FAR SIDE OF THE DOLLAR, Ross Macdonald, 1965
THE GOODBYE LOOK, Ross Macdonald, 1969

John D. MacDonald (1916–86), author of the Travis McGee novels, signs books for fans at Bouchercon XIV in 1983.

BOGMAIL, Patrick McGinley, 1978
LAIDLAW, William McIlvanney, 1977
ABOVE SUSPICION, Helen MacInnes, 1941
THE VENETIAN AFFAIR, Helen MacInnes, 1963
SOUTH BY JAVA HEAD, Alistair MacLean, 1958
THE SATAN BUG, Alistair MacLean (as Ian Stuart), 1962
ENTER A MURDERER, Ngaio Marsh, 1935
THIN AIR, William Marshall, 1977
AN OXFORD TRAGEDY, J. C. Masterman, 1933
THE PASS BEYOND KASHMIR, Berkely Mather, 1960
ASHENDEN, W. Somerset Maugham, 1928
THE SEVEN PER CENT SOLUTION, Nicholas Meyer, 1974
BEAST IN VIEW, Margaret Millar, 1955
AN AIR THAT KILLS, Margaret Millar, 1957
THE RED HOUSE MYSTERY, A. A. Milne, 1922
THE THIRD POLICEMAN, Flann O'Brien, 1967
THE GREAT IMPERSONATION, E. Phillips Oppenheim, 1920
INDEMNITY ONLY, Sara Paretsky, 1982
GOD SAVE THE CHILD, Robert B. Parker, 1974
MORTAL STAKES, Robert B. Parker, 1975
LOOKING FOR RACHEL WALLACE, Robert B. Parker, 1980
THE OUTSIDE MAN, Richard North Patterson, 1981
DREAMLAND LAKE, Richard Peck, 1973
THE BUTCHER'S BOY, Thomas Perry, 1982
ONE CORPSE TOO MANY, Ellis Peters, 1979
VERDICT OF TWELVE, Raymond Postgate, 1940
OTHER PATHS TO GLORY, Anthony Price, 1974
THE PUB CRAWLER, Maurice Procter, 1956
THE STALKER, Bill Pronzini, 1971
THE ROMAN HAT MYSTERY, Ellery Queen, 1929
THE TRAGEDY OF X, Ellery Queen (as Barnaby Ross), 1932
CALAMITY TOWN, Ellery Queen, 1942
DEATH IN THE MORNING, Sheila Radley, 1978
THE EURO-KILLERS, Julian Rathbone, 1979
A DEMON IN MY VIEW, Ruth Rendell, 1976
THE BAT, Mary Roberts Rinehart, 1926
THE RED RIGHT HAND, Joel Townsley Rogers, 1945
SACRIFICIAL PAWN, Francis Ryck, 1973

THE FIRST DEADLY SIN, Lawrence
Sanders, 1973

STRONG POISON, Dorothy L. Sayers, 1930

THE NINE TAILORS, Dorothy L.
Sayers, 1934

GAUDY NIGHT, Dorothy L. Sayers,
1935

THE LISTENING HOUSE, Mabel
Seeley, 1938

THE MAN WHO WATCHED THE
TRAINS GO BY, Georges
Simenon, 1942

THE BIG FIX, Roger L. Simon,
1973

ROSEANNA, Maj Sjöwall and Per
Wahlöö, 1967

THE FIRE ENGINE THAT DISAP-
PEARED, Maj Sjöwall and Per
Wahlöö, 1971

Dorothy L Sayers (1893–1957),
creator of the ineffable Lord Peter
Wimsey.

THE BALLAD OF THE RUNNING MAN, Shelley Smith, 1961

THE DAY OF THE DEAD, Bart Spicer, 1955

TOO MANY COOKS, Rex Stout, 1938

AND BE A VILLAIN, Rex Stout, 1948

PLOT IT YOURSELF, Rex Stout, 1959

THE 31ST OF FEBRUARY, Julian Symons, 1950

THE MAN WHO KILLED HIMSELF, Julian Symons, 1967

A CRIMINAL COMEDY, Julian Symons, 1986

THE DUTCH BLUE ERROR, William G. Tapply, 1985

THE MARINE CORPSE, William G. Tapply, 1986

A SHILLING FOR CANDLES, Josephine Tey, 1936

THE DAUGHTER OF TIME, Josephine Tey, 1951

THE FAMILY ARSENAL, Paul Theroux, 1976

THE COLD WAR SWAP, Ross Thomas, 1966

THE SEERSUCKER WHIPSAW, Ross Thomas, 1967

THE BRASS GO-BETWEEN, Ross Thomas (as Oliver Bleeck), 1969

THE KILLER INSIDE ME, Jim Thompson, 1952

DEATH CAP, June Thomson, 1973

THE EIGER SANCTION, Trevanian, 1972
DEEP AND CRISP AND EVEN, Peter Turnbull, 1981
THE BACHELORS OF BROKEN HILL, Arthur Upfield, 1950
THE NEW SHOE, Arthur Upfield, 1951
LIFE'S WORK, Jonathan Valin, 1986
FIRE LAKE, Jonathan Valin, 1987
THE MIND-MURDERS, Janwillem van de Wetering, 1981
STATELINE, John van der Zee, 1976
THE BENSON MURDER CASE, S. S. Van Dine, 1926
THE CHINESE BELL MURDERS, Robert van Gulik, 1958
THE DEPARTMENT OF DEAD ENDS, Roy Vickers, 1947
THE FOUR JUST MEN, Edgar Wallace, 1905
LAST SEEN WEARING, Hillary Waugh, 1952
DEATH AND CIRCUMSTANCE, Hillary Waugh, 1963
THE HOT ROCK, Donald E. Westlake, 1970
VICTIMS, Colin Wilcox, 1984
NEW HOPE FOR THE DEAD, Charles Willeford, 1985
THE CATFISH TANGLE, Charles Williams, 1951
TREE FROG, Martin Woodhouse, 1966

Edgar Wallace (1875–1932) founded his own publishing company to bring out his first book. He went on to become a hugely successful writer of almost two hundred books.

THE BRIDE WORE BLACK, Cornell Woolrich, 1940
SMOKE DETECTOR, Eric Wright, 1984
THE SUSPECT, L. R. Wright, 1985
THE FIFTH PASSENGER, Edward Young, 1963
HAZELL PLAYS SOLOMON, P. B. Yuill, 1974

15. The Armchair Detective
Readers' Survey

In 1994, *The Armchair Detective* conducted a survey of its readers asking them for their favorites in several categories. Bear in mind that these are devoted—and extremely knowledgeable—mystery fans!

ALL-TIME FAVORITE MYSTERY WRITERS

1. Rex Stout
2. Agatha Christie
3. Sir Arthur Conan Doyle
4. Raymond Chandler
5. Ross Macdonald
6. Dorothy L. Sayers
7. Dashiell Hammett
8. Ngaio Marsh
9. Josephine Tey
10. P. D. James
11. Robert B. Parker
12. John Dickson Carr
13. Erle Stanley Gardner
14. Dick Francis
15. James Lee Burke

Rex Stout (1886–1975), creator of Nero Wolfe.

FAVORITE CURRENTLY ACTIVE MYSTERY WRITERS

1. P. D. James
2. Lawrence Block
3. Robert B. Parker
4. Sue Grafton
5. Dick Francis
6. Tony Hillerman
7. Ed McBain
8. James Lee Burke
9. Martha Grimes
10. Elizabeth George

P. D. James.

FAVORITE MYSTERY NOVELS

1. THE MALTESE FALCON by Dashiell Hammett
2. THE MURDER OF ROGER ACKROYD by Agatha Christie
3. THE HOUND OF THE BASKERVILLES by Sir Arthur Conan Doyle
4. GAUDY NIGHT by Dorothy L. Sayers
5. THE DAUGHTER OF TIME by Josephine Tey

FAVORITE MYSTERY SERIES CHARACTER

1. Sherlock Holmes, created by Sir Arthur Conan Doyle
2. Nero Wolfe, created by Rex Stout
3. Hercule Poirot, created by Agatha Christie
4. Miss Marple, created by Agatha Christie
5. Lew Archer, created by Ross Macdonald

Frederic Dorr Steele

WRITER WHO WILL STILL BE READ FIFTY YEARS FROM NOW

1. P. D. James
2. Tony Hillerman
3. Dick Francis
4. Robert B. Parker
5. (tie) Ruth Rendell
   Lawrence Block

16. The Drood Review's Editors' Choice Lists

The Drood Review is well-known in the mystery community for the exceptionally high quality of its reviews and commentary. In selecting the Editors' Choice List for each year, the editorial staff gives special consideration to work by talented newcomers. For more information on *The Drood Review* see the "Mystery Periodicals" listing.

1994
TRACK OF THE CAT by Nevada Barr
TO DIE LIKE A GENTLEMAN by Bernard Bastable (aka Robert Barnard)
BUCKET NUT by Liza Cody
THE WAY THROUGH THE WOODS by Colin Dexter
SARATOGA HAUNTING by Stephen Dobyns
THE POISON POOL by Patricia Hall
THE RED, WHITE, AND BLUES by Rob Kantner

1993
AUNT DIMITY'S DEATH by Nancy Atherton
A WALK AMONG THE TOMBSTONES by Lawrence Block
LULLABY TOWN by Robert Crais
BOOKED TO DIE by John Dunning
FOR THE SAKE OF ELENA by Elizabeth George

PROTECTION by Bill James
EVERY CROOKED NANNY by Kathy Hogan Trocheck
THE ICE HOUSE by Minette Walters

1992
DEATH AND OTHER LOVERS by Jo Bannister
A SCANDAL IN BELGRAVIA by Robert Barnard
MESSITER'S DREAM by Brian Cooper
THE DECEIVER by Frederick Forsyth
HOPE AGAINST HOPE by Susan B. Kelly
A GERMAN REQUIEM by Philip Kerr
THE NINE GIANTS by Edward Marston
ORIGINAL SIN by Mary Monica Pulver
THE SHADOW OF THE SHADOW by Paco Ignacio Taibo II
THE RANSOM by Brian Tobin
DEATH QUALIFIED by Kate Wilhelm

1991
MURDER MISREAD by P. M. Carlson
BONES AND SILENCE by Reginald Hill
STILL AMONG THE LIVING by Zachary Klein
C.A.T. CAPER by Margaret Logan
IF EVER I RETURN, PRETTY PEGGY-O by
    Sharyn McCrumb
DEVIL IN A BLUE DRESS by Walter Mosley
DEAD IN THE SCRUB by B. J. Oliphant
BURN MARKS by Sara Paretsky
THE SCARRED MAN by Keith Peterson
FORCED ENTRY by Stephen Solomita

1990
NOT AS FAR AS VELMA by Nicolas Freeling
THE FOUR LAST THINGS by Timothy Hallinan
SKIN TIGHT by Carl Hiaasen
THE MOTHER SHADOW by Melodie Johnson Howe
BURN SEASON by John Lantigua

A MOUTHFUL OF SAND by M. R. D. Meek
LITTLE BOXES OF BEWILDERMENT by Jack Ritchie
THE RIPPER'S APPRENTICE by Donald Thomas
THE FOURTH DURANGO by Ross Thomas
DEATH BY DECEPTION by Anne Wingate

17. The Sunday Times
100 Best Crime Stories, Selected by Julian Symons in 1957–58

Julian Symons has not only been awarded the British Crime Writers' Association Cartier Diamond Dagger for lifetime achievement, he has also been named a Grand Master by the Mystery Writers of America and served as president of the prestigious Detection Club in London. In additon to his highly praised crime novels, he is a distinguished critic of the genre.

THE BEGETTERS
1. William Godwin, CALEB WILLIAMS, 1794
2. Edgar Allan Poe, TALES OF MYSTERY AND IMAGINATION, 1845
3. Wilkie Collins, THE WOMAN IN WHITE, 1860
4. Sheridan Le Fanu, UNCLE SILAS, 1864
5. Wilkie Collins, THE MOONSTONE, 1868
6. Charles Dickens, THE MYSTERY OF EDWIN DROOD, 1870
7. Robert Louis Stevenson, THE NEW ARABIAN NIGHTS, 1882
8. Fyodor Dostoyevsky, CRIME AND PUNISHMENT, 1886
9. Emile Gaboriau, THE MYSTERY OF ORCIVAL, 1887
10. Fergus Hume, THE MYSTERY OF A HANSOM CAB, 1887
11. A. Conan Doyle, THE MEMOIRS OF SHERLOCK HOLMES, 1894
12. Arthur Machen, THE THREE IMPOSTORS, 1895
13. E. W. Hornung, RAFFLES, 1899
14. A. Conan Doyle, THE HOUND OF THE BASKERVILLES, 1902

15. Jacques Futrelle, THE THINKING MACHINE, 1907
16. Maurice Leblanc, THE SEVEN OF HEARTS, 1907
17. Gaston Leroux, THE MYSTERY OF THE YELLOW ROOM, 1909
18. Baroness Orczy, THE OLD MAN IN THE CORNER, 1909
19. A. E. W. Mason, AT THE VILLA ROSE, 1910
20. G. K. Chesterton, THE INNOCENCE OF FATHER BROWN, 1911
21. R. Austin Freeman, THE SINGING BONE, 1912
22. E. C. Bentley, TRENT'S LAST CASE, 1913
23. Ernest Bramah, MAX CARRADOS, 1914

Literary tradition has it that Wilkie Collins (1824–89) met his longtime mistress, Caroline Graves, under much the same circumstances as described in *The Woman in White*.

THE AGE OF THE GREAT DETECTIVE

24. Edgar Wallace, THE CRIMSON CIRCLE, 1922
25. A. A. Milne, THE RED HOUSE MYSTERY, 1922
26. Freeman Wills Crofts, THE PIT-PROP SYNDICATE, 1922
27. A. E. W. Mason, THE HOUSE OF THE ARROW, 1924
28. Agatha Christie, THE MURDER OF ROGER ACKROYD, 1926
29. C. S. Forester, PAYMENT DEFERRED, 1926
30. S. S. Van Dine, THE GREENE MURDER CASE, 1928
31. Frances Noyes Hart, THE BELLAMY TRIAL, 1928
32. Anthony Berkeley, THE POISONED CHOCOLATES CASE, 1929
33. H. C. Bailey, MR. FORTUNE SPEAKING, 1929
34. Ellery Queen, THE GREEK COFFIN MYSTERY, 1932

35. Dorothy L. Sayers, MUR-
    DER MUST ADVERTISE,
    1933
36. Margery Allingham,
    DEATH OF A GHOST,
    1934
37. Rex Stout, FER-DE-
    LANCE, 1934
38. Ellery Queen, THE
    ADVENTURES OF ELLERY
    QUEEN, 1935
39. Dorothy L. Sayers,
    GAUDY NIGHT, 1935
40. John Dickson Carr, THE
    HOLLOW MAN, 1935
41. Erle Stanley Gardner,
    THE CASE OF THE SLEEP-
    WALKER'S NIECE, 1936
42. Michael Innes, HAMLET,
    REVENGED!, 1937
43. Philip MacDonald, THE
    NURSEMAID WHO DIS-
    APPEARED, 1938
44. Ngaio Marsh, OVERTURE
    TO DEATH, 1939
45. Cyril Hare, TRAGEDY AT LAW, 1942
46. Agatha Christie, DEATH COMES AS THE END, 1945
47. Edmund Crispin, THE MOVING TOYSHOP, 1946
48. Georges Simenon, MAIGRET IN MONTMARTRE, 1951

Margery Allingham (1904–66). Most of her novels feature Albert Campion, who was originally something of a con man but in later novels is one of Scotland Yard's trusted advisors.

NOVELS OF ACTION
49. Dashiell Hammett, THE GLASS KEY, 1931
50. William Faulkner, SANCTUARY, 1931
51. James M. Cain, THE POSTMAN ALWAYS RINGS TWICE, 1934
52. Jonathan Latimer, THE LADY IN THE MORGUE, 1937
53. Raymond Chandler, THE HIGH WINDOW, 1943
54. William Irish, PHANTOM LADY, 1945
55. W. R. Burnett, THE ASPHALT JUNGLE, 1950

Above left: Dashiell Hammett (1894–1961) created the legendary Sam Spade. He himself worked for some years as a private detective for The Pinkerton Agency. *Above right:* In addition to his classic Philip Marlow novels, Raymond Chandler (1888–1959) also had a distinguished screenwriting career. He either wrote or co-wrote such classics as *Double Indemnity, Strangers on a Train* and *The Blue Dahlia.*

56. Raymond Chandler, THE LONG GOODBYE, 1953
57. John Ross Macdonald, THE IVORY GRIN, 1953
58. Hillary Waugh, LAST SEEN WEARING, 1953

THE ENGLISH SCHOOL
59. John Buchan, THE THIRTY-NINE STEPS, 1915
60. "Sapper," BULL-DOG DRUMMOND, 1920
61. W. Somerset Maugham, ASHENDEN, 1928
62. Thomas Burke, THE PLEASANTRIES OF OLD QUONG, 1931
63. Ethel Lina White, THE WHEEL SPINS, 1933
64. Daphne du Maurier, REBECCA, 1938
65. Eric Ambler, THE MASK OF DIMITRIOS, 1939
66. Geoffrey Household, ROGUE MALE, 1939

67. John Mair, NEVER COME BACK, 1941
68. Georges Simenon, THE LODGER, 1943
69. Victor Canning, VENETIAN BIRD, 1951
70. Michael Innes, THE MAN FROM THE SEA, 1955
71. Ian Fleming, FROM RUSSIA WITH LOVE, 1957

THE MODERN CRIME NOVEL

72. Francis Iles, MALICE AFORETHOUGHT, 1931
73. Hugh Walpole, ABOVE THE DARK CIRCUS, 1931
74. F. Tennyson Jesse, A PIN TO SEE THE PEEP-SHOW, 1934
75. Ernest Raymond, WE, THE ACCUSED, 1935
76. Graham Greene, A GUN FOR SALE, 1936 (U.S.: THIS GUN FOR HIRE)
77. Raymond Postgate, VERDICT OF TWELVE, 1940
78. Patrick Hamilton, HANGOVER SQUARE, 1941
79. Vera Caspary, LAURA, 1944
80. Helen Eustis, THE HORIZONTAL MAN, 1946
81. Kenneth Fearing, THE BIG CLOCK, 1947
82. Edgar Lustgarten, A CASE TO ANSWER, 1947
83. Roy Fuller, WITH MY LITTLE EYE, 1948
84. John Franklin Bardin, DEVIL TAKE THE BLUE-TAIL FLY, 1948
85. Roy Vickers, THE DEPARTMENT OF DEAD ENDS, 1949
86. Michael Gilbert, SMALLBONE DECEASED, 1950
87. Christianna Brand, CAT AND MOUSE, 1950
88. Charlotte Armstrong, MISCHIEF, 1950
89. Josephine Tey, THE DAUGHTER OF TIME, 1951
90. John Bingham, MY NAME IS MICHAEL SIBLEY, 1952
91. Edward Grierson, REPUTATION FOR A SONG, 1952
92. Ira Levin, A KISS BEFORE DYING, 1954
93. Margot Bennett, THE MAN WHO DIDN'T FLY, 1955
94. Margaret Millar, A BEAST IN VIEW, 1955
95. Patrick Quentin, THE MAN WITH TWO WIVES, 1955
96. Shelley Smith, THE LORD HAVE MERCY, 1956
97. Nicholas Blake, A TANGLED WEB, 1956
98. Patricia Highsmith, THE BLUNDERER, 1956
99. Stanley Ellin, MYSTERY STORIES, 1957
100. Meyer Levin, COMPULSION, 1957

18. The Hard-Boiled Dick:
A Personal Checklist by James Sandoe

James Sandoe was a book reviewer for the *Chicago Sun-Times* and the *New York Herald-Tribune,* among others, during the forties, fifties and sixties. He was twice awarded the Edgar Allan Poe Award for Outstanding Mystery Criticism, in 1949 and 1961. He compiled this list in 1952.

James Sandoe comments: "It is convenient to date the birth of the detective story from 1841, the year in which Poe's *Murders in the Rue Morgue* was first published. It is convenient to date the hard-boiled detective story from 1929 with the publication in book form of Dashiell Hammett's *Red Harvest,* although Hammett and the tradition had been established in the pages of *Black Mask* for half a dozen years by that time.

"Since 1929 the hard-boiled sort has proliferated, making a jungle through which readers may reasonably find it hard to hack their way and in which recalling the mark of a blaze some yards or years back may be difficult. The reader who, having Hammett and Spillane to choose between, prefers the former, may find some use in the titles and notes which follow. The list is selective, not comprehensive, and some celebrated names are absent by design, but I hope that none is absent by chance. Readers will make their own case for writers or books not listed here."

Adams, Cleve Franklin. SABOTAGE (1940). Adams's first book, by all odds his best and the only one I know to recommend with the exception of "John Spain's" DIG ME A GRAVE, q.v. Detective: Rex McBride.

Ard, William. THE DIARY (1952). Sex and sadism after the latter-day mode but set forth with some sense of style. Detective: Timothy Dane.

Avery, A. A. ANYTHING FOR A QUIET LIFE (1942). A thriller, derived in some degree from the McKesson and Robbins scandal of 1940: a long and involved chase rather remarkably sustained. Narrator: Donovan.

Ballard, Willis Todhunter. DEALING OUT DEATH (1948), about Bill Lennox, executive vice president of General-Consolidated (films), who doesn't have to flex his biceps to prove that he's strong. A little corpse-heavy at the end.

Berkeley, Anthony, pseud. "The Policeman Only Taps Once" in SIX AGAINST SCOTLAND YARD (1936), the happy consequence of Mr. Berkeley's reading of James M. Cain and his faux naïf passes at fate.

Black, Thomas B. THE 3-13 MURDERS (1946). Familiar and competent pre-Spillane pyrotechnicality with an avoidance of incidental clichés. Irritating habit of referring to women as "hairpins." Detective: Al Delaney.

Brackett, Leigh. NO GOOD FROM A CORPSE (1944). Chandleresque and a sound chase which bogs down somewhat in plot before it stops. Detective: Edmond Clive.

Cain, Paul, pseud. (Peter Ruric) FAST ONE (1933). Leanly observed violence centering about one Kells, a fast man with a gun. Sheer narrative astonishingly sustained.

Also, Cain's SEVEN SLAYERS (Hollywood: Saint Enterprises, 1946) is a paperback collection of seven short stories in much the same mode.

Chandler, Raymond. THE HIGH WINDOW (1942), THE LADY IN THE LAKE (1943), and THE LITTLE SISTER (1949) with THE SIMPLE ART OF MURDER (1950) containing one essay, Chandler's apologia, and twelve short stories. Detective: Philip Marlowe (although in the short stories he is sometimes given other names). It is usual to cite Chandler's earlier novels, THE BIG SLEEP (1939) and FAREWELL, MY LOVELY (1940), and they are as clearly readable as they are apprentice pastiche through which Chandler was developing past pastiche and a nervous tic of purple similitude to the assurance of THE HIGH WINDOW.

Cheyney, Peter. DARK DUET (1943). Three related novelettes about Michael Kane and Ernest Buelvada, secret agents, and the only volume of Mr. Cheyney's many I've found any reason to keep.

Dent, Lester: see Shaw, Joseph T., ed., THE HARD-BOILED OMNIBUS. There are probably more of Dent's tales worth rediscovery if only on the evidence of "Angelfish" in BLACK MASK for December 1936.

Dodge, David. DEATH AND TAXES (1941), SHEAR THE BLACK SHEEP (1942), and IT AIN'T HAY (1946). Detective: James Whitney, CPA.

Finnegan, Robert, pseud. (Paul Ryan, alias "Mike Quin") THE BANDAGED NUDE (1947) and MANY A MONSTER (1948). Detective: Dan Banion.

Gunn, James. DEADLIER THAN THE MALE (1942). A story of murder rather than of detection.

Hammett, Dashiell. THE MALTESE FALCON (1930), preferably in the Modern Library edition, which contains Hammett's introduction, and THE GLASS KEY (1931). Detectives: Sam Spade and Ned Beaumont, respectively. These seem to me decidedly the best of his novels, and choosing between them is impossible. Most readers will want to find the other novels and the volumes of short stories.

Heberden, Mary Violet. MURDER OF A STUFFED SHIRT (1944). Competent and relatively restrained among the Desmond Shannon tales, as is SUBSCRIPTION TO MURDER (1940). See also Leonard, Charles L., pseud.

Herrington, Lee. CARRY MY COFFIN SLOWLY (1951). Barney Moffatt, chief investigator for a Midwestern county attorney, investigates a very rapid set of incidents indeed. The rush of business is nicely plotted and sustained.

Homes, Geoffrey, pseud. (Daniel Mainwaring) BUILD MY GALLOWS HIGH (1946). The brief history of a wary if doomed cat's-paw.

Kane, Henry. A HALO FOR NOBODY (1947) was Peter Chambers's first case and the only one in which I could discover any pleasure.

King, Sherwood. IF I DIE BEFORE I WAKE (1938).

Leonard, Charles L. (pseud. of M. V. Heberden, q.v.) THE STOLEN SQUADRON (1942). Wildly silly but so rapidly managed from little excitements to large-scale ones that you're sufficiently bound up with the personnel to gulp down the absurdities. The author wrote less successful thrillers with her hard-boiled private

eye (the despairing expedient of Military Intelligence) and she wrote much soberer and more probable pieces in which he was involved. (SEARCH FOR A SCIENTIST, 1947, or SINISTER SHELTER, 1949.)

Macdonald, John Ross, pseud. (Kenneth Millar) THE WAY SOME PEOPLE DIE (1951) and THE IVORY GRIN (1952), with at least an agreeable nod at THE MOVING TARGET (1949) and THE DROWNING POOL (1950). Like Chandler, Mr. Macdonald began in pastiche cleverly and grew into his own statement. Detective: Lew Archer.

Masur, Harold Q. BURY ME DEEP (1947). Fast and tough by rote but played so effectively that it slips past the eyes. Detective: Scott Jordan.

Millar, Kenneth (see above, John Ross Macdonald, pseud.) THE THREE ROADS (1948). Not to be confused with anything Mr. Millar produced before it, least of all with a hard-boiled phony called BLUE CITY.

Miller, Wade, pseud. (Robert Wade and William Miller) Max Thursday's adventures in GUILTY BYSTANDER (1945), FATAL STEP (1948), MURDER CHARGE (1950), and SHOOT TO KILL (1951): synthetic but effective.

Morgan, Murray C. THE VIEWLESS WINDS (1949). Violence in a coastal logging town, more thriller than mystery but conceived and set down with some bite.

Nielson, Helen. OBIT DELAYED (1952), which I found considerably more persuasive in its plot and management than its predecessors.

Perelman, Sidney Joseph. "Somewhere a Roscoe" in CRAZY LIKE A FOX (1945) and "Farewell, My Lovely Appetizer" in KEEP IT CRISP (1946). Two devastatingly perceptive notes on the hard-boiled detective story, the first in its SPICY detective version, the second discerning almost unbearable sentimentality beneath the brassy exterior of Hammett and (especially) Chandler. Two vital little exercises that no admirer of the hard-boiled school (nor any of its enemies) should miss.

Philips, James Atlee. PAGODA (1951). A fierce, abrupt, fragmentary little thriller set in Hong Kong and Rangoon, and probably one of its predecessors, SUITABLE FOR FRAMING (1949), which shares the same untidy ferocity.

Presnell, Frank G. NO MOURNERS PRESENT (1940). The best of the disorderly cases of John Webb, an unscrupulous attorney-at-law.

Quinn, Eleanor Baker. ONE MAN'S MUDDLE (1937). Told by "James Strange," whose toughness of mind is compellingly evident and unexpectedly transatlantic and whose acrid observation is a curious anticipation of Chandler.

Reeves, Robert. DEAD AND DONE FOR (1939). Celebrating Cellini Smith, detective, and a considerable improvement over his first case.

Shaw, Joseph Thompson, ed. THE HARD-BOILED OMNIBUS (1946). Stories selected from BLACK MASK by its most distinguished editor. The authors include J. J. des Ormeaux (Forrest Rosaire), Reuben Jennings Shaw, Dashiell Hammett, Ramon Decolta (and his alter ego, Raoul Whitfield), Raymond Chandler, Norbert Davis, George Harmon Coxe, Lester Dent (whose "Sail" is as exciting as anything in the volume), Charles G. Booth, Thomas Walsh, Roger Torrey, and Theodore Tinsley. Not all of the writers are represented at their best.

Spain, John, pseud. (Cleve F. Adams) DIG ME A GRAVE (1942). Bill Rye, related to Hammett's Ned Beaumont, is the legman in this. It is fast, hard, and credible as its sequel (DEATH IS LIKE THAT, 1944) is not.

Spicer, Bart. Mr. Spicer seems one of the more considerable writers in the vein for a succession of substantially sound tales about Carney Wilde, a detective with muscles and a conscience, a nice set of wits (a little too much given to spending themselves in the wisecrack), and no clear determination to stay within the boundaries of the hard-boiled sort, although his first novel was sound and independent of allegiances in striking degree. THE DARK LIGHT (1949), BLUES FOR A PRINCE (1950), THE GOLDEN DOOR (1951), and THE LONG GREEN (1952) are all worth attention, but the first and latest are perhaps most effective.

Stuart, William L. THE DEAD LIE STILL (1945). A thriller compounded of, but dashing successfully through, its clichés, and NIGHT CRY (1948), about an angry cop in grave difficulties.

Walsh, Thomas. THE NIGHT WATCH (1952), about

a cop's slip and fall. By the author of a good many BLACK MASK stories, a lot of softer ones in the SATURDAY EVENING POST, as well as an admirable melodrama called NIGHTMARE IN MANHATTAN (1950).

Whitfield, Raoul. DEATH IN A BOWL (1931). Try this just after Chandler's FAREWELL, MY LOVELY and see if its toughness isn't more compelling. The bowl is Hollywood's and the death that of a motion picture director. Whitfield, a prolific and vigorous contributor to the pulps, published two other novels, GREEN ICE (1930) and THE VIRGIN KILLS (1932), neither as satisfactory as this one.

19. H. R. F. Keating's 100 Best Crime and Mystery Books

H. R. F. Keating was the crime-books reviewer for *The Times* (London) for fifteen years. Former chairman of the British Crime Writers' Association, as well as a past president of the Detection Club, he is also the award-winning author of the Inspector Ghote mysteries set in Bombay, India. He compiled this list in 1987.

1. TALES OF MYSTERY AND IMAGINATION by Edgar Allan Poe (1845)
2. THE MOONSTONE by Wilkie Collins (1868)
3. THE MYSTERY OF EDWIN DROOD by Charles Dickens (1870)
4. THE ADVENTURES OF SHERLOCK HOLMES by A. Conan Doyle (1892)
5. THE AMATEUR CRACKSMAN by E. W. Hornung (1899)
6. THE HOUND OF THE BASKERVILLES by A. Conan Doyle (1902)
7. THE THINKING MACHINE by Jacques Futrelle (1907)
8. THE CIRCULAR STAIRCASE by Mary Roberts Rinehart (1908)
9. THE INNOCENCE OF FATHER BROWN by G. K. Chesterton (1911)
10. UNCLE ABNER by Melville Davisson Post (1918)

Charles Dickens (1812–70).

11.   THE MIND OF MR. J. G. REEDER by Edgar Wallace (1925)
12.   THE MURDER OF ROGER ACKROYD by Agatha Christie (1926)
13.   RED HARVEST by Dashiell Hammett (1929)
14.   DEATH OF MY AUNT by C. H. B. Kitchin (1929)
15.   THE DOCUMENTS IN THE CASE by Dorothy L. Sayers (1930)
16.   THE MALTESE FALCON by Dashiell Hammett (1930)
17.   THE SANDS OF WINDEE by Arthur W. Upfield (1931)
18.   BEFORE THE FACT by Francis Iles (1932)
19.   THE CASE OF THE SULKY GIRL by Erle Stanley Gardner (1933)
20.   MURDER ON THE ORIENT EXPRESS by Agatha Christie (1934)
21.   THE POSTMAN ALWAYS RINGS TWICE by James M. Cain (1934)
22.   THE NINE TAILORS by Dorothy L. Sayers (1934)
23.   THE HOLLOW MAN by John Dickson Carr (1935)
24.   THE LEAGUE OF FRIGHTENED MEN by Rex Stout (1935)
25.   THE WHEEL SPINS by Ethel Lina White (1936)
26.   THE BEAST MUST DIE by Nicholas Blake (1938)
27.   THE BRIDE WORE BLACK by Cornell Woolrich (1940)
28.   SURFEIT OF LAMPREYS by Ngaio Marsh (1940)
29.   CALAMITY TOWN by Ellery Queen (1942)
30.   TRAGEDY AT LAW by Cyril Hare (1942)
31.   THE HIGH WINDOW by Raymond Chandler (1942)
32.   GREEN FOR DANGER by Christianna Brand (1944)
33.   APPLEBY'S END by Michael Innes (1945)
34.   MURDER AMONG FRIENDS by Elizabeth Ferrars (1946)
35.   THE HORIZONTAL MAN by Helen Eustis (1946)
36.   THE MOVING TOYSHOP by Edmund Crispin (1946)

Ngaio Marsh (1895–1982). Marsh's love of theater forms the backdrop to many of her Inspector Roderick Alleyn mysteries.

37. THE FABULOUS CLIPJOINT by Fredric Brown (1947)
38. THE FRANCHISE AFFAIR by Josephine Tey (1948)
39. DEVIL TAKE THE BLUE-TAIL FLY by John Franklin Bardin (1948)
40. MORE WORK FOR THE UNDERTAKER by Margery Allingham (1948)
41. MY FRIEND MAIGRET by Georges Simenon (1949)
42. THE ASPHALT JUNGLE by W. R. Burnett (1949)
43. SMALLBONE DECEASED by Michael Gilbert (1950)
44. THE STAIN ON THE SNOW by Georges Simenon (1950)
45. THE DAUGHTER OF TIME by Josephine Tey (1951)
46. LAST SEEN WEARING . . . by Hillary Waugh (1952)
47. THE TIGER IN THE SMOKE by Margery Allingham (1952)
48. FIVE ROUNDABOUTS TO HEAVEN by John Bingham (1953)
49. THE LONG GOODBYE by Raymond Chandler (1953)
50. POST MORTEM by Guy Cullingford (1953)
51. THE PARTY AT NO. 5 by Shelley Smith (1954)
52. THE TALENTED MR. RIPLEY by Patricia Highsmith (1955)
53. BEAST IN VIEW by Margaret Millar (1955)
54. GIDEON'S WEEK by John Creasey (1956)
55. MYSTERY STORIES by Stanley Ellin (1956)
56. MAIGRET IN COURT by Georges Simenon (1960)
57. THE NEW SONIA WAYWARD by Michael Innes (1960)
58. GUN BEFORE BUTTER by Nicolas Freeling (1963)
59. THE EXPENDABLE MAN by Dorothy B. Hughes (1963)
60. POP. 1280 by Jim Thompson (1964)
61. R.S.V.P. MURDER by M. G. Eberhart (1966)
62. THE MAN WHO KILLED HIMSELF by Julian Symons (1967)
63. MURDER AGAINST THE GRAIN by Emma Lathen (1967)
64. ROSEANNA by Maj Sjöwall and Per Wahlöö (1967)
65. THE LAST BEST FRIEND by George Sims (1967)
66. THE GLASS-SIDED ANTS' NEST by Peter Dickinson (1968)
67. MR. SPLITFOOT by Helen McCloy (1968)
68. THE PRIVATE WOUND by Nicholas Blake (1968)
69. THE TREMOR OF FORGERY by Patricia Highsmith (1969)
70. BLIND MAN WITH A PISTOL by Chester Himes (1969)
71. YOUNG MAN, I THINK YOU'RE DYING by Joan Fleming (1970)
72. BEYOND THIS POINT ARE MONSTERS by Margaret Millar (1970)

73. SADIE WHEN SHE DIED
by Ed McBain (1972)
74. THE FRIENDS OF EDDIE
COYLE by George V. Higgins (1972)
75. THE PLAYERS AND THE
GAME by Julian Symons (1972)
76. MIRROR, MIRROR ON THE
WALL by Stanley Ellin (1972)
77. DANCE HALL OF THE
DEAD by Tony Hillerman (1973)
78. THE POISON ORACLE by
Peter Dickinson (1974)
79. FLETCH by Gregory
Mcdonald (1974)
80. THE BLACK TOWER by
P. D. James (1975)
81. THE LONG SHADOW by
Celia Fremlin (1975)

Agatha Christie (1890–1976).
According to her publisher, she has
over two *billion* books in print.

82. THE NAKED NUNS by Colin Watson (1975)
83. THE BLUE HAMMER by Ross Macdonald (1976)
84. SLEEPING MURDER by Agatha Christie (1976)
85. A DEATH IN THE LIFE by Dorothy Salisbury Davis (1976)
86. THE INVESTIGATION by Dorothy Uhnak (1976)
87. A JUDGEMENT IN STONE by Ruth Rendell (1977)
88. LAIDLAW by William McIlvanney (1977)
89. NOBODY'S PERFECT by Donald E. Westlake (1977)
90. A PINCH OF SNUFF by Reginald Hill (1978)
91. SKINFLICK by Joseph Hansen (1979)
92. KILL CLAUDIO by P. M. Hubbard (1979)
93. THE GREEN RIPPER by John D. MacDonald (1979)
94. ALL ON A SUMMER'S DAY by John Wainwright (1981)
95. DEATH IN A TENURED POSITION by Amanda Cross (1981)
96. THE GLITTER DOME by Joseph Wambaugh (1981)

97. TO MAKE A KILLING by June Thomson (1982)
98. THE FALSE INSPECTOR DEW by Peter Lovesey (1982)
99. THE ARTFUL EGG by James McClure (1984)
100. A TASTE FOR DEATH by P. D. James (1986)

20. Most Frequently Taught Crime and Mystery Writers

Murder Is Academic is a newsletter that focuses on the teaching and criticism of crime fiction on campus. The editor, B. J. Rahn, compiled this list of most commonly assigned writers and titles in 1993 based on syllabi submitted by professors from the United States and Great Britain. For more information on *Murder is Academic,* please see the "Mystery Periodicals" section.

THE MOST COMMONLY TAUGHT WRITERS IN CRIME FICTION COURSES (IN DESCENDING ORDER)

Sir Arthur Conan Doyle
Agatha Christie
Raymond Chandler
Dashiell Hammett
P. D. James
Edgar Allan Poe
Sara Paretsky
Dorothy L. Sayers

Wilkie Collins
Tony Hillerman
Robert B. Parker
Josephine Tey
Amanda Cross
Charles Dickens
Maj Sjöwall/Per Wahlöö
Chester Himes
Ed McBain
Ruth Rendell
Joseph Wambaugh

THE MOST COMMONLY ASSIGNED NOVELS IN CRIME FICTION COURSES

1. THE MALTESE FALCON by Dashiell Hammett
2. THE MURDER OF ROGER ACKROYD by Agatha Christie
3. THE BIG SLEEP by Raymond Chandler
4. THE LONG GOODBYE by Raymond Chandler

THE MOST COMMONLY ASSIGNED TEXTBOOKS ABOUT MYSTERY FICTION

1. DETECTIVE FICTION: CRIME AND COMPROMISE, Dick Allen and David Chacko
2. ADVENTURE, MYSTERY, ROMANCE: FORMULA STORIES AS ART, John Cawelti

21. The Ten Best Mystery Reference Works, Selected by Jon L. Breen

Jon L. Breen is a well-known mystery novelist and critic who has twice won Edgar Awards for his critical work in the mystery field. His regular column, "What About Murder?" in *The Armchair Detective,* reviews critical and reference works in the mystery genre.

Jon Breen notes: "Works on individual authors have been excluded. Titles are not ranked but listed alphabetically by author or compiler."

1. Albert, Walter. DETECTIVE AND MYSTERY FICTION: AN INTERNATIONAL BIBLIOGRAPHY OF SECONDARY SOURCES. Madison, Ind.: Brownstone, 1985.
2. Barzun, Jacques, and Wendell Hertig Taylor. A CATALOGUE OF CRIME. rev. ed. New York: Harper and Row, 1989.
3. Conquest, John. TROUBLE IS THEIR BUSINESS: PRIVATE EYES IN FICTION, FILM, AND TELEVISION, 1927–1988. New York: Garland, 1990.
4. Contento, William G., with Martin H. Greenberg. INDEX TO CRIME AND MYSTERY ANTHOLOGIES. Boston: G. K. Hall, 1990.
5. Haycraft, Howard. MURDER FOR PLEASURE: THE LIFE AND TIMES OF THE DETECTIVE STORY. New York: Appleton-Century, 1941.
6. Hubin, Allen J. CRIME FICTION II: A COMPREHENSIVE BIBLIOGRPAHY, 1749–1990. New York: Garland, 1994.

7. Pronzini, Bill, and Marcia Muller. 1001 MIDNIGHTS: THE AFICIONADO'S GUIDE TO MYSTERY AND DETECTIVE FICTION. New York: Arbor, 1986.

8. Queen, Ellery (Frederic Dannay and Manfred B. Lee). THE DETECTIVE SHORT STORY: A BIBLIOGRAPHY. Boston: Little, Brown, 1941.

9. Steinbrunner, Chris, and Otto Penzler. ENCYCLOPEDIA OF MYSTERY AND DETECTION. Marvin Lachman and Charles Shibuk, sr. eds. New York: McGraw-Hill, 1976.

10. TWENTIETH CENTURY CRIME AND MYSTERY WRITERS. 3rd ed. Chicago: St. James, 1991.

AND TEN RUNNERS-UP

11. Adey, Robert C. S. LOCKED ROOM MURDERS, rev. ed. Minneapolis: Crossover, 1991.

12. Cook, Michael L. MONTHLY MURDERS. Westport, Conn.: Greenwood, 1982.

13. East, Andy. THE COLD WAR FILE. Metuchen, N.J.: Scarecrow, 1983.

14. Keating, H. R. F., ed. WHODUNIT. New York: Van Nostrand, 1982.

15. Kramer, John E. Jr., and John E. Kramer III. COLLEGE MYSTERY NOVELS. New York: Garland, 1983.

16. Lachman, Marvin. A READER'S GUIDE TO THE AMERICAN NOVEL OF DETECTION. New York: G. K. Hall, 1993.

17. Menendez. THE SUBJECT IS MURDER. New York: Garland, 1986; supplement 1990.

18. Nehr, Ellen. DOUBLEDAY CRIME CLUB COMPENDIUM 1928–1992. Martinez, Calif.: Offspring, 1992.

19. Niebuhr, Garry Warren. A READER'S GUIDE TO THE PRIVATE EYE NOVEL. New York: G. K. Hall, 1993.

20. Queen, Ellery. QUEEN'S QUORUM. Boston: Little, Brown, 1951.

22. The Ten Best First Mystery Novels, Selected by Marvin Lachman

Marvin Lachman is a noted critic within the mystery genre and author of several reference works (most recently the Edgar-nominated *A Reader's Guide to the American Novel of Detection*). He is also a longtime contributor to the pages of *The Armchair Detective* where he regularly reviews first-time novelists in his column, "Original Sins."

Marvin Lachman comments: "Some readers may be surprised to find few recent books, and they may also note the absence of many 'big' names. I took my assignment literally and tried to select best *first* efforts."

TRENT'S LAST CASE (1913) by
   E. C. Bentley
THE CASK (1920) by Freeman
   Wills Crofts
THE ROMAN HAT MYSTERY
   (1929) by Ellery Queen
PICK YOUR VICTIM (1946) by
   Patricia McGerr
WILDERS WALK AWAY (1948) by
   Herbert Brean

Ira Levin won an Edgar Award for his first novel *A Kiss Before Dying* in 1954. He's shown here with his Edgar for the mystery play *Deathtrap* in 1980.

A KISS BEFORE DYING (1953) by Ira Levin
DEAD MEN DON'T SKI (1959) by Patricia Moyes
FROM DOON WITH DEATH (1964) by Ruth Rendell
THE FIDELIO SCORE (1965) by Gerald Sinstadt
THE RELIGIOUS BODY (1966) by Catherine Aird

23. James Corbett's Ten Greatest Lines, Retrieved by William F. Deeck

Unsung, unread, some would say unintelligible—James Corbett has long lurked in the shadows of literary obscurity. But for the past few years, noted mystery critic William F. Deeck has devoted himself to resuscitating the reputation of this literary criminal—er, crime writer. *The Armchair Detective* asked him to select, as Corbett himself might have phrased it, "the cream of the cream."

Deeck comments: "Corbett's ten greatest lines? Selecting them is an impossible task among the richness he has provided us. Still, I gritted my teeth and girded my loins and did other strange things, and enclosed are my choices."

"Your steps are feline and catlike."
—THE MERRIVALE MYSTERY

"The two half-brothers are developing into congenital idiots."
—THE MERRIVALE MYSTERY

She frowned, as if the subject were distasteful to her, and her tone was coldly if normative.
—THE BODY IN THE BUNGALOW

She laid a hand on the doorknob and turned it, went inside and stopped, as though galvanized into sudden immobility.
—THE SOMERVILLE CASE

It somewhat resembled the French villas found at Paris Plage, except that the design was entirely English, while in that respect it was unique.

—Vampire of the Skies

Not a flicker on his face moved.

—Death Comes to Fanshawe

Treat gave a guttural grin.

—Murder at the Palace

Nothing could have surprised the astonishment on his countenance.

—The Man with Nine Lives

Peterson knew him as a trustworthy colleague, his chief fault being failure to see the obvious, which meant he possessed no originality.

—Murder at Red Grange

"I wish you would not speak so loud," she cautioned. "There is no guarantee that one of those Yard men may not be a lip-reader."

—Red Dagger

24. The Most Fiendishly Ingenious Locked-Room and Impossible-Crime Novels of All Time, Selected by Douglas G. Greene

Douglas G. Greene is a widely recognized authority on detective and mystery fiction. In 1994, he started his own small mystery press, Crippen & Landru, Publishers. He is also the author of the recent biography *John Dickson Carr: The Man Who Explained Miracles,* as well as the editor of several anthologies of Carr's work.

Douglas G. Greene comments: "Any list of locked-room and similar novels must be divided into two groups. The first includes the most ingenious solutions devised by John Dickson Carr (aka Carter Dickson), who made the impossible crime his own domain. The second contains the greatest impossible-crime novels by other authors. Both lists are arranged by 'ingenuity'—a task which is almost as impossible as the crimes themselves."

BOOKS BY JOHN DICKSON CARR OR CARTER DICKSON
THE JUDAS WINDOW
THE THREE COFFINS
HE WOULDN'T KILL PATIENCE
TILL DEATH DO US PART
THE PEACOCK FEATHER MURDERS
HE WHO WHISPERS
THE CROOKED HINGE

THE WHITE PRIORY MURDERS
SHE DIED A LADY
THE HOUSE AT SATAN'S ELBOW

BOOKS BY OTHER AUTHORS

RIM OF THE PIT, Hake Talbot
THE HANGMAN'S HANDYMAN, Hake Talbot
NINE TIMES NINE, H. H. Holmes (Anthony
   Boucher)
THE BIG BOW MYSTERY, Israel Zangwill
DEATH FROM A TOP HAT, Clayton Rawson
THE CHINESE ORANGE MYSTERY, Ellery
   Queen
SCATTERSHOT, Bill Pronzini
THE TALKING SPARROW MURDERS, Darwin
   L. Teilhet
TOO MANY MAGICIANS, Randall Garrett
INVISIBLE GREEN, John Sladek

John Dickson Carr
(1906–77) also wrote
under the name Carter
Dickson.

25. Firsts *Magazine's List of 25 Rapidly Appreciating Mystery Books*

Firsts: Collecting Modern First Editions is an attractive magazine with lively, informative articles about book collecting. They have a strong focus on mysteries, so we asked *Firsts* publisher Robin H. Smiley to compile a list of the most collectible mystery titles. (See the "Mystery Periodicals" section for more information.)

Robin H. Smiley notes: "I limited this list to one title per author and tried to include a mix of classic and contemporary books."

Ambler, Eric, THE MASK OF DIMITRIOS
Burnett, W. R., LITTLE CAESAR
Cain, James M., THE POSTMAN ALWAYS RINGS TWICE
Carr, John Dickson, IT WALKS BY NIGHT
Cornwell, Patricia, POSTMORTEM
Chandler, Raymond, THE BIG SLEEP
Davis, Lindsey, SILVER PIGS
Deighton, Len, THE IPCRESS FILE
Fleming, Ian, CASINO ROYALE
Francis, Dick, DEAD CERT
Gardner, Erle Stanley, THE CASE OF THE VEL-
    VET CLAWS
Grafton, Sue, "A" IS FOR ALIBI
Greene, Graham, BRIGHTON ROCK
Grisham, John, A TIME TO KILL
Hammett, Dashiell, THE MALTESE FALCON
Hillerman, Tony, THE BLESSING WAY

James, P. D., COVER HER FACE
Le Carré, John, CALL FOR THE DEAD
Marquand, J. P., THANK YOU, MR. MOTO
Millar, Kenneth, THE DARK TUNNEL
Paretsky, Sara, INDEMNITY ONLY
Stout, Rex, FER-DE-LANCE
Van Dine, S. S., THE BENSON MURDER CASE
Van Gieson, Judith, NORTH OF THE BORDER
Walters, Minette, THE ICE HOUSE

26. The Top Ten Mystery Movies of All Time, Selected by Ric Meyers

Ric Meyers is *The Armchair Detective* magazine's movie and television columnist. He has served as a consultant for CBS's recent *Twilight Zone* series and ABC's new *Columbo*. He is also the author of such books as *TV Detectives* and the Edgar-nominated *Murder on the Air*.

1. THE ADVENTURES OF SHERLOCK HOLMES (1939)
Written by Edwin Blum and William Drake, based on a story by
   Arthur Conan Doyle
Directed by Alfred Werker
Starring Basil Rathbone as Sherlock Holmes, Nigel Bruce as Dr.
   Watson, and George Zucco as Professor Moriarty

2. AND THEN THERE WERE NONE (1945)
Written by Dudley Nichols, based on the novel by Agatha Christie
Directed by René Clair
Starring Barry Fitzgerald, C. Aubrey Smith, Louis Hayward, Walter
   Huston, Roland Young, Judith Anderson, and Mischa Auer

3. CHINATOWN (1974)
Written by Robert Towne
Directed by Roman Polanski
Starring Jack Nicholson as Jake Gittes, Faye Dunaway, and John
   Huston

Paul Newman starred in *Harper* based on Ross Macdonald's Lew Archer novels.

4. HARPER (1966)
Written by William Goldman, based on the novel THE MOVING TARGET by Ross Macdonald
Directed by Jack Smight
Starring Paul Newman as Lew Harper (née Archer), Lauren Bacall, Arthur Hill, Julie Harris, Robert Wagner, and Janet Leigh

5. THE LAST OF SHEILA (1973)
Written by Anthony Perkins and Stephen Sondheim
Directed by Herbert Ross
Starring James Mason, Dyan Cannon, James Coburn, Raquel Welch, Richard Benjamin, Joan Hackett, and Ian McShane

6. THE LIST OF ADRIAN MESSENGER (1963)
Written by Anthony Veiller, based on the novel by Philip MacDonald
Directed by John Huston

Starring George C. Scott as Anthony Gethryn, Dana Wynter, Clive
Brook, Gladys Cooper, Herbert Marshall, John Merivale, Tony
Curtis, Kirk Douglas, Burt Lancaster, Robert Mitchum, and Frank
Sinatra

7. THE MALTESE FALCON (1941)

Written by John Huston, based on the novel by Dashiell Hammett
Directed by John Huston
Starring Humphrey Bogart as Sam Spade, Mary Astor, Peter Lorre,
Gladys George, and Sydney Greenstreet

8. MURDER MY SWEET (1944)

Written by John Paxton, based on the novel FAREWELL, MY LOVELY by
Raymond Chandler
Directed by Edward Dmytryk
Starring Dick Powell as Philip Marlowe, Claire Trevor, Mike Mazurki,
Anne Shirley, and Otto Kruger

9. MURDER ON THE ORIENT EXPRESS (1974)

Written by Peter Schaffer, based on the novel MURDER IN THE CALAIS
COACH by Agatha Christie
Directed by Sidney Lumet
Starring Albert Finney as Hercule Poirot,
Lauren Bacall, Sean Connery, Ingrid
Bergman, Wendy Hiller, John Gielgud,
Vanessa Redgrave, Richard Widmark,
Jacqueline Bisset, Michael York, Rachel
Roberts, and Anthony Perkins

10. PSYCHO (1960)

Written by Joseph Stefano, based on the
novel by Robert Bloch
Directed by Alfred Hitchcock
Starring Anthony Perkins as Norman Bates,
Janet Leigh, Martin Balsam, Vera Miles,
and John Gavin

Alfred Hitchcock's
famous silhouette.

27. The Top Ten Mystery TV Series of All Time, Selected by Ric Meyers

1. COLUMBO (1971–PRESENT)
Created by Richard Levinson and William Link
Starring Peter Falk as Lieutenant Columbo

2. DRAGNET (1949–70)
Created by Jack Webb
Starring Jack Webb as Joe Friday, Barton Yarborough as Ben Romero, Barney Phillips as Ed Jacobs, Herb Ellis as Frank Smith, Ben Alexander as Frank Smith, and Harry Morgan as Frank Gannon

Peter Falk in *Columbo.*

3. HAWAII FIVE-O (1968–80)
Created by Leonard Freeman
Starring Jack Lord as Steve McGarrett, James MacArthur as Danny "Dan-O" Williams, Kam Fong as Chin Ho Kelly, Zulu as Kono, Richard Denning as Governor Grey, Al Harrington as Ben Kokua, Herman Wedemeyer as Duke Lukela, Moe Keale as Truck Kealoha, Sharon Farrell as Lori Wilson, and William Smith as James "Kino" Carew

4. HILL STREET BLUES (1981–88)
Created by Stephen Bochco and Michael Kozoll

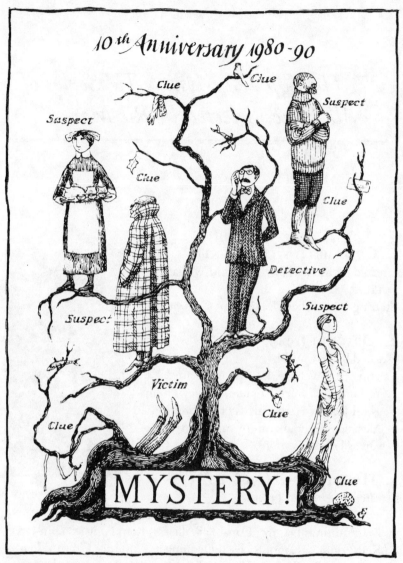

The *Mystery!* tenth anniversary poster by Edward Gorey.

Starring Daniel J. Travanti as Frank Furillo, Veronica Hamel as Joyce
Davenport, Michael Conrad as Phil Esterhaus, Bruce Weitz as
Mick Belker, James B. Sikking as Howard Hunter, Kiel Marin as
Johnny LaRue, Joe Spano as Henry Goldblume, Taurean Blacque
as Neal Washington, Rene Enriquez as Ray Calletano, Charles
Haid as Andrew Renko, Michael Warren as Robert Hill, Betty
Thomas as Lucy Bates, and Dennis Franz as Norm Buntz

5. LAW & ORDER (1990–PRESENT)
Created by Dick Wolf
Starring Michael Moriarty, Sam Waterston, Steven Hill, Jill Hennessy,
Richard Brooks, Chris Noth, George Dzundza, Paul Sorvino, and
Jerry Orbach

6. MURDER, SHE WROTE (1984–PRESENT)
Created by Richard Levinson, William Link, and Peter Fischer
Starring Angela Lansbury as Jessica Beatrice Fletcher

7. MYSTERY! (1980–PRESENT)

8. PERRY MASON (1957–94)
Created by Erle Stanley Gardner
Starring Raymond Burr as Perry Mason, Barbara Hale as Della Street,
William Hopper as Paul Drake, William Talman as Hamilton
Burger, and Ray Collins as Arthur Tragg

9. THE PRISONER (1968)
Created by Patrick McGoohan
Starring Patrick McGoohan as Number Six

10. THE ROCKFORD FILES (1974–PRESENT)
Created by Roy Huggins and Stephen J. Cannell
Starring James Garner as Jim Rockford, Noah Beery Jr. as Rocky, Joe
Santos as Dennis Becker, and Stuart Margolin as Angel

Some Famous Authors Pick
Their Favorite Mysteries

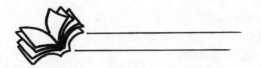

28. Famous Authors Pick Their Favorite Mystery Writers and Novels

We asked some prominent mystery writers to give us their lists of favorite mysteries and/or writers. Their responses to our query letter are included to explain their choices. Numbers are only included if used by the author.

ISAAC ASIMOV
(Isaac Asimov, 1920–92, sent this contribution for our first edition of *The Armchair Detective Books of Lists.* —ed.)

Isaac Asimov noted in 1989: "Please don't make it appear that I think these are the ten best mysteries ever written. I don't consider myself a judge of such things. I advance the following list only as ten mysteries that affected me strongly at the time I first read them. They are not in order of merit. They are in alphabetical order of the authors. Please note I didn't include anything of my own."

WILDERS WALK AWAY by Herbert Brean
CASE FOR THREE DETECTIVES by Leo Bruce
THE INNOCENCE OF FATHER BROWN by G. K. Chesterton
THE MURDER OF ROGER ACKROYD by Agatha Christie
AND THEN THERE WERE NONE by Agatha Christie
THE JUDAS WINDOW by Carter Dickson
THE HORIZONTAL MAN by Helen Eustis
PICK YOUR VICTIM by Pat McGerr
MURDER MUST ADVERTISE by Dorothy L. Sayers
THE DAUGHTER OF TIME by Josephine Tey

ROBERT BARNARD

"If you put me on the spot and demand the ten best ever, I would come up with some such list."

BLEAK HOUSE by Charles Dickens
EMMA by Jane Austen
THE HOUND OF THE BASKERVILLES by Sir Arthur Conan
  Doyle
FIVE LITTLE PIGS by Agatha Christie
STRONG POISON by Dorothy L. Sayers
MORE WORK FOR THE UNDERTAKER by Margery Allingham
TOUR DE FORCE by Christianna Brand
HOW LIKE AN ANGEL by Margaret Millar
A JUDGMENT IN STONE by Ruth Rendell
DOVER ONE by Joyce Porter

"I compiled for CRIME AND DETECTION a list of my top ten crime books published in the last twenty years."

DEAD ROMANTIC by Simon Brett
A TALENT FOR DESTRUCTION by Sheila Radley
A JUDGMENT IN STONE by Ruth Rendell
THE NEAPOLITAN STREAK by Timothy Holme
DEADHEADS by Reginald Hill
THE ROSE IN DARKNESS by Christianna Brand
THE BLOND BABOON by Janwillem van de Wetering
SPIDER WEBS by Margaret Millar
THE KILLINGS AT BADGER'S DRIFT by Caroline Graham
LIFE'S WORK by Jonathan Valin

JACQUES BARZUN

"It is nice to have a chance of listing the Top Ten among the crime fiction classics, but considering the great output since Poe, ten is a pitifully small number. I find myself going round and round among at least two dozen works of the highest merit. Still, in deference to the assigned limits, I propose the following, in random order; they are equal in rank—"

TRENT'S LAST CASE by E. C. Bentley
THE PALE HORSE by Agatha Christie
SALT IS LEAVING by J. B. Priestley
STRONG POISON by Dorothy L. Sayers
THE LADY IN THE LAKE by Raymond Chandler
GAMBIT by Rex Stout
FURIOUS OLD WOMEN by Leo Bruce
A FUNERAL IN EDEN by Paul McGuire
THE HOUND OF THE BASKERVILLES by Arthur Conan Doyle
THE KILLING OF KATIE STEELSTOCK by Michael Gilbert

GEORGE BAXT
"Here are my ten favorite mysteries with a theatrical theme."

DEATH AND THE CHASTE APPRENTICE by Robert Barnard
DEAD HEAT by Linda Barnes
MURDER IN THE TITLE by Simon Brett
DEATH MASK by Jane Dentinger
MURDER IN THE WINGS by Edward Gorman
THE SKULL BENEATH THE SKIN by P. D. James
THE G-STRING MURDERS by Gypsy Rose Lee
SHOW RED FOR DANGER by Richard Lockridge
THE DARK WHEEL by Philip MacDonald
REPEAT PERFORMANCE by William O'Farrell

LAWRENCE BLOCK
"16 Favorite (Deceased) Writers"

Anthony Boucher
Fredric Brown
James M. Cain
Raymond Chandler
Stanley Ellin
Erle Stanley Gardner
Dashiell Hammett

Chester Himes
John D. MacDonald
Ross Macdonald
Ellery Queen
Jack Ritchie
Rex Stout
Jim Thompson
Charles Willeford
Cornell Woolrich

DOROTHY SALISBURY DAVIS

"Here are my choices, in no particular order except for Number 1."

BRIGHTON ROCK by Graham Greene
GAUDY NIGHT by Dorothy L. Sayers
WE HAVE ALWAYS LIVED IN THE CASTLE by Shirley Jackson
A COFFIN FOR DIMITRIOS by Eric Ambler
BEAST IN VIEW by Margaret Millar
DEVIL TAKE THE BLUE-TAIL FLY by John Franklin Bardin
THE MAN WHO WATCHED THE TRAINS GO BY by Georges Simenon
THE DARK FANTASTIC by Stanley Ellin
SKINFLICK by Joseph Hansen
DEADLOCK by Sara Paretsky

AARON ELKINS

"Would you believe I've never before sat down and done this? All the same, it took no more than ten minutes, so I guess the list was there all along, just waiting to be asked for. The order is chronological."

THE MOONSTONE by Wilkie Collins
THE HOUND OF THE BASKERVILLES by Arthur Conan Doyle
THE ABC MURDERS by Agatha Christie
THE MOVING TOYSHOP by Edmund Crispin
THE CASE OF SONIA WAYWARD by Michael Innes
FORFEIT by Dick Francis
TIED UP IN TINSEL by Ngaio Marsh
DANCE HALL OF THE DEAD by Tony Hillerman
CROCODILE ON THE SANDBANK by Elizabeth Peters
DEATH OF MYSTERY WRITER by Robert Barnard

JAMES ELLROY
"In approximate chronological order."

RED HARVEST by Dashiell Hammett
DOUBLE INDEMNITY by James M. Cain
FAREWELL, MY LOVELY by Raymond Chandler
COMPULSION by Meyer Levin
THE CHILL by Ross Macdonald
THE DIGGER'S GAME by George V. Higgins
NO BEAST SO FIERCE by Edward Bunker
THE CHOIRBOYS by Joseph Wambaugh
TRUE CONFESSIONS by John Gregory Dunne
RED DRAGON by Thomas Harris

JOHN GARDNER
"You ask for my top ten books. I fear they are, in the main, novels of espionage, but, as that is my field, I suppose it is only to be expected."

THE TEARS OF AUTUMN by Charles McCarry
THE SECRET LOVERS by Charles McCarry
THE BETTER ANGELS by Charles McCarry
THE SPY WHO CAME IN FROM THE COLD by John le Carré
TINKER, TAILOR, SOLDIER, SPY by John le Carré

SMILEY'S PEOPLE by John le Carré
BERLIN GAME by Len Deighton
FUNERAL IN BERLIN by Len Deighton
THE BERIA PAPERS by Alan Williams
AGENTS OF INNOCENCE by David Ignatius

MICHAEL GILBERT

"Here is my list of the (to me) ten best mystery novels. Perhaps 'crime novels' would be an even better description. I have set them out in alphabetical order to avoid any sign of favoritism."

THE FASHION IN SHROUDS by Margery Allingham
THE LADY IN THE LAKE by Raymond Chandler
THE MURDER OF ROGER ACKROYD by Agatha Christie
THE MOONSTONE by Wilkie Collins
THE HOUND OF THE BASKERVILLES by Arthur Conan Doyle
THE BIG CLOCK by Kenneth Fearing
THE GLASS KEY by Dashiell Hammett
A KISS BEFORE DYING by Ira Levin
STRONG POISON by Dorothy L. Sayers
THE FRANCHISE AFFAIR by Josephine Tey

SUE GRAFTON

"In alphabetical order."

DOUBLE INDEMNITY by James M. Cain
THE HIGH WINDOW by Raymond Chandler
THE MYSTERIOUS AFFAIR AT STYLES by Agatha Christie
BERLIN GAME by Len Deighton
NERVE by Dick Francis
DEATH DROP by B. M. Gill
BEYOND A REASONABLE DOUBT by C. W. Grafton
CAT CHASER by Elmore Leonard
THE DROWNING POOL by Ross Macdonald
TALKING TO STRANGE MEN by Ruth Rendell

REGINALD HILL

"My definition of mystery is broad, but unless we claim the best, who's going to give them to us?

"These are not in any order of preference except that the last could have been two or three other authors; and of course the Simenon could have been almost any title!"

ROXANA by Daniel Defoe
THE MOONSTONE by Wilkie Collins
BLEAK HOUSE by Charles Dickens
THE LAST CHRONICLE OF BARSET by Anthony Trollope
TRENT'S LAST CASE by E. C. Bentley
THE GLASS KEY by Dashiell Hammett
MAIGRET IN MONTMARTRE by Georges Simenon
AT THE BACK OF THE NORTH WIND by Nicolas Freeling
THE NAME OF THE ROSE by Umberto Eco
THE KILLER INSIDE ME by Jim Thompson

TONY HILLERMAN

THE LITTLE SISTER by Raymond Chandler
A COFFIN FOR DIMITRIOS by Eric Ambler
THE THIRD MAN by Graham Greene
ROGUE MALE by Geoffrey Household
TINKER, TAILOR, SOLDIER, SPY by John le Carré
UNKNOWN MAN #89 by Elmore Leonard
THE WILL OF THE TRIBE by Arthur Upfield
NEW HOPE FOR THE DEAD by Charles Willeford
THE ALVAREZ JOURNAL by Rex Burns
THE LIMITS OF PAIN by K. Arne Blom

H. R. F. KEATING

"Oh, why isn't the number ten expandable?"

THE MOONSTONE by Wilkie Collins
THE ADVENTURES OF SHERLOCK HOLMES by Arthur Conan Doyle
UNCLE ABNER by Melville Davisson Post
MY FRIEND MAIGRET by Georges Simenon

BEYOND THIS POINT ARE MONSTERS by Margaret Millar
THE PRIVATE WOUND by Nicholas Blake
MIRROR, MIRROR ON THE WALL by Stanley Ellin
THE POISON ORACLE by Peter Dickinson
THE ARTFUL EGG by James McClure
A TASTE FOR DEATH by P. D. James

ELMORE LEONARD

"My all-time favorite, the one book that has made a lasting impression, is *The Friends of Eddie Coyle* by George V. Higgins. That would be my list."

PETER LOVESEY

THE ADVENTURES OF SHERLOCK HOLMES by Arthur Conan Doyle
MALICE AFORETHOUGHT by Francis Iles
THE POSTMAN ALWAYS RINGS TWICE by James M. Cain
THE LONG GOODBYE by Raymond Chandler
THE DEADLY PERCHERON by John Franklin Bardin
STRANGERS ON A TRAIN by Patricia Highsmith
MY FRIEND MAIGRET by Georges Simenon
TINKER, TAILOR, SOLDIER, SPY by John le Carré
STRONGHOLD by Stanley Ellin
FLETCH by Gregory Mcdonald
"If the short story collections have to be excluded, please substitute THE HOUND OF THE BASKERVILLES for THE ADVENTURES OF SHERLOCK HOLMES."

CHARLOTTE MACLEOD

"My first thought would have been to list any ten books by Elizabeth Peters or Michael Innes . . . my second was to think, 'But there are so many great mysteries, how do I choose?'

"They're more or less in order of preference but it's not so easy to choose among some of them."

CROCODILE ON THE SANDBANK by Elizabeth Peters
CASE OF THE JOURNEYING BOY by Michael Innes
MORE WORK FOR THE UNDERTAKER by Margery Allingham
DEATH OF A FOOL by Ngaio Marsh

TRAGEDY AT LAW by Cyril Hare
THE PALE HORSE by Agatha Christie
RIDDLE OF THE SANDS by Erskine Childers
THE TRAGEDY OF PUDD'NHEAD WILSON by Mark Twain
CORPSE IN A GILDED CAGE by Robert Barnard
MISS MELVILLE REGRETS by Evelyn Smith

MICHAEL MALONE

"This list is in no particular order—indeed, it's finally arbitrary. I could, quite as truthfully, have listed books by other favorites: Margery Allingham, Anthony Price, Emma Lathen, Nicholas Blake, Michael Innes, Josephine Tey, Jonathan Gash, or Ed McBain. I might have mentioned Dreiser's *An American Tragedy* or Warren's *All The King's Men;* they're murder mysteries too."

BLEAK HOUSE by Charles Dickens
The novels of Dashiell Hammett
INTRUDER IN THE DUST by William Faulkner
FAREWELL, MY LOVELY by Raymond Chandler
THE NINE TAILORS by Dorothy L. Sayers
THE LEAGUE OF FRIGHTENED MEN by Rex Stout
THE DEEP BLUE GOODBYE by John D. MacDonald
CHINAMAN'S CHANCE by Ross Thomas
CRIME AND PUNISHMENT by Fyodor Dostoyevsky
WHO IS TEDDY VILLANOVA? by Thomas Berger

ELIZABETH PETERS (AKA BARBARA MICHAELS)

"I hate lists and I hate 'Bests' and I particularly hate 'Lists of Bests.' How can anyone whittle down her favorites to only ten? However, here are ten books concerning which I can truthfully say 'I wish I had written that.'

THE BURNING COURT by John
   Dickson Carr
THE PALE HORSE by Agatha
   Christie
THE HOUND OF THE BASKERVILLES
   by Arthur Conan Doyle

THE DARK PLACE by Aaron Elkins
THROUGH A GLASS DARKLY by Helen McCloy
THE FAMILY VAULT by Charlotte MacLeod
CALAMITY TOWN by Ellery Queen
STRONG POISON by Dorothy L. Sayers
THE DAUGHTER OF TIME by Josephine Tey
PHANTOM LADY by Cornell Woolrich

MARCIA MULLER

"Tough stuff, trying to whittle it down to ten; finally I just decided to list my most long-term favorites, since there are too many among my contemporaries!"

THE LADY IN THE LAKE by Raymond Chandler
THE LONG GOODBYE by Raymond Chandler
THE MALTESE FALCON by Dashiell Hammett
RIPLEY UNDERGROUND by Patricia Highsmith
LISTENING WOMAN by Tony Hillerman
IN A LONELY PLACE by Dorothy B. Hughes
RIDE THE PINK HORSE by Dorothy B. Hughes
DARKER THAN AMBER by John D. MacDonald
BLACK MONEY by Ross Macdonald
THE WYCHERLY WOMAN by Ross Macdonald

SARA PARETSKY

"Ten favorites are pretty hard to select out of a lifetime of mystery reading, but here goes in more or less chronological order—"

THE LEAVENWORTH CASE by Anna Katharine Green
THE HOUND OF THE BASKERVILLES by Arthur Conan Doyle
THE MALTESE FALCON by Dashiell Hammett
THE SMILER WITH THE KNIFE by Nicholas Blake
MORE WORK FOR THE UNDERTAKER by Margery Allingham
JOHNNY UNDERGROUND by Patricia Moyes
THE SPOILT KILL by Mary Kelly
THE POISON ORACLE by Peter Dickinson
THE ASSAULT by Harry Mulisch
UNDER CONTRACT by Liza Cody

ROBERT B. PARKER
"Favorites in no particular order—"

THE BIG SLEEP by Raymond Chandler
FAREWELL, MY LOVELY by Raymond Chandler
THE HIGH WINDOW by Raymond Chandler
THE LADY IN THE LAKE by Raymond Chandler
THE LITTLE SISTER by Raymond Chandler
THE LONG GOODBYE by Raymond Chandler
THE MALTESE FALCON by Dashiell Hammett
Most of Rex Stout
Most of Elmore Leonard
THE DIGGER'S GAME by George V. Higgins

PETER STRAUB
"I guess, if pressed, I would come up with the following books. On another day, it might not be quite the same, but here goes anyhow—"

THE LONG GOODBYE by Raymond Chandler
THE LADY IN THE LAKE by Raymond Chandler
LIVE FLESH by Ruth Rendell
MORTAL STAKES by Robert B. Parker
TRENT'S LAST CASE by E. C. Bentley
WHEN THE SACRED GINMILL CLOSES by Lawrence Block
PALE GREY FOR GUILT by John D. MacDonald
THE JAMES JOYCE MURDER by Amanda Cross
THE FIRST DEADLY SIN by Lawrence Sanders
RED DRAGON by Thomas Harris

JULIAN SYMONS
"I've imposed one or two rules on myself. 1) The whole spectrum of crime stories is considered, thrillers and spy stories included 2) No more than one book by any writer may be chosen 3) I've regarded a *Collected Works* as cheating, e.g., *The Complete Sherlock Holmes Stories* is ruled out."

THE GLASS KEY by Dashiell Hammett
THE WOMAN IN WHITE by Wilkie Collins

THE MEMOIRS OF SHERLOCK HOLMES by Arthur Conan Doyle
THE TWO FACES OF JANUARY by Patricia Highsmith
DOCTOR FRIGO by Eric Ambler
THE SPY WHO CAME IN FROM THE COLD by John le Carré
COGAN'S TRADE by George V. Higgins
THE LONG GOODBYE by Raymond Chandler
TALES OF MYSTERY AND IMAGINATION by Edgar Allan Poe
THE MURDER OF ROGER ACKROYD by Agatha Christie

DONALD E. WESTLAKE

"What you ask is, of course, impossible. I could give you my Top
Three or my Top Twenty-five, but once you go past three there's no
way to stop at ten; partly because, in only doing ten, I wouldn't feel
right listing one author more than once (which is why *A Coffin for
Dimitrios* isn't here).

"So I've cheated; two of my selections are series, the complete series.
And I've done the list in alphabetical order: *my* alphabetical order."

The Hoke Mosely series by Charles Willeford
THE RED RIGHT HAND by Joel Townsley Rogers
KILL THE BOSS GOODBYE by Peter Rabe
The Gravedigger/Coffin Ed series by Chester Himes
THE MALTESE FALCON by Dashiell Hammett
INTERFACE by Joe Gores
THE EIGHTH CIRCLE by Stanley Ellin
SLEEP AND HIS BROTHER by Peter Dickinson
THE LIGHT OF DAY by Eric Ambler

PHYLLIS A. WHITNEY

"There are few detective stories on my list, but they are all mysteries.
I've begun with those I read and loved when I was in my teens."

THE SECRET GARDEN by Frances Hodgson Burnett
THE SCARLET PIMPERNEL by Baroness Orczy
THE PRISONER OF ZENDA by Anthony Hope
BRAT FARRAR by Josephine Tey
THE NINE TAILORS by Dorothy L. Sayers

REBECCA by Daphne du Maurier
NINE COACHES WAITING by Mary Stewart
NIGHT OF THE JUGGLER by William P. McGivern
ACT OF DARKNESS by Francis King
A THIEF OF TIME by Tony Hillerman

29. Sir Arthur Conan Doyle's Favorite Sherlock Holmes Stories

In March of 1927, Sir Arthur Conan Doyle invited readers of the *Strand* magazine to pick their favorite Sherlock Holmes stories. In June, when the competition ended, Doyle selected his own favorite twelve stories.

1. "The Speckled Band"
2. "The Red-Headed League"
3. "The Dancing Men"
4. "The Final Problem"
5. "A Scandal in Bohemia"
6. "The Empty House"

Doyle noted that he was less confident about the last half dozen selections, but his choices were

7. "The Five Orange Pips"
8. "The Second Stain"
9. "The Devil's Foot"
10. "The Priory School"
11. "The Musgrave Ritual"
12. "The Reigate Puzzle"

Mystery Booksellers Make Their Recommendations

30. Mystery Booksellers' Favorite Mystery Books/Authors

According to a recent, unofficial *TAD* count, over seventy-five bookstores in the United States specialize in mystery fiction (and there are many more mail-order companies). These independent booksellers are the backbone of the mystery world and are generally the best source of intelligent, informed, and up-to-the-minute recommendations. Would Aunt Mary love a mystery about an Egyptologist in the Victorian era? Do you have a special interest in southern fiction or forensic pathology? Do you want to immerse yourself in 1940s-era Los Angeles? These are the folks who can point you in the right direction. Many mystery booksellers also sponsor author signings and events, and almost all of them make a specialty of old-fashioned customer service.

The following is certainly not a complete listing of all the mystery booksellers in the country, but it is a good sampling. Stores are arranged in alphabetical order by name. With the many new stores that open yearly, it's worth a look in your local telephone directory to find the mystery bookseller nearest you.

THE BLACK ORCHID BOOKSHOP
303 E. 81st Street
New York, NY 10028
(212) 734-5980
Owners Bonnie Claeson and Joe Guglielmelli comment: "Although the Black Orchid Bookshop is our new business venture, we have both been selling mysteries for many years. Our list includes novels that we not only enjoyed reading but enjoy selling. We have regretfully exclud-

ed authors—such as Rex Stout and Ross Macdonald—whose work we so admire we could not choose among their novels, and authors—such as Sue Grafton and James Lee Burke—whom we believe new readers should approach beginning with the first novel in their series. We have listed the novels alphabetically by author."

A TROUBLE OF FOOLS by Linda Barnes
EIGHT MILLION WAYS TO DIE by Lawrence Block
THE BLACK ECHO by Michael Connelly
THE LAST GOOD KISS by James Crumley
BOOKED TO DIE by John Dunning
TIME AND AGAIN by Jack Finney
CUTTING EDGE by John Harvey
AN UNSUITABLE JOB FOR A WOMAN by P. D. James
SPLIT IMAGES by Elmore Leonard
CHILD OF SILENCE by Abigail Padgett
GALLOWS VIEW by Peter Robinson
THE ICE HOUSE by Minette Walters
TRUST ME ON THIS by Donald E. Westlake

BOOK CARNIVAL
Mystery & Science Fiction
348 S. Tustin Avenue
Orange, CA 92666
(714) 538-3210
Ed Thomas, owner: "It was a hard choice to just name ten but here goes—"

Sue Grafton
James Lee Burke
Dick Francis
Ross Macdonald
Colin Dexter
Ross Thomas
James W. Hall
Arthur Lyons
Charles Willeford
Michael Connelly

CARDINAL BOOKS
1508 NW 136th Street
Vancouver, WA 98685
(206) 576-9070
Larry and Linda Johnson, owners: "Our 'Top Ten' Favorite Mystery Authors List has undergone some revisions from our original contribution. For this second edition of *TAD Book of Lists,* we submit our current 'Top Ten' favorites in alphabetical order":

Lawrence Block
James Lee Burke
James Crumley
Dick Francis
Sue Grafton
Tony Hillerman
Jonathan Kellerman
Elmore Leonard
Marcia Muller
Walter Satterthwait

THE FOOTPRINTS OF A GIGANTIC HOUND
16 Broadway Village
123 S. Eastbourne
Tucson, AZ 85716
(602) 326-8533
Elaine and Joseph Livermore: "We debated just as long for the new *TAD Book of Lists* as for the first edition. Ultimately we made only one change."

CHINAMAN'S CHANCE by Ross Thomas
"E" IS FOR EVIDENCE by Sue Grafton
A THIEF OF TIME by Tony Hillerman
A COFFIN FOR DIMITRIOS by Eric Ambler
SOME BURIED CAESAR by Rex Stout
FLYING FINISH by Dick Francis
DEATH IN A TENURED POSITION by Amanda Cross
BOOTLEGGER'S DAUGHTER by Margaret Maron
LONG JOURNEY HOME by Michael Gilbert
FAREWELL, MY LOVELY by Raymond Chandler

KATE'S MYSTERY BOOKS
2211 Massachusetts Avenue
Cambridge, MA 01240
(617) 491-2660
Kate Mattes, owner: "Alphabetically—"

CONTENTS UNDER PRESSURE by Edna Buchanan
DEADHEADS by Reginald Hill
HAVE HIS CARCASS by Dorothy L. Sayers
THE IMMEDIATE PROSPECT OF BEING HANGED by Walter Walker
JUDGEMENT IN STONE by Ruth Rendell
THE LANDING by Howard Simons And Haynes Johnson
THE MOONSTONE by Wilkie Collins
ONE CORPSE TOO MANY by Ellis Peters
PHILOSOPHICAL ENQUIRY by Philip Kerr
A THIEF OF TIME by Tony Hillerman

MORDIDA BOOKS
PO Box 79322
Houston, TX 77279
(713) 467-4280
Dick Wilson, owner.

Ross Thomas
Raymond Chandler
Elmore Leonard
Dashiell Hammett
Colin Dexter
Charles McCarry
Charles Willeford
Len Deighton
Michael Gilbert
Patricia Highsmith

MURDER BY THE BOOK
2348 Bissonet
Houston, TX 77005
(713) 524-8597

David Thompson, manager: "Being a fan of John D. MacDonald's Travis McGee, these are the books that I most often recommend to my customers who have similar tastes."

A MORNING FOR FLAMINGOS by James Lee Burke
THE MONKEY'S RAINCOAT by Robert Crais
BODY SCISSORS by Jerome Doolittle
FOURSOME by Jeremiah Healy
ART OF SURVIVAL by A. E. Maxwell
WHITE BUTTERFLY by Walter Mosley
A LONG COLD FALL by Sam Reaves
TIGHT LINES by William Tapply
THE HEAT ISLANDS by Randy Wayne White
BLOOD UNDER THE BRIDGE by Bruce Zimmerman

MURDER BY THE BOOK
1281 N. Main Street
Providence, RI 02904
(401) 331-9140
Kevin J. Barbero, owner: "The 'Top Ten' best authors is something that is frequently asked and I am always surprised to see how the lists change with time. The first five seem to always be on any list I make while the bottom five fluctuate somewhat with what I've been reading. I tend to favor the older writers."

John Dickson Carr (and as Carter Dickson)
Arthur Conan Doyle
Raymond Chandler
Dashiell Hammett
Rex Stout
Tony Hillerman
P. D. James
Dick Francis
Colin Dexter
Michael Gilbert

MURDER ONE
71-73 Charing Cross Road
London WC2H OAA
Phone: 071-734-3483
Fax: 071-734-3429

Maxim Jakubowski, owner: "One's tastes do not change too much over five years or so, at least if you've reached middle age as I now have for good or for worse. Comments on my initial selection: at least Crumley has written a further novel, and a terrific modern western it is. Thornburg has been sadly silent and Marc Behm has published another four incredibly idiosyncratic novels, however only published in French translation; when will he be published again in English?

"As Murder One has grown in size between the two editions, can I increase my list to a top twelve? Two talents have emerged over this period that I feel I cannot ignore":

Cornell Woolrich. More the short stories than the novels, because of the dark, brooding, obsessive atmosphere, the muted eroticism, and the delicacy of the man/woman relationships. Romantic, old-fashioned, but gripping.

Jim Thompson. Even darker than Woolrich, at times psychopathic. But a fascinating writer I never seem to tire of.

David Goodis. The third in my top trinity of poets of the night and despair.

Jerome Charyn. Picaresque, touching, contemporary, and unlike any other modern practitioner of the genre. A beautiful stylist and creator of mood and feelings.

James Crumley. If only he wrote more . . . but then I suppose he'd have to drink less and lead more of a normal life, and as we all know, life feeds the fiction in insidious ways.

Charles Willeford. The modern master of the hard-boiled, but with a heart.

Newton Thornburg. Underrated author of *Cutter and Bone* and others. His latest novel can't even find a publisher in the USA. A criminal state of affairs.

Horace McCoy. A bigger influence than any of the *Black Mask* boys on today's scene.

Marc Behm. If only for one book, *The Eye of the Beholder,* the best private-eye book ever written.

Raymond Chandler. They might be clichés today, but he was the man who created them.

Carl Hiaasen. He looks and acts like a junior CIA trainee, but the humor is dark, sardonic, and when the violence is in such bad taste, I cannot but smile with all the mischief I can muster.

Paul Mayersburg. With two novels only, he is stretching the crime map into dangerous areas where sex rears its troubling head. Unique, brooding, and fascinating.

MYSTERIES & MORE
11139 N. IH35, #178
Austin, TX 78753
(512) 837-6768
Jan Grape, owner: "A dozen of our favorite mystery writers—because we can sell the heck out of whatever they write. In alphabetical order, not in order of sales. A heavy emphasis on local and Southwestern writers."

Susan Rogers Cooper
Bill Crider
Earl Emerson
Sue Grafton
Jan Grape
Carolyn Hart
Joan Hess
Tony Hillerman
J. A. Jance
D. R. Meredith
Marcia Muller
Bill Pronzini

MYSTERIOUS BOOKSHOP
129 W. 56th Street
New York, NY 10019
(212) 765-0900
Otto Penzler, owner: "My all-time favorite
mystery writers—"

Arthur Conan Doyle
Wilkie Collins
Ross Thomas
Elmore Leonard
Ruth Rendell
Cornell Woolrich
Raymond Chandler
Donald Westlake
Fredric Brown
Rex Stout

Robert Miller, manager: "Here are my Top Ten Golden Age crime/
mystery novels in chronological order."

THE MUCKER, Edgar Rice Burroughs (1921)
THE MURDER OF ROGER ACKROYD, Agatha Christie (1926)
THE LIVING SHADOW, Walter B. Gibson (1931)
THE CASE OF THE VELVET CLAWS, Erle Stanley Gardner (1933)
THE SAINT IN NEW YORK, Leslie Charteris (1935)
THE DEAD DON'T CARE, Jonathan Latimer (1938)
MURDERS IN VOLUME 2, Elizabeth Daly (1941)
BLACK ORCHIDS, Rex Stout (1942)
LAURA, Vera Caspary (1943)
CAT OF MANY TAILS, Ellery Queen (1949)

Cordelia Wilson, assistant manager: "My top five favorite authors and
their books. All are contemporary female writers":

   Patricia Highsmith, LITTLE TALES OF MISOGYNY. My all-time
favorite writer. This title is out of print. I make friends grovel before I
loan the book to them.

Anne Billson, SUCKERS. A first novel. Suppose present-day London were plagued with vampires? Suppose people got what they deserved? A vicious send-up of artists, theater people, and yuppies.

Sarah Andrews, TENSLEEP. This is also a first novel. "Ed" is a most accurate depiction of the vile subspecies "white middle-management male"!

Joan Hess, MORTAL REMAINS IN MAGGODY. All of the Maggody books have horrifying glimpses of trailer park life and many shrewd observations about human nature in general.

Minette Walters, THE ICE HOUSE. Another first novel. Stories repeated enough times become truths. This is a cozy with enough malice to satisfy a true-crime fan. Minette Walters won an Edgar for her second book, THE SCULPTRESS.

Joe Bitowf, paperback manager: "My all-time favorite mystery writers":

Dorothy L. Sayers
Nicolas Freeling
Donald Westlake
Ruth Rendell
Patricia Moyers
Ellery Queen
Michael Gilbert
Stanley Ellin
Nicholas Blake
Michael Innes

MYSTERIOUS BOOKSHOP WEST
8763 Beverly Boulevard
West Hollywood, CA 90048
(310) 659-2959
Sheldon MacArthur, manager: "It is almost impossible to put things in categories, so here are my ten favorite authors: old, new, and up-and-coming, in no order. I could give another ten times ten. I hate not to mention every book or author I have loved."

Ross Thomas
Dick Francis
James Lee Burke
James D'Alessandro
Lawrence Block
Raymond Chandler
Brian Tobin
Charles Willeford
Sara Paretsky
George Chesbro

MYSTERY BOOKSHOP
7700 Old Georgetown Road
Bethesda, MD 20814
(301) 657-2665

Jean R. McMillen, owner: "I love almost every mystery book I have ever read and recommend hundreds of them to my customers. At Mystery Bookshop we try to describe books rather than evaluate them because, as we say at the store, 'we're all different, we like different things, and that's what makes America great.' The following is a whimsical list of some of my favorites."

CARDS ON THE TABLE by Agatha Christie
FLEE FROM THE PAST by Carolyn G. Hart
SHATTERED SILK by Barbara Michaels
IF EVER I RETURN, PRETTY PEGGY-O by Sharon McCrumb
THE CEREAL MURDERS by Diane Mott Davidson
BOOTLEGGER'S DAUGHTER by Margaret Maron
THE BODY IN THE BELFRY by Katharine Hall Page
A DIET TO DIE FOR by Joan Hess
WILD KAT by Karen Kijewski
WOLF IN THE SHADOWS by Marcia Muller
TIME AND AGAIN by Jack Finney

PARTNERS & CRIME
44 Greenwich Avenue
New York, NY 10011
(212) 243-0440
"Here's our ten Best 'Nobody-Heard-
of-'Em-Just-a-Few-Years-Ago' List":

James Lee Burke
Michael Connelly
Patricia Cornwell
Cynthia Harrod-Eagles
Carl Hiaasen
Jon A. Jackson
Philip Kerr
Laurie R. King
Walter Mosley
Minette Walters

THE POISONED PEN
7100B E. Main Street
Scottsdale, AZ 85251
(602) 947-2974
Barbara Peters, owner: "We specialize in spotting up-and-coming
authors. Our current picks are":

Nevada Barr
Michael Connelly
Phillip R. Craig
Deborah Crombie
Janet Neel
Sharan Newman
Abigail Padgett
Ronald Querny
Steven Saylor
Minette Walters

PRIME CRIME
891 Bank Street
Ottawa, Canada K1S 3W4
(613) 238-2583
Jim Reicker, owner: "I took 'favorite author' to mean an author whose work I have read with such great personal pleasure that someday I hope to have read their entire output. I excluded authors with only two to three books published or those with only single titles I have enjoyed. . . . In alphabetical order":

James Lee Burke
Raymond Chandler
Stephen Greenleaf
Carl Hiaasen
Reginald Hill
James McClure
Richard N. Patterson
Dorothy L. Sayers
Maj Sjöwall and Per Wahlöö
Eric Wright

THE RAVEN BOOKSTORE
8 East 7th Street
Lawrence, KS 66044
(913) 749-3300
Mary Lou Wright and Pat Kehde, owners: "Certainly our list has changed, as tastes change, writers develop (or stop publishing), and new exciting authors come on the scene. A short list of up-and-coming authors would be interesting also. Pat and Mary Lou's list (as of February 1994; try us in April and it will probably be different already!)":

Lawrence Block
James Lee Burke
Agatha Christie
Aaron Elkins
Tony Hillerman
Sara Paretsky
Nancy Pickard

Josephine Tey
Ross Thomas
Arthur Upfield

THE RUE MORGUE
A Mystery Bookstore
946 Pearl Street
Boulder, CO 80302
(303) 443-8346
Tom and Enid Schantz, owners: "Here're our picks of the most promising mystery writers whose first book in a new series was published since 1990."
The women:
Nevada Barr, TRACK OF THE CAT
Minette Walters, THE ICE HOUSE
Nancy Atherton, AUNT DIMITY'S DEATH
Abigail Padgett, CHILD OF SILENCE
Dana Stabenow, A COLD DAY FOR MURDER
The men:
John Dunning, BOOKED TO DIE
Randy Wayne White, SANIBEL FLATS
Michael Connelly, THE BLACK ECHO
Walter Mosley, DEVIL IN A BLUE DRESS
John Straley, THE WOMAN WHO MARRIED A BEAR

SAN FRANCISCO MYSTERY BOOKSTORE
746 Diamond Street
San Francisco, CA 94114
(415) 282-7444
Bruce Taylor, owner: "In no particular order—"

Individual books of special merit:
A KISS BEFORE DYING by Ira Levin
THE LONG GOODBYE by Raymond Chandler
THE MURDER OF MY AUNT by Richard Hull
LISTENING WOMAN by Tony Hillerman
THE BEAST MUST DIE by Nicholas Blake
MYSTERY STORIES by Stanley Ellin

Authors with a body of work with special merit:
Joyce Porter
Cornell Woolrich
Donald Westlake
John Dickson Carr

SLEUTH OF BAKER STREET
1595 Bayview Avenue
Toronto, Ontario
Canada M4G 3B5
(416) 483-3111
J. D. Singh, owner: "Talk about a challenge! Being the alpha book-seller, and inclined to push my weight around, I retained the right to have the last say, but what follows is indeed a cooperative venture between Marian Misters and I (owners) and Jill Abrams (manager).

"This is a list of books that all three of us would happily reread and reread, There are no books by Peter Robinson, Reginald Hill, or Michael Malone on the list because their entire bodies of work would qualify under the above criterion. So in no particular order . . ."

THE MIRRORMAKER, David Thompson
BY EVIL MEANS, Sandra West Prowell
A PHILOSOPHICAL INVESTIGATION, Philip Kerr
BLACK CHERRY BLUES, James Lee Burke
A GREAT DELIVERANCE, Elizabeth George
"A" IS FOR ALIBI, Sue Grafton
BUCKET NUT, Liza Cody
POSTMORTEM, Patricia D. Cornwell
BRIARPATCH, Ross Thomas
THE SUSPECT, L. R. Wright

UNCLE EDGAR'S MYSTERY BOOKSTORE
2864 Chicago Avenue S.
Minneapolis, MN 55407
(612) 824-9984
Jeff Hatfield, manager: "Favorite authors were out since I couldn't jus-tify Patrick O'Brian and Terry Pratchett as crossover mystery writers. What may be useful is a top ten titles list combining personal favorites,

most recommended, and bestselling mystery and detective titles at Uncle Edgar's over the past fifteen years. An overwhelming (it's amazing) number was reduced to fifty, then ten, and continues to change. Unranked, many of these went on to attract nominations or win awards, and so will be mentioned on other lists."

BONES AND SILENCE by Reginald Hill
DOUBLE NEGATIVE by David Carkeet
DOUBLE WHAMMY by Carl Hiaasen
THE JUDAS PAIR by Jonathan Gash
MARCH VIOLETS by Philip Kerr
PICTURE MISS SEETON by Heron Carvic
THE PROMISED LAND by Robert B. Parker
THE SILENCE OF THE LAMBS by Thomas Harris
TAPPING THE SOURCE by Ken Nunn
THUS WAS ADONIS MURDERED by Sarah Caudwell

Mystery Organizations, Conventions, and Publications

31. Organizations

AMERICAN CRIME WRITERS LEAGUE

Professional organization formed to address the needs and concerns of mystery writers. Membership limited to published writers only. Meetings held at various mystery conferences. Monthly newsletter. For information contact: Jay Brandon, 219 Tuxedo, San Antonio, TX 78209.

MYSTERY WRITERS OF AMERICA

The major organization for American mystery writers. Founded in 1945, this group bestows the coveted Edgar Allan Poe Awards. Members receive a monthly national newsletter, *The Third Degree*. Local chapters organize workshops, lectures, etc. Membership limited to published writers and some publishing professionals. For information on membership contact: Priscilla Ridgway, Executive Director, MWA, 17 E. 47th Street, 6th floor, New York, NY 10017.

CRIME WRITERS' ASSOCIATION

Britain's national organization for crime writers, founded in 1953. Membership is open to published writers of crime fiction and nonfiction. Application for associate membership may be made by publishers, agents, producers, or reviewers associated with crime fiction. Publishes a newsletter, *Red Herrings*. Annual awards are given in several categories. Contact: Anthea Fraser, Secretary, "Owlswick," 22 Chiltern Way, Tring, Herts. HP23 5JX

THE DETECTION CLUB

Founded in 1928 in London, the membership of this prestigious writers' club is relatively small, but includes the most distinguished names in British detective fiction. Election to membership is a highly coveted professional honor.

SISTERS IN CRIME

Writer *and* fan organization dedicated to the promotion of mysteries by women—although they also promote male writers who join the group. SIS publishes a useful newsletter, a bibliography of books by all SIS members, and detailed self-promotion guides for writers. This group also sponsors booths at trade conferences such as the annual American Library Association convention. Local chapters throughout the country offer many services including speakers' bureaus. For membership information, contact: Sisters in Crime, Box 442124, Lawrence, KS 66044-8933.

INTERNATIONAL ASSOCIATION OF CRIME WRITERS

Organization of professional writers whose primary goals are to promote communication among writers of all nationalities, to encourage translation of crime fiction and nonfiction into other languages, and to speak out against censorship and other forms of tyranny. Branches throughout Europe and Latin America with other branches currently being organized in Asia and Africa. Sponsors the popular Semana Negra Conference in Spain and the annual Four Frontiers (Canada/U.S./Mexico/Cuba) Conference. IACW-at-large contact: K. Arne Blom, President, Smaskolevagen 22, S-224-67 Lund, Sweden.

IACW, North American Branch (U.S. and Canada) is open to published writers only. Publishing professionals and booksellers may join by invitation. The North American Branch sponsors the annual North American Hammett Prize for a work of literary excellence in the crime-writing field by a U.S. or Canadian author. North American members receive a quarterly newsletter and invitations to regional and international conferences. North American Branch contact: Mary A. Frisque, Executive Director, IACW/NA, JAF Box 1500, New York, NY 10116.

PRIVATE EYE WRITERS OF AMERICA

An organization devoted to private-eye detective fiction. Membership open to fans, writers, and publishing professionals. Gives the annual Shamus Awards and THE EYE Life Achievement Award. Quarterly newsletter, *Reflections in a Private Eye*. Sponsors the new EyeCon convention. For membership information, please contact: Martha L. Derickson, 407 W. 3rd Street, Moorestown, NJ 08057.

CRIME WRITERS OF CANADA

Canada's national association of authors and industry professionals active in the field of crime writing. They give the Arthur Ellis Awards annually. Contact: David Skene-Melvin, CWC, 225 Carlton Street, Toronto, Ontario, Canada M5A 2L2

MYSTERY READERS INTERNATIONAL

Publishes the quarterly *Mystery Readers Journal* and organizes activities for mystery readers. Open to all readers, fans, critics, publishing professionals, and writers. Gives the annual Macavity Awards, which are determined by a vote of the general membership. Contact: Janet A. Rudolph, Director, Mystery Readers International, Box 8116, Berkeley, CA 94707.

INDEPENDENT MYSTERY BOOKSELLERS ASSOCIATION

For owners of independent bookshops specializing in mystery fiction. Periodic meetings at mystery conventions and publishing events. This organization also gives annual book awards. Contact: Barbara Peters, Poisoned Pen, 7100B E. Main St., Scottsdale, AZ 85251.

32. Author Fan Clubs and Newsletters

This is a listing of clubs and periodicals that are devoted to the work of a single author. Periodicals that cover a broader range of mystery writers are listed in the "Mystery Periodicals" section.

MARGERY ALLINGHAM

THE BOTTLE STREET GAZETTE (U.S.)
The Margery Allingham Society
c/o Maryell Cleary
1183 Arbor Drive, Apt. B
E. Lansing, MI 48823
(2 issues/year for $5)

THE BOTTLE STREET GAZETTE (U.K.)
Mrs. Pat Watt
3 Corringham Road
Wembley
Middlesex HA9 9PX
England

PAUL BISHOP

PAUL BISHOP NEWSLETTER
5480 Butterfield Street
Camarillo, CA 93012
The author's newsletter.

LAWRENCE BLOCK

LAWRENCE BLOCK NEWSLETTER
299 W. 12th Street
New York, NY 10014
This chatty personal newsletter—written by Block himself—is free, but a check in any amount is appreciated. Proceeds go to God's Love We Deliver (which supplies meals to homebound AIDS patients) or the Village Nursing Home (a NYC facility for the elderly).

LILIAN JACKSON BRAUN

THE LILIAN JACKSON BRAUN NEWSLETTER
Helen McCarthy
4 Tamarack Road
Natick, MA 01760
(2 issues/year; donations welcome)

JOHN BUCHAN

JOHN BUCHAN JOURNAL
Limpsfield, Ranfurly Road
Bridge of Wir
Renfrewshire PA113EL
Scotland

G. K. CHESTERTON

CHESTERTON REVIEW
Ian Boyd, St. Thomas Moore College

1437 College Drive
Saskatoon, Sask. S7N 0W6
Canada

AGATHA CHRISTIE

WOMAN OF MYSTERY
Amy Lubelski
P.O. Box 1616, Canal Street Station
New York, NY 10013
(monthly/$30)

MAX ALLAN COLLINS

MAX ALLAN COLLINS NEWSLETTER
301 Fairview Avenue
Muscatine, IA 52761
A newsletter written by Max Allan Collins.

WILKIE COLLINS

WILKIE COLLINS SOCIETY (U.S.)
Kirk Beetz, President
1307 F Street
Davis, CA 95616

WILKIE COLLINS SOCIETY (U.K.)
Andrew Gasson, Secretary
3 Merton House
36 Belsize Park
London NW3 4EA
England

BILL CRIDER

BILL CRIDER NEWSLETTER
1606 S. Hill Street
Alvin, TX 77511-4356

Written by Crider himself. To receive this newsletter send some stamps to the above address. Alligator jokes, news items, and paraphernalia also appreciated.

FREEMAN WILLS CROFTS

FREEMAN WILLS CROFTS SOCIETY
Paul Moy
Flat, 82 Bedford Road
Horsham
West Sussex RH13 5BH
U.K.

ARTHUR CONAN DOYLE/SHERLOCK HOLMES

There are literally hundreds of groups and newsletters devoted to Sherlock Holmes and his creator, Arthur Conan Doyle. For simplicity's sake only the major American and British organizations are listed here. Please write to them for information on a society near you.

THE BAKER STREET IRREGULARS
Thomas L. Stix Jr., "Wiggins"
34 Pierson Avenue
Norwood, NJ 07648
The Baker Street Irregulars is the world's largest Sherlockian fan organization. In addition there are more than five hundred Scion Societies around the world. The BSI organizes events and an annual dinner as well as publishing *The Baker Street Journal.* Only the address of the main society is included here; there are many affiliated groups around the United States.

THE BAKER STREET JOURNAL
(Editorial address)

William R. Cochran, Editor
517 N. Vine Street
Du Quoin, IL 62832
(Subscriptions)
P.O. Box 465
Hanover, PA 17331
(4 issues/yr., $17.50)

THE SHERLOCK HOLMES SOCIETY OF LONDON
Geoffrey Stavert
3 Outram Road
Southsea
Hampshire PO5 1QP
England
This is the largest Sherlockian society in England. It publishes *The Sherlock Holmes Journal.*

THE SHERLOCK HOLMES JOURNAL
Nicholas Utechin and Heather Owen, Editors
Highfield Farm House
23 Highfield Avenue
Headington
Oxford OX3 7LR
U.K.

R. AUSTIN FREEMAN

THORNDYKE FILE
John McAleer
121 Follen Road
Lexington, MA 02173
(2 issues/yr., $7.50)

ERLE STANLEY GARDNER (PERRY MASON)

NAAPM NEWSLETTER
(National Association for the Advancement of Perry Mason)
Jim Davidson

2735 Benvenue Avenue, #3
Berkeley, CA 94705
(4 issues/yr., $10)

RON GOULART

RON GOULART'S WEEKLY
Goulart Publishing Empire
30 Farrell Road
Weston, CT 06883
An irregular (in many senses of the word) newsletter written by Ron Goulart. Write to the above address for more information.

ELIZABETH LININGTON/DELL SHANNON

THE LININGTON LINEUP
Rinehart Potts
1223 Glen Terrace
Glassboro, NJ 08028
(6 issues/yr., $15)

JOHN D. MACDONALD

JDM BIBLIOPHILE
Ed Hirschberg
English Department
University of Florida
Tampa, FL 33620

CHARLOTTE MACLEOD

CHARLOTTE MACLEOD NEWSLETTER
Ann Weisman, Editor
P.O. Box 481
Brunswick, ME 04011
(3 issues/yr., free)

NGAIO MARSH

THE NGAIO MARSH SOCIETY
Prof. B. J. Rahn
Department of English
Hunter College
695 Park Avenue
New York, NY 10021

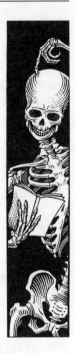

ED MCBAIN

87TH PRECINCT REPORT
Russell W. Hultgren, Editor
1136 Silverleaf Drive
Arnold, MD 21012

JOHN MORTIMER

RUMPOLE SOCIETY
William Sears
P.O. Box 906
San Mateo, Ca 94403

ELIZABETH PETERS/BARBARA MICHAELS

FRIENDS OF ELIZABETH PETERS NEWSLETTER
Mary Mormon
1802 Sanford Road
Silver Spring, MD 20902
(2 issues/yr., free but stamps/donations appreciated)

ELLIS PETERS

MOST LOVING MERE FOLLY
Sue Feder
7815 Daniels Avenue
Parkville, MD 21234
(4 issues/yr., $15, checks payable to Sue Feder)

DOROTHY L. SAYERS

DOROTHY L. SAYERS SOCIETY
Christopher Dean, Chairman
Rose Cottage
Malthouse Lane
Hurstpierpoint
Sussex BN6 9JY
England

WALTER SORRELLS

WALTER SORRELLS NEWSLETTER
2605 Bentley Road, #3209
Marietta, GA 30067
This newsletter is written by legal-thriller writer Sorrells.

REX STOUT

THE GAZETTE
The Wolfe Pack
P.O. Box 822
Ansonia Station
New York, NY 10023
The $25 membership fee for The Wolfe Pack (a fan organization
devoted to Rex Stout's creation Nero Wolfe) will also get you four
issues of *The Gazette*. This group organizes the annual Black Orchid
Banquet in October and Shad Roe Banquet each spring, both held in
New York City. There are a few regional branches around the U.S. The
Wolfe Pack annually gives the Nero Wolfe Awards.

REX STOUT JOURNAL
John McAleer
121 Follen Road
Lexington, MA 02173
(2 issues/yr., $7.50)

ARTHUR UPFIELD

THE BONY BULLETIN
Philip T. Asdell
5719 Jefferson Boulevard
Frederick, MD 21701

EDGAR WALLACE

THE EDGAR WALLACE SOCIETY
Neil Clark
9 Hurst Rise Road
North Hinksey
Oxford OX2 9HE
U.K.
This society has events and yearly meetings and publishes *The Crimson Circle Magazine*.

THE CRIMSON CIRCLE MAGAZINE
Ms. Betty Hogan
7 Devonshire Close
Amersham
Bucks HP6 5JG
England

33. Mystery Fan Conventions

Mystery conventions—whether small or large, devoted to "cozy mysteries," private-eye novels, or the full gamut of crime fiction—are an excellent way to meet writers in person, get acquainted with new books and topics, have books signed, and generally share a good time with like-minded fans. The following are some of the conventions that are currently held around the United States and beyond. Many mystery periodicals provide regular listings of upcoming conventions.

BOUCHERCON (THE WORLD MYSTERY CONVENTION)

Named after the distinguished mystery critic Anthony Boucher, this is the largest of all mystery-fan conventions. The location varies from year to year as do the organizers; occasionally this event travels from the United States to England or Canada. Three-track panel scheduling, special events, films, bookdealers room, signings, readings, cocktail party, banquet. Generally over a thousand fans, writers, agents, editors and bookdealers attend. In 1995, Bouchercon will be held September 28–October 1 in Nottingham, England. In 1996, Bouchercon will be held October 9–13 in St. Paul, Minnesota.

BOUCHERCON 26 (1995)
Broadway
14 Broad Street
Nottingham NG1 3AL
England

BOUCHERCON 27 (1996)
P.O. Box 8296
Minneapolis, MN 55408-0296

CLUEFEST

An annual (since 1992) mystery reader's book fair with various mystery writers as guests. Dealers room, two-track panel scheduling, book signings, Sunday buffet luncheon. This event is generally held in late August in Dallas, Texas.

CON & DAGGER PRODUCTIONS
c/o The Book Tree
702 University Village
Richardson, TX 75081

EYECON

This is a brand-new convention organized by The Private Eye Writers of America and focusing on that particular subgenre. Bookdealers room, media events, author talks, fan panels, presentation of the PWA Shamus Awards and the St. Martin's Press Award for Best First Private Eye Novel. Writers, fans, editors, agents. In 1995, this convention will be held June 15–18 in Milwaukee, Wisconsin.

GARY WARREN NIEBUHR
3734 W. Ohio Avenue
Milwaukee, WI 53215

LEFT COAST CRIME

This is an annual (since 1990) regional mystery convention held in the western portion of the United States in February or March. Two-track panel scheduling, a banquet. Writers, fans, agents, editors. The site and organizers vary from year to year. In 1996, this convention will be held in Boulder, Colorado, in early March.

LCC 6, c/o The Rue Morgue Bookstore
946 Pearl Street
Boulder, CO 80302

Magna Cum Murder

This small mystery conference made its debut in October 1994, over Halloween weekend. Sponsored by Ball State University, it offers panels, signings, seminars, a bookdealers room, the presentation by *The Armchair Detective* magazine of the Armchair Detective Award for best scholarship in the mystery genre, and a banquet. Fans, writers, editors, and agents.

Magna Cum Murder
c/o Joanna Wallace
Ball State University
Carmichael Hall 201
Muncie, IN 47306

Malice Domestic Mystery Convention

This is a small annual convention devoted to "cozy crime." Three-track panel programming, presentation of the Agatha Awards and of the St. Martin's Press Award for Best First Malice Domestic Novel, banquet, cocktail party, bookdealers room, signings, readings, events. Limited to around four hundred attendees. Held annually at the Bethesda Hyatt Regency (outside Washington, D.C.), usually near the end of April. It generally sells out well in advance.

Malice Domestic
P.O. Box 31137
Bethesda, MD 20824-1137

Mid-Atlantic Book Fair and Convention

A three-day annual (since 1990) convention that covers all aspects of the mystery genre. Panels, special events, bookdealers room, signings, Friday night cocktail party. Limited to four hundred registrants. Fans, authors, editors, booksellers, and agents. Generally held the first weekend of November.

DEEN KOGAN
Detecto-Mysterioso Books
Society Hill Playhouse
507 South 8th Street
Philadelphia, PA 19147
(215) 923-0211

DOROTHY L. SAYERS CONVENTION

Held annually in the summer months in England.

CHRISTOPHER DEAN
Rose Cottage
Malthouse Lane
Hurstpierpoint
Sussex BN6 9JY
England

SHOTS ON THE PAGE

This yearly English convention runs in conjunction with Shots in the Dark, an international film, television, and arts festival with a crime and mystery theme.

SHOTS ON THE PAGE
Broadway
14 Broad Street
Nottingham NG1 3AL
England

34. Mystery Periodicals

In the last twenty-five years there has been a virtual explosion of periodicals devoted to the mystery genre. Subscribing to one or more of these publications is the easiest way to enter mystery fandom.

Please note that periodicals that are devoted to a single author are listed under "Author Fan Clubs and Newsletters."

COLLECTING

FIRSTS: COLLECTING MODERN FIRST EDITIONS
P.O. Box 65166
Tucson, AZ 85728-5166
This lively, colorful, and informative monthly (bimonthly in July and August) offers information to book collectors of all genres, but has an especially strong interest in mysteries. ($35/11 issues; $50, Mexico and Canada; $75, all other countries)

MFE COLLECTORS BOOKLINE
P.O. Box 150119
San Rafael, CA 94915
Phone/Fax: (415) 457-LINE
Internet address: BookLine@aol.com
Editor and publisher: David M. Brown
This newsletter is published monthly and offers information on collecting modern first editions and recent fiction. They cover mysteries also, several of which are usually included on their year-end top instant collectibles list. ($135/12 issues)

CRITICISM/REVIEWS

AMERICAN MYSTERY NEWS
Box 5343
Winston-Salem, NC 27113
Editor: Janet Loo
Reviews. Members nominate authors and titles to be featured in future issues. (Published quarterly: $14/year)

THE ARMCHAIR DETECTIVE (TAD)
129 W. 56th Street
New York, NY 10019
Editor: Kate Stine
Founded in 1967, *TAD* is a large-sized glossy magazine featuring in-depth critical articles, author interviews, commentary, regular colum-nists, reviews of novels, film, and TV, audio books, reference works, Sherlockiana, and a regular feature on collecting mystery fiction by Otto Penzler. ($26/4 issues; $30 elsewhere; after July 1, 1995: $31/4 issues; $35 elsewhere)

CEMETERY DANCE
"The Magazine of Dark Mystery, Suspense and Horror"
(Editorial)
P.O. Box 858
Edgewood, MD 21040
Subscriptions—please make all checks payable to CDP Publications)
CDP Publications
P.O. Box 18433
Baltimore, MD 21237
($15/4 issues)
Editor and Publisher: Richard T. Chizmar
Interviews with writers, articles, commentary, and reviews focusing on the darker side of mystery fiction as well as the horror genre.

CLUES: A JOURNAL OF DETECTION
Bowling Green State University Popular Press
Bowling Green, OH 43403
Editor: Pat Browne

This twice yearly, digest-sized publication contains academic criticism, commentary, and interviews. ($12.50/2 issues)

CRIME AND DETECTIVE STORIES (CADS)
9 Vicarage Hill
South Benfleet
Essex 5S7 1PA
England
Editor: Geoff Bradley
In-depth articles, opinion pieces, along with reviews, new-release information. Large-format size, irregular publishing schedule.

THE CRIMINAL RECORD
3131 E. Seventh Avenue Parkway
Denver, CO 80206
Editor: Ann M. Williams
($7/6 issues; $1/sample copy)

DEADLY PLEASURES
Box 839-EP
Farmington, UT 84025-0839
Editor: George A. Easter
Newsletter with commentary, essays, reviews. Send subscription checks to George Easter. ($12/4 issues; $14, Canada; $22, overseas)

DEADLY SERIOUS
"References for Writers of Mystery, Detective & Crime Fiction"
P.O. Box 1045
Cooper Station
New York, NY 10276-1045
Editor: Sharon Villines
Each issue provides a brief introduction to a topic such as poisons, crime-scene investigation, or art fraud, and discusses the best sources on that subject including reference works and telephone numbers of professional associations. Digests of journal articles, letters from readers, and notes from talks and panel discussions are also included. ($36/10 issues; $41, Canada; $47 elsewhere)

THE DROOD REVIEW OF MYSTERY
Box 50267
Kalamazoo, MI 49005
Editor and publisher: Jim Huang
Both in-depth and capsule book reviews and commentary, publication checklists, yearly Editor's Choice lists. Bimonthly. ($14/6 issues; $18, Canada/Mexico; $24, overseas)

THE GOTHIC JOURNAL
19210 Forest Road N.
Forest Lake, MN 55025-9766
A bimonthly publication covering romantic suspense, women-in-jeopardy, gothic romance, and supernatural romance. Reviews, author profiles, market news articles, etc. ($30/11 issues; $16.50/6 issues; $3/single issue)

KRACKED MIRROR MYSTERIES
370 E. Woodlaws
Le Center, MN 56057
Editor: Debbie Gish
Triannual digest featuring fiction and nonfiction mystery and suspense. ($11.50/year; $4/single issue)

MDM (MYSTERY & DETECTIVE MONTHLY)
5601 N. 40th Street
Tacoma, WA 98407
Editor: Bob Napier
A "letterzine" devoted to mystery-related topics. Contributors are generally knowledgeable fans and/or writers. Topics include latest books read, opinions on publishing, events in the fan world. ($30/11 issues; $16.50/6 issues; $3/single issue)

MEAN STREETS
214 Hat Hill Road
Blackheath, NSW 2785
Australia
Editor: Stuart Coupe

Magazine for fans of hard-boiled mysteries. (U.S. subscriptions *in Australian dollars:* $35/surface mail; $45/airmail. Check payable to What Goes On Pty. Ltd.)

MOSTLY MURDER
(subscriptions)
P.O. Box 191207
Dallas, TX 75219
(editorial)
2614 Hood Street
Dallas, TX 75219
Editor: Jay W. K. Setliff
Tabloid-format review newspaper. ($8/4 issues. No foreign orders)

MURDER & MAYHEM
P.O. Box 415024
Kansas City, MO 64141
Editors: Elly Ann & Fiske Miles
Interviews, articles, in-depth reviews. This lively magazine recently expanded in size. ($15/6 issues; $30 outside U.S.)

MURDER IS ACADEMIC
Department of English
Hunter College
695 Park Avenue
New York, NY 10021
Editor: Professor B. J. Rahn
Newsletter devoted to the discussion of teaching and criticism of crime fiction on campus. Information on academic gatherings, research resources, course syllabi. Book reviews of special interest to scholars.

MYSTERY FORUM MAGAZINE
P.O. Box 138
Independence, MO 64051
Editor: Bob Myers
Fiction, features, and reviews including serialized novels and comic-strip art. ($18/year)

MYSTERY NEWS
P.O. Box 1201
Port Townsend, WA 98368-0901
Editor: Harriet Stay
Tabloid-format periodical featuring mainly reviews, also some interviews and essays. Bimonthly. ($15/6 issues)

MYSTERY READERS JOURNAL
P.O. Box 8116
Berkeley, CA 94707
Editor: Janet Rudolph
A quarterly thematic mystery journal containing articles, reviews, and author essays on a specific theme as well as special columns, a calendar of events, etc. Membership in Mystery Readers International entitles members to a year's subscription of this journal. ($22.50/year; $35, libraries/overseas airmail)

THE MYSTERY REVIEW
P.O. Box 233
Colborne, Ontario KOK 1SO
Canada
Editor: Barbara Davey
Reviews, articles, "Kid's Corner." ($20/4 issues; $21.50, Canada)

MYSTERY SCENE
P.O. Box 669
Cedar Rapids, IA 52406-0669
Editor: Joe Gorman
Published bimonthly this lively fan/mystery-writer magazine features interviews, publishing/market news, regional news, columns, reviews, and short articles by mystery writers about their upcoming books. ($35/6 issues; $63.50, foreign)

MYSTERY STREET MAGAZINE
P.O. Box 1378
Eugene, OR 97440
Features eight to twelve original mystery short stories of all types in each issue. Some articles and book reviews.

OVER MY DEAD BODY!
"The Mystery Magazine"
P.O. Box 1778
Auburn, WA 98071
Fiction, author profiles, reviews. This is a new magazine format for the popular on-line computer mystery forum. ($12/4 issues)

PI MAGAZINE
755 Bronx
Toledo, OH 43609
Academic criticism, commentary on private-eye fiction.

FICTION

ALFRED HITCHCOCK MYSTERY MAGAZINE
(subscriptions)
P.O. Box 5124
Harlan, IA 51593
(editorial)
Dell Magazines
1540 Broadway
New York, NY 10036
Editor: Cathleen Jordan
Digest-sized magazine devoted to mystery short stories. ($34.97 year, U.S.; $44.97 elsewhere)

ELLERY QUEEN'S MYSTERY MAGAZINE
(subscriptions)
P.O. Box 5127
Harlan, IA 51593
(editorial)
Dell Magazines
1540 Broadway
New York, NY 10036
Editor: Janet Hutchings
Digest-sized magazine devoted to mystery short stories. ($34.97/year; $44.97, elsewhere)

THE NEW HARDBOILED
Gryphon Publications
P.O. Box 209
Brooklyn, NY 11228
Editor: Gary Lovisi
A quarterly digest of original hard-boiled fiction, classic reprints, some nonfiction, and reviews. ($30/6 issues; $36, elsewhere)

NEW MYSTERY MAGAZINE
175 Fifth Avenue
Suite 2001
The Flatiron Building
New York, NY 10010-7703
($27.77/year)

TRUE CRIME

THE LIZZIE BORDEN QUARTERLY
P.O. Box 1823
Fall River, MA 02722
Editors: Jules Ryckebusch and Kenneth J. Souza
Devoted to the infamous murder mystery that made Lizzie Borden a legend. ($8/4 issues)

MURDER CAN BE FUN
P.O. Box 640111
San Francisco, CA 94109
Editor: John Marr
Fanzine dedicated not only to murder but all kinds of death and destruction—mostly bizarre. Write for subscription information.

REAL CRIME BOOK DIGEST
1029 W. Wilson Avenue
Chicago, IL 60640
Editor: Jim Agnew
Reviews of true-crime books, features on true-crime writers. ($12/6 issues)

PHOTO/ART CREDITS